Managerialism and
the Public Services

For Hazel

Managerialism and the Public Services

Cuts or Cultural Change in the 1990s?

Second Edition

Christopher Pollitt

BLACKWELL
Business

Copyright © Christopher Pollitt 1990, 1993

First published 1990
Second edition published 1993
Reprinted 1994

Blackwell Publishers
108 Cowley Road, Oxford, OX4 1JF, UK

238 Main Street, Cambridge,
Massachusetts 02142, USA

British Library Cataloguing in Publication Data

A CIP catalogue record for this book is available from the British Library.

Library of Congress Cataloging in Publication Data
Pollitt, Christopher.
    Managerialism and the public services / Christopher Pollitt.—
2nd ed.
        p.   cm.
    Includes bibliographical references (p.   ) and index.
    1. Administrative agencies—Great Britain—Management.
2. Government productivity—Great Britain. 3. Administrative
agencies—United States—Management. 4. Government productivity-
-United States.   I. Title.
JN425.P63   1993
354.4104—dc20   92–26772
                                                            CIP

ISBN 0–631–18837–1

Designed by Chase Production Services, Chipping Norton
Typeset in 11 on 13 pt Ehrhardt
by Setrite Typesetters Limited, Hong Kong
Printed in Great Britain by Athenæum Press Ltd, Newcastle upon Tyne
This book is printed on acid-free paper

Contents

Preface

Efficient management is a key to the (national) revival . . . . And the management ethos must run right through our national life — private and public companies, civil service, nationalized industries, local government, the National Health Service.

(Michael Heseltine, then Conservative Secretary of State for the Environment, 1980)

We shall shortly be aware of the devastating effects of the loss of one quarter of the Senior Executive Service through early retirement and the expressed desire of another 20 per cent to leave government.

(Senior US public official, 1981)

Management? As far as I'm concerned it's bad habit left over from the Army and the Church.

(National Health Service Manager, 1986)

This book examines how the British and the Americans aspire to run their public services. It suggests that the dominant approach to thinking about this gargantuan task has changed significantly since the 1970s and that, albeit more slowly, practices have begun to change too. A new set of assumptions and techniques, here termed 'managerialism', has grown enormously in salience. Managerialism, it is argued, needs to be understood as an ideology, and one with some concrete and immediate consequences. In the first four chapters the content, context and early impacts of managerialism are described and analysed. I then move to, first, a theoretical critique and subsequently, a forward-looking section in which some alternatives are assessed. In the concluding chapter I attempt to draw together an overview, and then to look ahead.

The ideas for the book, and the urge to put them together in this particular form have come from several sources. One has been my awareness, as an academic with strong interests in health care, education, local authority social services and the civil service, of the remarkable similarities between what − in the UK − 'has happened' to these quite disparate public services since the late 1970s. Activity costing, devolved budgeting, performance indicators, staff appraisal schemes, merit pay − all these and more have been introduced in the name of strengthening 'management' and improving 'efficiency'. Beneath these banners the routines of hundreds of thousands of British public servants have been transformed. Significantly, the very terms many of these individuals use to describe themselves have changed. Formerly they were called 'administrators', 'principal officers', 'finance officers' or 'assistant directors'. Now they are 'managers'. Even head teachers/ principals, hospital consultants and police chief inspectors are frequently being given the same label, though some (not all) remain uncomfortable with it.

In the United States, also, the working lives of many public officials have been disturbed, re-routed, and in some cases truncated. Budgetary and personnel reductions have been concentrated on domestic agencies, the contracting-out of many previously public service activities has begun, staff appraisal and merit pay systems have proliferated and evidence of declining morale has accumulated for a variety of federal and state agencies. Some of the American terminology has been significantly different from that current in the UK, but much of the detailed practice has been surprisingly similar, given differences in political culture and institutions.

A second source of motivation was probably even stronger than the first. For six years I was a civil servant myself. I often lecture to civil service audiences (sometimes on 'management' courses), to NHS administrators, doctors and a variety of other public servants. Within my own university, and many others in which friends and colleagues work, one would need to be singularly inattentive not to notice the spreading rash of management boards, management training, performance indicators, staff counselling and appraisal schemes. My many contacts with persons actually 'doing management' have convinced me that there is much confusion and uncertainty as to its essential character and significance. The rapid expansion of management training has not done much to lessen this unease. In my view this is because − in both the UK and US − 90 per cent of such training remains a discourse in 'how to do it', and most of the people delivering that discourse are ill-equipped, if not also temperamentally unsuited, to delve into the political, philosophical and ethical status of management itself. So this is a book addressed not only to academics and their students, important though that audience is. It is also intended for public officials of all kinds who wish to reflect on the nature of managerialism as well as learn how to manage. If my experience of teaching on management courses is any guide there are many − at all levels − whose appetite for such discussion remains unsatisfied. To this end I have tried to write most of the book simply and with a minimum of academic 'apparatus'. Readers who wish to pursue the 'academic' dimension in greater detail should find they can do so through the extensive references to other scholarly sources.

CJP
Eaglescliffe, January 1990

Preface to Second Edition

The past two and a half years have made the book's subject matter if anything even more salient. British academics have decided that there is something called the 'New Public Management' and the British Prime Minister has declared that raising the quality of public services is to be 'one of the central themes of public life in the 1990s'. I have modified the text to take account of these recent developments, not least by adding a new chapter specifically addressed to the themes of quality, decentralization and the spread of market-like mechanisms.

CJP
Eaglescliffe, September 1992

Acknowledgements

Like most academic authors, I have accumulated intellectual debts so numerous and tangled that I shall never have sufficient time or space to pay most of them off. A few of the larger borrowings do, however, stand out. I am especially grateful to Michael Connolly, Patricia Day, Andrew Dunsire, Stuart Hall, Steve Harrison, Rod Rhodes and Phil Strong. Finally, in this as in most of my other work, I have been massively dependent on the organizing and keyboarding skills — and the consistent good humour — of Mary Dicker, Anne Hunt and Lin Clark.

1
Naming the Parts: the Content of Managerialism

The elements

Managerialism is a set of beliefs and practices, at the core of which burns the seldom-tested assumption that better management will prove an effective solvent for a wide range of economic and social ills. In one way it seems a glaringly obvious, almost tautologous proposition — if things are better organized, they will improve. Surely this *must* be true, in the public services as in business and commerce? From another standpoint, however, 'managerialism' has become a term of abuse. It is hurled at those who, in the eyes of their critics, pretend that problems which really need new policies or additional resources can be solved merely by more effort or efficiency within the structural and budgetary status quo. Then again, from a third perspective, managerialism appears an optimistic, almost a romantic creed. For it suggests that solutions lie within our own hands, that determined, clear-sighted leadership (a common refrain in contemporary managerialist rhetoric) can achieve fundamental changes and can give a new sense of purpose and achievement.

In this first chapter the ingredients of managerialism will be examined, and an attempt will be made to trace its intellectual parentage. Initially this will entail some fairly general and abstract discussion, but this is a necessary precursor to the examination of the concrete cases and circumstances to which the book will soon proceed. The principal territory of the book will be the application of managerialism to the welfare state (particularly the federal/civil service, health care and education) but an understanding of its nature demands some inquiry into other sectors, especially the worlds of big business and the military from which many key management ideas and attitudes have come.

The question 'what is managerialism?' can be pursued on several different levels. One response might be to try to identify a set of specific beliefs and practices which 'are' managerialism. As will be seen, however, such an attempt — though useful — soon runs into limitations. Some of these can only be resolved by moving onto a different level and asking '*how* are these beliefs linked, combined and deployed?' This in turn quickly raises questions of context — the same specific belief may have rather different meanings (and practical consequences) according to the time, place and circumstances in which it is expressed. To take an extreme example, the belief that efficiency should be one of the dominant goals of human activity may be entirely non-controversial among the managers of a canning factory yet evoke powerful resistance when transferred to a discussion of possible euthanasia for those born with severe handicaps. In this first chapter a relatively undifferentiated (though not, I hope, ahistorical) identification of managerialism will be advanced. In later chapters this will be reconsidered, 'unpacked' and separated out into different strands.

At the most general level the specific beliefs routinely found in managerialist analyses are the following:

- The main route to social progress now lies through the achievement of continuing increases in economically defined productivity.
- Such productivity increases will mainly come from the application of ever-more-sophisticated technologies. These include information and organizational technologies as well as the technological 'hardware' for producing material goods. Organizationally, the large, multi-functional corporation or state agency has rapidly emerged as a dominant form.
- The application of these technologies can only be achieved with a labour force 'disciplined in accordance with the productivity ideal' (Alvesson, 1987, p. 158).
- 'Management' is a separate and distinct organizational function and one that plays the crucial role in planning, implementing and measuring the necessary improvements in productivity. 'Business success will depend increasingly on the qualities and professionalism of managers' (Reid, 1988, p. i).

- To perform this crucial role managers must be granted reasonable 'room to manoeuvre' (i.e. the 'right to manage').

Taken together these beliefs envisage a large, sometimes almost apocalyptic role for management. This is clear from some of the most widely cited management texts. For example, Peter Drucker, having asserted that ours is now a 'pluralist society in which every major social task has been entrusted to large organizations' (1974, p. ix) goes on to observe that: 'But it is managers and management that make institutions perform. Performing, responsible management is the alternative to tyranny and our only protection against it .... For management is the organ, the life-giving, acting, dynamic organ of the institution it manages' (p. x).

This hyperbole is matched by another popular management guru, Alfred Chandler, when he writes of management that: 'Rarely in the history of the world has an institution grown to be so important in so short a period of time' (Chandler, 1977, p. 4).

Politicians, too, have construed these matters in a grand manner. Michael Heseltine, the then British Secretary of State for the Environment, said in 1980 that: 'Efficient management is a key to the [national] revival .... And the management ethos must run right through our national life — private and public companies, civil service, nationalized industries, local government, the National Health Service' (Heseltine, 1980).

Academic commentators are scarcely more cautious. Koontz and O'Donnell, authors of a standard textbook, speculate that 'Perhaps there is no more important area of human activity than managing' (Koontz and O'Donnell, 1978, p. 1). They go on to explain that:

While the culture of present day society is characterized by revolutionary improvements in the physical and biological sciences, the social sciences have lagged far behind. Yet, unless we can learn to harness human resources and co-ordinate the activities of people, inefficiency in applying technical discoveries will continue .... Managing is essential in all organized co-operation, as well as at all levels of organization in an enterprise. It is the function not only of the corporation president and the army general but also of the shop supervisor and the company commander. (p. 5)

The elements of managerialism thus far identified are pitched at a high level of generality — indeed, they are so general that they are often taken for granted as truths and therefore not subjected to critical discussion. From them, however, more specific beliefs appear to follow. These cluster around the authority and techniques necessary for the effective discharge of the special functions allocated to managememt. That is, what does the 'right to manage' actually involve? Here there is a considerable and quite specific literature. One very well-known formulation, from Gulick and Urwick's classic papers on the science of administration, is POSDCORB:

- Planning
- Organizing
- Staffing
- Directing
- Co-ordinating
- Reporting
- Budgeting.   (Gulick and Urwick, 1937)

Interestingly POSDCORB was originally coined in a public-sector context — as a memorandum for the US President's Committee on Administrative Management. In the 1970s Koontz and O'Donnell still used a fairly similar list — planning, organizing, staffing, leading and controlling — and claimed that their prescriptions applied as much to government agencies, hospitals and universities as to business organizations (Koontz and O'Donnell, 1978, pp. 1 and 5). More recently still one finds a slightly different approach in Margaret Thatcher's Financial Management Initiative (FMI). Here the improved management of Whitehall departments was held to depend on developing a system in which managers at all levels would have:

a) a clear view of their objectives; and means to assess, and wherever possible measure, outputs or performance in relation to those objectives;
b) well-defined responsibility for making the best use of their resources, including a critical scrutiny of output and value for money; and
c) the information (particularly about costs), the training and the access to expert advice which they need to exercise their responsibilities effectively. (Cmnd 9058, 1983)

In this case the implicit scope of management appears somewhat narrower than in Gulick's POSDCORB. The emphasis is more on control, and less on planning; more on finance and less on establishing formal organizational structures. These differences may have something to do with the particular political context in which a British Conservative government had set its face against 'planning' in favour of the market, and was according the highest political priority to the reduction of public expenditure. Even so, there is a good deal of common ground with the earlier formulation. Management is clearly an activity which is intimately concerned with directing flows of resources so as to achieve defined objectives. These objectives are defined predominantly in the language of economics − 'output' and 'value for money'.

There are many, many other lists of key management tasks which could be cited, but perhaps enough of their flavour has been given for present purposes (for an intricate discussion of the historical variations see Dunsire, 1973). There is one, however, which deserves special mention here, because it provides an early example of a changing mood in the UK civil service. Writing in 1972 Keeling sought to distinguish 'management' − the 'coming thing' in Whitehall as he and others saw it − from 'administration', the traditional way of doing things. For him administration meant: 'The review, in an area of public life, of law, its enforcement and revision; and decision-making on cases in that area submitted to the public service.' Whereas, by contrast, management was: 'The search for the best use of resources in pursuit of objectives subject to change' (Keeling, 1972).

From lists of key tasks or functions may then be derived more prescriptive formulae for how to be a good manager. These have been published beyond number and, although showing some interesting variations, usually include the need to set clear objectives, communicate them throughout the organization, allocate resources to ensure their achievement, control costs, motivate staff, improve efficiency and, especially for senior managers, move strategically and proactively to shape external relationships with customers, suppliers and other organizations. During the 1980s there has also been much discussion of the need for senior managers to mould appropriate 'organizational cultures' (one of the most spectacularly successful such texts was Peters and Waterman, 1982; for applications to, respectively, the federal bureaucracy and the British civil service see Williams, 1986, and Metcalfe and Richards, 1984).

Ideologies

We have proceeded very rapidly from global generalizations about the significance of management in western societies in the late twentieth century to more specific lists of the functions of management and then to relatively detailed prescriptions for optimal management performance. I am about to deem this cluster of beliefs and associated recommendations an 'ideology', but before doing so it is necessary to address some possible confusions about that term. Like 'management', 'ideology' has been used in a variety of ways (Alvesson, 1987, pp. 143–86). In this book it will *not* be used to mean false or highly politically partisan beliefs (as is sometimes the case when authors or speakers wish to contrast 'ideological' views with their own supposedly objective or 'non-political' positions). Nor do I intend the reader to conceive of the managerialist ideology as some tightly defined package of items, each one of which will be clearly and firmly held in the minds of all managers. Ideologies are much looser, messier and more contradictory creatures than that. They may be firmly or weakly adhered to by particular individuals. Some elements may be rejected while the remainder of the 'package' is, however inconsistently, still maintained. Furthermore the elements and the relations between them may change over time: at one point the 'humanistic', consultative or integrative functions of management may be stressed while at another emphasis may be on 'drive', efficiency and wealth creation. In what follows I will try to adhere to the definition offered by Hartley (1983, pp. 26–7):

The essential characteristics of ideology are, first, that it consists of values and beliefs or ideas about the state of the world and what it should be. Second, these cognitive and affective elements form a framework. In other words, ideology is not simply a summation of a set of attitudes, but consists of some kind of relatively systematic structuring (though the structuring may be psychological rather than logical). Third, ideologies concern social groups and social arrangements – in other words, politics in its widest sense of being concerned with the distribution and ordering of resources. Fourth, an ideology is developed and maintained by social groups, and thus is a socially-derived link between the individual and the group .... Fifth, ideology provides a justification for behavior.

It may be worth going through this definition point by point, both in order to unravel its meaning in slightly more concrete terms and to illustrate the ideological character of managerialism.

First, ideology is said to consist of values, ideas and beliefs about the state of the world. That managerialism consists of a set of ideas and beliefs has already been established, but what of *values*? These are not hard to find. The most obvious valuation is of management itself — it is not only important, it is also good. Better management will make institutions perform, provide the key to national revival, 'help to identify and eliminate waste, to concentrate resources where benefits can be seen to be greatest, and give a clearer display of how the money is spent' (Cmnd 9058, p. 3). Also, as Hartley suggests, it indicates how the world *should* be. Evidently, the world should be a place where objectives are clear, where staff are highly motivated to achieve them, where close attention is given to monetary costs, where bureaucracy and red tape are eliminated. If one asks *how* this is to be achieved the managerialist answer is, overwhelmingly, through the introduction of good management practices, which are assumed to be found at the highest pitch and most widely distributed in the private sector. Equally important, these benefits will not be secured through 'politics', an activity which — by contrast — is portrayed as, at best, inefficient and sectional and, at worst, irrelevant and conflictual. As Ronald Reagan suggested when announcing his President's Private Sector Survey on Cost Control (The Grace Commission or PPSSCC): 'The private sector survey will give us an *objective* outsider's view on improving management and reducing federal costs' (House sub-committee on investigations, 1981, p. 94 — my italics).

Second, managerialism, however indefinite at the edges, is a systematically structured set of beliefs, not just a random assemblage of attitudes and superstitions. The belief in the potential of better management is connected to a favourable analysis of the achievements of the corporate sector during the last half century. The suspicions of public administration and politics are justified by the 'bad press' that politicians frequently receive and by the way in which government appears to have grown in size and cost without any obvious evidence of correspondingly large gains in productivity or effectiveness. Much state activity — especially in the welfare sector — is seen as insulated from competition and therefore tending to chronic inefficiency (predicted by the classical economists's model of monopoly behaviour — see, e.g., Minford, 1987). Furthermore there is a sense in which the authority of politicians (in both the USA and UK) has diminished since 1945, while the authority of the senior corporate manager or chief executive has risen — is this not testimony to the superior effectiveness of the methods of the second group?

Hartley's third point is that ideologies concern social groups and social arrangements. This is certainly true of managerialism, which obviously privileges certain groups and, by implication if not explicitly, marginalizes or negatively values others. Managers themselves are the heroes (and there is an important gender issue here because, by media image and by statistical estimate, most of them *are* heroes — white middle-class heroes — and not heroines — see Hennig and Jardim, 1978; Winter and Robert, 1980). The popularity of biographies of corporate heroes (all white males) in the 1980s was one manifestation of this (Harvey-Jones, 1988; Iacocca, 1984; Edwardes, 1984). These paragons are called upon to pronounce not merely on business affairs, but (in one American text) on the press, the school 'crisis', gun control and defence expenditure (Iacocca, 1988). The villains are more various. They include, on occasions, trade unions (with their restrictive work practices), professions (ditto), politicians (who meddle and fudge) and bureaucrats (who slow everything down and are usually inefficient). All these groups may, on occasion, block the path to greater productivity. These may be stereotypes, but stereotypes are indeed common ideological building blocks not least because of their powerful function in encouraging the appropriate popular attitudes.

From the late 1960s in the US, and five years or so later in the UK, the propagation of such 'villain' stereotypes became more intense. By 1981 Herbert Kaufman was able to write of fear of bureaucracy as a 'raging pandemic' in the USA (Kaufman, 1981). In 1984 the chairman of the PPSSCC published a popular book on the federal government with the ('objective'?) title *Burning money: the waste of your tax dollars* (Grace, 1984). Meanwhile, on both sides of the Atlantic many politicians and other public commentators attacked professional educationalists for fostering ill-discipline and anti-business attitudes, and for failing to teach the basic language and mathematical skills (see, e.g., for the USA Bunzel, 1985; and for the UK, Margaret Thatcher's comments as reported in English, 1988). At the same time surveys indicated that the public's confidence in politicians continued to decline, as did its participation rates in general (UK) and presidential (US) elections. Surveys also encouraged the Thatcher government to believe that it would attract popular support for its several pieces of legislation limiting the activities of trade unions. Ministerial references back to the 1978−9 'winter of discontent' (when many public-sector unions took industrial action) were both frequent and scathing. Ronald Reagan, too, was not averse to playing on the public's suspicions of unions, especially those in the public services which had grown so rapidly in membership and confidence from the mid 1960s to the mid 1970s. Most notable, perhaps, was his administration's sustained attack on the air traffic controllers. All this contrasted sharply with the confidence both governments expressed in business leaders and the scope for improving management.

Hartley's fourth contention is that ideologies are developed and maintained by social groups. Again, it is not hard to see these processes at work in the case of managerialism. Perrow (1979) describes how, historically, management ideologies have sought to justify the authority of one group (the managers) over another (the workers). Writing of Chester Barnard's classic text *The functions of the executive* (1938) Perrow argues that: 'Barnard's central concepts, which are so widely used today, combine to legitimize and justify what should forever remain problematic − the value of imperatively co-ordinated systems of human effort' (Perrow, 1979, p. 87).

Thus it is very much in the interests of managers themselves to promote a set of beliefs which highlight the special contribution of management and thereby justify management's special rights and powers. Further, beyond the managers there may be other groups which also stand to benefit: owners, governments, even, occasionally, trade-union officials who, by conceding a certain 'sphere' to management, can then disown any responsibility for certain awkward decisions. These groups may find it convenient to adopt, at least rhetorically, certain elements of managerialism, even if they do not subscribe to the full 'package'. This is not the place to enter upon a full-blown sociological analysis of the gainers and losers, promoters and opponents of different brands of managerialism, but the fact that ideologies do not simply spring into being but are rather the product of active dissemination and reinforcement by particular individuals and organizations will receive more detailed attention in later chapters.

Finally, there is the point that ideology provides a justification for behaviour. This is not as simple as it sounds, for the links between beliefs, attitudes and behaviour are complex. Notoriously, words may be a poor guide to deeds. In the late 1970s John Kotter conducted a study of a group of successful senior US executives. He compared their actual behaviour with the business school model of the calm, logical, strategic-minded professional manager who could successfully apply generic management skills in almost any organization. His conclusion was that: 'While such knowledge is important, much more is involved in the production of effective executive behaviour. A large number of motivational, temperamental, interpersonal, and other experiences, literally starting from birth are important; some degree of specialisation, commitment, and fit with the local environment is important; complex, subtle, and informal behaviours are important' (Kotter, 1982, p. 131).

Yet some divergence between normative models and actual behaviour — in management as in every other walk of life — does not destroy the point that ideology can, and often does, provide the *justification* for some particular course of action. The justification may be pre- or post-hoc, but it is legitimation none the less. Individuals who say 'I did this as a matter of good management practice' are tapping into a wider, socially shared paradigm of approved actions. Like doctors who cite 'customary medical practice' they are trying to clothe themselves in the garb of warranted professional procedure. Like 'clinical freedom' the 'right to manage' is a claim to justified, socially beneficial autonomy. Even when management actions at first sight appear misguided, the actors concerned may seek the shelter of this protected sphere — to cite the textbook tends to be a less compelling defence than worldly success, but it is better than no defence at all.

The development of management thought

It will not have escaped the reader that the discussion thus far has made little reference to the welfare state or the characteristic modes of thought of its policymakers, administrators and service providers. There has been no mention, for example, of social needs, professional standards, deprivation, community or equity. They have not entered the 'story so far' precisely because, historically, they played little or no part in the development of managerialist ideologies (Perrow, 1979). Thus the transfer, during the last decade or two, of managerialism from private-sector corporations to welfare-state services represents the injection of an ideological 'foreign body' into a sector previously characterized by quite different traditions of thought. This confluence of managerialism and (for want of a better term) 'welfarism' forms the subject matter of most of the rest of this book. Before turning to that examination, however, one final preliminary remains to be tackled. While the general contents of managerialism have been set out (above), as yet little sense of its history has been given. This is necessary, however, if the particular timing and character of the managerialist incursion on welfarism is to be properly understood. For while the broad assumptions of managerialism may change only slowly, the more specific content of management thought has developed rather fast. The managerialism of the 1980s and 1990s is therefore not simply a set of broad assumptions about the unique potentials and rights of management. It is also a much more specific set of models of efficient organizational functioning and of techniques through which such smooth functioning may be realized. There is, then, a middle level to the ideology of managerialism, one subject to variety, controversy and sometimes quite rapid change. At this level lie specific theories and models and techniques which in turn are set within the framework of the broader assumptions and attitudes we have already discussed. Thus the whole corpus of ideas is structured 'vertically' as well as 'horizontally'. As one moves from the level of deep assumptions to these middle-range theories the overtly ideological element tends to diminish and ostensibly more 'technical' elements come to the fore. Finally — though only limited attention can be given to this within the present work — there is the most detailed level, that of specific techniques and practices. Here the ideological component is frequently difficult to discern. Particular perform-ance indicators (bed turnover interval in hospitals for example, or staff/student ratios in education) appear by themselves to be relatively neutral, technical artefacts. Yet to appreciate their full significance one has also to take account of the other techniques which accompany them, the model of management within which they are deployed and the broad assumptions about the role of management underlying both. As Child put it in a seminal study twenty years ago:

For the development of management thought, and the awareness of the management role which it reflects, cannot be understood merely through reference to the technical aspects of managing. This is because, in addition to its technical function, management is 'a system of authority through which policy is translated into the execution of tasks; and ... an elite social grouping which acts as an economic resource and maintains the associated system of authority. (Child, 1969, p. 13)

In this final section, therefore, the intention is to offer enough of a potted history to enable the reader to see how management thought has itself developed through several historical phases. Once this has been accomplished chapter 2 can return to con-temporary circumstances, and show how they help explain the 'forced feeding' of managerialism to the public services. Those who wish for a fuller treatment of the history of management and administrative thought are advised to seek it through the more specialist references, particularly Child (1969), Dunsire (1973), Perrow (1979) and Thomas (1978).

Pushing simplification somewhere near to the point where its drawbacks begin to overtake its advantages, one may say that managerial thought grew up hastily in the final decades of the nineteenth century and has since moved through at least six broad phases. (Not too much should be made of these, since, in practice, they frequently ran side by side. The sequence here depicted is a logically neat summary of what was actually a fairly untidy process).

In the first phase theorists struggled to come to terms with the process of industrialization, and the concomitant creation of large workforces concentrated at particular sites of production. How

were these workforces to be selected, controlled, paid and prevented from endangering the increase in production and the
accumulation of capital?

Factory work involves specialization, sub division and fragmentation. Decisions about the general rules and procedures and detailed work specifi-
cations are vested in experts, managers or machinery. The speed and quality
of work cannot remain with the individual workers .... These features
required a new 'rational' work ethic on the part of the hands. (Salaman,
1981, p. 33)

Explicit theorizing on these questions was perhaps most noticeable in the US, which industrialized later and even faster than
Germany or the UK. In the US in the 1870s and 1880s doctrines
of Social Darwinism were widely expounded. Ideas of competition and natural selection suggested that entrepreneurs and
owners need have little regard for the active welfare of their
workers. Nature's 'laws' would in any case ensure the survival of
the fittest, and the sensible employer should therefore go with the
grain of this 'legislation' by retaining the healthiest, strongest
workers and not paying too much attention to the rest (Perrow,
1979, pp. 60–1).

By the beginning of the twentieth century, however, fresh
theories were beginning to suggest that far more initiative lay in
the hands of the owners and managers themselves. In the US the
New Thought Movement emphasized not biology but the power
of positive thinking. It spawned advisory texts with what now
sound preposterously exhortatory titles such as *Your forces and
how to use them* or *Pushing to the front* (Perrow, 1979, pp. 61–2).
The emphasis was on willpower and mental energy – if individuals applied themselves keenly enough then wealth and success
lay within reach (one can detect echoes of this in many popular
expressions of contemporary 'new right' political and economic
thought, for example Michael Heseltine's *Where there's a will*
(1987), or the Conservative Party's 1987 slogan *The resolute
approach*).

Hard on the heels of the New Thought Movement came the
considerably more detailed and practical body of thought most
commonly associated with the name of Frederick Winslow Taylor.
His *Principles and methods of scientific management* (1911) became

enormously influential, and its basic approach remains with us to this day. Though countless social scientists have subsequently criticized or scorned Taylor's techniques:

A successful and durable business of management consulting and an endless series of successful books rest upon the basic principles of the classical management school. These principles have worked and are still working, for they addressed themselves to the very problems of management, problems more pressing than those advanced by social science. (Perrow, 1979, p. 59; see also Merkle, 1980)

Taylor's work was so seminal that it is worth quoting from it at some length:

This paper has been written:
FIRST. To point out through a series of simple illustrations, the great loss which the whole country is suffering through inefficiency in almost all of our daily acts.
SECOND. To try to convince the reader that the remedy for this inefficiency lies in systematic management, rather than in searching for some unusual or extraordinary man.
THIRD. To prove that the best management is a true science, resting upon clearly defined laws, rules and principles, as a foundation. And further to show that the fundamental principles of scientific management are applicable to all kinds of human activities, from our simplest individual acts to the work of our great corporations, which call for the most elaborate cooperation. (Taylor, 1911, pp. 5–7)

Taylor is perhaps best known as a pioneer of time and motion techniques, and for his studies of the detailed movements of workers dealing with particular, well-defined tasks. As the above manifesto clearly shows, however, his ambitions ran far beyond this and it is indeed the broader aspects of his creed which are of the greatest relevance to the present book. Scientific management constituted: 'a clearly-marked complex that ties together patterns of technological innovation with techniques of organization and larger designs for social change, unifying its entire structure with an ideology of science as a form of puritanism' (Merkle, 1980, p. 11).

Two of his claims are of particular importance. First, there is the assertion that management can be a 'true science' (with all the connotations of discovering precise, impersonal laws). Second, a parallel claim is made for universality of application — *all* human activities are subject to the laws thus discovered. Both these claims, but perhaps especially the second one can still be heard today — *anything* can, and should, be managed.

Taylor's ideas had considerable influence on both sides of the Atlantic, and in both private and public sectors. The notion that management could be divided off as a separate and scientific field of study combined very neatly with what was by the 1920s a popular view of public administration in the US. As long ago as 1887 Woodrow Wilson had written what later became an influential paper, *The study of administration*. Here Wilson urged that 'administrative questions are not political questions' (Wilson, 1887). This had been widely interpreted as marking out a distinct sphere of 'administration' in which politics constituted an unwelcome and improper intrusion (Dunsire, 1973, pp. 87—94). Within this sphere, therefore, 'scientific' methods could be applied. Various attempts were made to do just this, especially among the 'progressive' reformers of municipal government (Schliesl, 1977, especially pp. 163—5).

In Britain the impact of Taylorism was less pervasive, but its spirit was nevertheless clearly present in some influential quarters. The Haldane Committee report on the machinery of government espoused the general idea of a set of functional principles by which the optimal pattern of government departments could be determined (Cd 9230, 1918). In 1922 the first issue of *Public Administration*, journal of the newly-founded Institute of Public Administration (now RIPA) carried an article entitled 'Public administration: a science', and editorialized in favour of this stance. Then, as now, it was supposed that, if only management and administration could be established as a scientific discipline, then public officials would be better protected against the irrationalities of 'political interference'.

Taylorism has a special importance for the present analysis because in subsequent chapters it will be suggested that the particular species of managerialism which Reaganite Washington and Thatcherite Whitehall sought to introduce to the public services in the 1980s had a certain 'neo-Taylorian' character. Of course there are major differences. Taylor was concerned to divide 'brain work' (planning) from manual work (doing), whereas recent reforms in the public services have been aimed at a predominantly non-manual workforce. The similarities are, however, intriguing. Taylorism was centrally concerned with 'the processes of determining and fixing effort levels' and can be seen as 'the bureaucratization of the structure of control but *not* the employment relationship' (Littler, 1978, pp. 199 and 185 respectively). It proceeded on the basis that previously unmeasured aspects of the work process could and should be measured, by management, and then used as the basis for controlling and rewarding effort. In the 1880s and 1890s it was Carl Barth's slide rule for calculating machine speeds. This is not so far, in principle, from the recent epidemic of electronically-mediated public-service systems of performance indicators, individual performance review and merit pay. The slide rule has been replaced by the microcomputer. And while this 'bureaucratization of the structure of control' has been proceeding there have also been some signs – though less marked – of the *de*-bureaucratization of employment relationships. The range of public-service jobs which are tenured and permanent has been contracting, while the proportion of short-term or consultancy appointments has increased. Central personnel controls over conditions and pay are being relaxed in favour of greater flexibility for line and local management (Mueller, 1986). In the UK the government has proposed the creation of more lightly-trained cadres of 'nurse helpers' and non-certificated teachers, raising the spectre of de-skilling and the undermining of defended professional territory. These and other 'neo-Taylorian' tendencies will be discussed in more detail in the later chapters.

From Taylorism flowed many attempts to identify and enumerate the correct principles for the design of organizations. This extensive literature, much of it published during the 1920s and 1930s, has become known as 'classical management theory'. Among its exponents was Luther Gulick, best known for the list of chief executive functions (POSDCORB) already referred to. However, scientific management was not without its rivals. From the early 1930s a new perspective was developed, one which has been retrospectively dubbed the 'human relations school'. The key difference from Taylorism was the advancement of a considerably more sophisticated model of the individual worker.

Whereas in early scientific management the worker was treated as an individual unit responding directly to some fairly simple incentives and punishments, the human relations school substituted a model of rather a complex being who responded to a much wider variety of environmental factors, including behavioural norms created and sustained by informal groups of fellow workers. Whilst Taylor had been aware of work group solidarity he seems to have seen it as an obstacle to be overcome rather than as phenomenon which needed to be understood and turned to management advantage. For human relations theorists, however what was required for a smoothly functioning organization was no less than a rational assessment of the whole person, set in a context of the social relations of the workplace (Perrow, 1979, p. 49).

The human relations approach grew from roots in the work of industrial psychologists during the First World War, but the investigations which established it as a major force in management were the 'Hawthorne Studies', carried out between 1926 and 1932. The classic text, *The human problems of an industrial civilisation*, was published by the leading researcher, Elton Mayo, in 1933 (Mayo, 1933). The significance of this work for managerialist ideologies today is that it established the idea that *informal* relations within and without the organization are of considerable importance. It is not only the formal organization chart, distribution of functions and systems of work measurement which are important, but also the feelings, values, informal group norms and family and social backgrounds of workers which help determine organizational performance. 'Man is not merely − in fact is very seldom − motivated by factors pertaining strictly to facts or logic' (Roethlisberger and Dickson, 1969, pp. 54−5). Subsequently this general message has been developed in many and various detailed applications − modern techniques of job enrichment, participative management styles and 'self-actualisation' (Argyris, 1960) are part of the intellectual heritage of the human relations school.

It should be noticed, however, that the genuinely 'humanizing' tendencies of the human relations movement have their limits. Many critics of the approach: 'point to the excessive concern of the authors with consensus and co-operation .... Conflict is given little attention, such instances as are noted being attributed to worker irrationality' (Salaman, 1981, p. 149).

Furthermore:

whereas management like [company] have a definite interest in recognizing more fully that production is social production – i.e. in recognizing that men are not simply commodities but thinking, social beings, with potentially valuable contributions to make, and with the potential to work together more productively – they also have an interest in limiting the development of these human potentials. And this is because, though it would suit workers to act as if there were really socialism inside work, managers themselves have to operate in a world in which market forces reign and impede the development of the very unstinted co-operation they wish to bring about (Nichols, 1980, p. 298)

One might add that, in a contemporary public-sector context, one could substitute, without diminishing the accuracy of Nichols' generalization, the words 'cash limits, performance indicators and staffcuts' for 'market forces'.

The fifth main phase in the development of management thought is even harder to summarize than the first four. One problem here is that the sheer volume of material grew enormously during the three decades after 1945. This was in large part due to the rapid growth of management-related disciplines (social psychology, sociology, organization theory etc.) in universities and business schools. This growth was itself related to the emergence of new dominant organizational forms, especially the large multi-national corporation in the private sector, and to the appearance in the UK, of very large nationalized industries (mainly created by the 1945–51 Labour government) which greatly enlarged the public sector. In the face of this flood of ideas I have decided to term the period up to the mid 1970s the 'decisions and systems' phase. I do this because, alongside continuing work in the scientific management and human relations traditions, two major new foci emerged: first, a concern with the cognitive processes of individual and group decision making in organizational contexts and, second, attempts to understand the macro-features of organizational performance by characterizing them as 'open, socio-technical systems' (Sayles, 1958).

The decision-making focus is most closely associated with the name of Herbert Simon, although it has now diversified into dozens of sub-approaches (Simon, 1947). The 'systems approach' enjoys many well-known advocates, but none quite so pre-eminent. Both perspectives share a concentration on goal-directed activity (Bourn, 1974). They are centrally concerned with the processes of objective setting, the review of alternative courses of action, the weighing and selection of these alternatives, the implementation of choices once made and the feedback (or lack of it) the decision makers receive about the consequences of the strategies which have been implemented. The decision-making approach concentrates more on the detailed cognitive and emotional processes at the individual and small-group levels, whereas the systems approach typically operates at the level of the organization as a whole, its major inputs and outputs, and the nature of the wider environment in which it is set. Neither approach denies the importance of the formal structures and behavioural processes which interested the Taylorists, nor do they ignore the social processes which were highlighted by the human relations school. Rather they incorporate and modify these insights, claiming to provide a more dynamic (action-oriented) synthesis.

For our purposes the nature of these modifications are of particular significance. Instead of searching for a timeless, 'one best way' of structuring any organization the decisions and systems perspective attempts to relate structures to organizational objectives, to the nature of the organizational environment (stable, unstable, highly competitive, oligopolistic etc.) and to the particular productive technologies employed within the organization. Thus, instead of arriving at a set of fixed 'administrative proverbs', as the classical school/Taylorists tended to do, decisions and systems writers were likely to adopt a much more relativistic stance. They say, in effect, 'If your objectives are so-and-so, and the environment you face is like this, and the technology you use is of type x, *then* you should design your organization as follows'. Because of this, one sub-school of the systems approach (which became particularly prominent in academic circles during the 1970s) is known as 'contingency theory', reflecting the idea that the optional internal structure for an organization will be determined by the 'setting' of key environmental contingencies (Clark, 1975; Pugh and Hickson, 1976.)

Nevertheless, some broad features of the classical school are still discernable. The decisions and systems paradigm is usually assumed to be universal in its applicability. All organizations are systems, with inputs, outputs etc. All set goals and then need to shape decision processes to serve those goals. Figure 1.1, or something similar, has appeared in dozens, probably hundreds of publications, some aimed at corporate executives, some at chemical plant managers, some at local government managers, some at hospital administrators and so on.

The second common feature with the classical school is a seeming distaste for any analysis of politics and power struggles. Systems and decisions can, it is usually assumed, be discussed in a detached, rational, scientific manner. Values, of course, have their place, but they enter the analysis preformed, from 'outside'. Once there, they can be slotted into the decision calculus, but − with a few honourable exceptions, including Simon himself − most writers in this genre do not spend much time discussing the origins, formation or substance of the values which provide fuel for the whole decision process. Furthermore, 'systems theorists, whether functionalist or not, have ... failed to provide a theoretically satisfactory framework for the satisfactory analysis of power relations' (Martin, 1977, p. 19). Clearly, therefore, if one regards the institutions of the welfare state as being imbued with a distinctive set of social and political values, values which are crucial to their modes of operation, then the decisions and systems corpus may be limited in its explanatory and diagnostic strengths.

Figure 1.1 Typical systems diagram

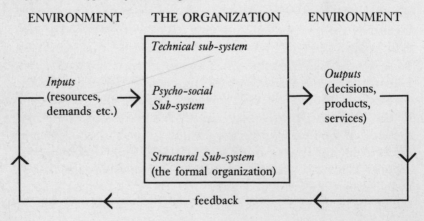

Decisions and systems ideas, like scientific management, extensively penetrated government and the public sector, as well as the world of business and commerce. Like Taylorism, however, it influenced some parts of the public sector more than others. Its presence was probably most noticeable in the training of general administrators, especially in central government/federal departments, and in the general administrative, planning and policy formulation units of state, local and city government. The language of systems — 'feedback', 'inputs', 'environment', 'interface', etc. — was widely learned and used, even where the impact of these concepts went little beyond rhetoric. In some areas, however, the influence of 'decisions and systems' went considerably further. In later chapters reference will be made to the introduction of planning, programming and budgeting systems (PPBS) in the federal government (from the early 1960s) and, later and on a smaller scale, in Whitehall (for brief summaries, see Patten and Pollitt, 1980; and Wildavsky, 1979, pp. 32—4). When British central government was restructured by Edward Heath's incoming government in 1970 the white paper *The reorganisation of central government* was redolent of this brand of thought. Its first aim was:

To improve the quality of policy formulation and decision-taking in government by presenting ministers, collectively in cabinet and individually within their departments, with well-defined options, costed where possible, and relating the choice between options to the contribution they can make to meeting national needs. (Cmnd 4506; for a detailed discussion see Pollitt, 1984, pp. 82—106)

Significantly, however, the parts of the public sector where these 'decisions and systems' approaches appear to have had least practical impact were precisely those public services with which this book is principally concerned. In the UK, for example, both the Department of Health and Social Services (DHSS) and the Department of Education and Science (DES) experimented with PPBS, but in the first instance the systems made little headway at the level of the health authorities, and in the second there was no discernible impact on budgeting and decision making within schools. Elaborate planning systems and data requirements were installed at the top of government but they made little change to the operating agencies and, it soon appeared, were not necessarily regarded as terribly interesting even by the ministers in whose departments they had been installed. In local government, too new management systems were more likely to be found in the departments of the new (post—1972) chief executives than in social services or education. The reasons for this, and the character of the managerialist incursions into these hitherto relatively undisturbed areas during the 1980s, will be explored in subsequent chapters. Suffice it to say here that the limited penetration of the operating arms of the welfare state by decisions and systems ideas seems to have been connected to both limitations in the ideas themselves and resistance (actual or anticipated) from the professional service deliverers. Doctors, teachers and social workers had their own practices, and their own professional cultures. The prospect of 'outsiders' refining *their* goals, streamlining *their* professional decision procedures and inspecting *their* 'feedback' was not an overwhelmingly attractive one.

If, however, specific borrowings could be made from this body of thought, and those borrowings could be kept under the control of the profession concerned, then that would be a different matter. Thus decision theory techniques have begun to be employed to assist doctors with problems in medical diagnosis. In other professions, too, the spread of computer-based 'expert systems' is widely predicted (for a survey of the techniques and their implications, see Dowie and Elstein, 1988).

From the beginning of the 1970s the decisions and systems perspective came under heavy attack. Criticisms centred on 'the incapacity of the dominent systems paradigm to deal with the inherent complexity of social action and the intellectual paralysis which this had produced within the field' (Reed, 1988, p. 36). An alternative 'social action' perspective was advanced which espoused a voluntaristic epistemology, emphasized the importance and legitimacy of differing perceptions of organizational 'realities' and rested 'on a moral philosophy which asserts the primacy of individual ethical choice over the normative imperatives entailed in institutions' (Reed, 1988, p. 37; for an influential early example see Silverman, 1970). Subsequently a more overtly 'political' critique directly attacked these normative imperatives by attempting to show that, far from being 'necessary' or unavoidable, they constituted a central element in a process of systematic domination by particular social groups (Burrell and Morgan, 1979). These methodological and ideological criticisms effectively dethroned the systems and decisions perspective (at least within the academic world) but they largely failed to provide a coherent new orthodoxy. Since the mid 1970s the field of organizational studies has been particularly kaleidoscopic — and therefore extremely hard to characterize in a brief summary such as this. Reed describes the situation as one in which there was a 'melee of competing theoretical perspectives that jockeyed for intellectual "pole position"'. (1988, p. 40).

There has, however, been one special recent trend which merits particular mention. This — my fifth and final key development in management thought — emerged during the 1970s, and became very fashionable in the 1980s. I am going to call it 'culture management', because it borrowed the concept of 'culture' from anthropology and sociology and attempted to make it central to the study of organizations. Just as the human relations school had reacted against the mechanistic model of the individual deployed by the Taylorists, so the culture management advocates believed that most decision-thoretic and systems analyses neglected the importance of symbolism and ritual in organizational life (see, e.g., March and Olsen, 1984; Meyer and Rowan 1977; Pettigrew 1985; Westerlund and Sjostrand, 1979). They aired this view in both academic journals such as *Dragon*, and in more popular formats such as *In search of excellence* (Peters and Waterman, 1982). A comprehensive and widely read text which integrated cultural aspects with other salient issues in management thought was Charles Handy's *Understanding organizations* (1976).

There are almost as many alternative definitions of 'culture' as of 'ideology' (indeed the two concepts are often used in overlapping ways). One useful and influential one was that offered by Donald Schon, who said that culture was the theoretical dimension of an organization which met the need for the 'inhabitants' of the organization to gain 'a view of itself, its role within some large system, the nature of its environment, its own operation and the norms which govern its behaviour' (Schon, 1971). Handy, similarly, refers to 'sets of values and norms and beliefs', and points out, far from there being 'one best culture', cultures may legitimately vary both between and within organizations (Handy, 1976, p. 176).

Peters and Waterman tended to be more prescriptive. They argued that the successful companies they studied were 'value-driven' — that their staffs were motivated by carefully maintained cultures of excellence. The task of shaping the organizational culture was seen as one for senior management. 'Even management's job becomes more fun. Instead of brain games in the sterile ivory tower, it's shaping values and reinforcing through coaching and evangelism in the field — with the worker and in support of the cherished product' (Peters and Waterman, 1982, p. xxv).

Subsequently this cry was taken up in the public-sector context, and writers in the field of public management began to argue that one of the tasks of top public officials was to change the old culture of advice and regulation in favour of a much more responsive and proactive style. Thus Metcalfe and Richards claimed that: 'The core values round which public management cultures should develop include learning, experimentation, adaptability and flexibility. The need for these values arises from the rate of change with which governments will have to cope in future' (Metcalfe and Richards, 1987, p. 85).

One problem with this approach is the generality of its key concepts. It is hard to derive very specific prescriptions for action from something as vague and elusive as 'culture'. Yet despite this vagueness the emphasis on culture also has its sinister side. For in crude or unscrupulous hands it is not hard to see how this line of thinking could be used to suppress dissent and harass staff who did not appear to have 'appropriate attitudes'. In the 'culture' movement one can see how Taylor's original attempt at direct, stick-and-carrot control of the workforce has long since given way to a much more subtle and indirect approach. Managers now work to create the right 'climate', to encourage identification with corporate goals, high motivation, internalization of 'constructive attitudes'. Those who can comply with these blandishments may be granted not simply higher pay but also discretion, status and other privileges (Salaman, 1981, pp. 172—4). Ultimately they may even cease to *see* contradictions or injustices within their employing organizations, to become what in political science terms might be termed the willing victims of the 'third dimension' of managerial power (Lukes, 1974).

Subtle managerial manipulations of organizational cultures may thus become a focus for growing concern. As yet, however, it is not clear that management possesses either the kinds of reliable theories or the kinds of inducements that would allow them to remould a given culture 'to order'. It will become plain during later chapters that such attempts as have been recently mounted in British and American public services have been either crude or contradictory or largely ineffective or some combination of all three. Part of the difficulty lies in the oft-made assumptions that management somehow 'owns' an organization's culture, and that that culture can be spread homogeneously throughout the various vertical and horizontal sub-divisions of the department or agency in question (Lynn Meek, 1988). Such assumptions are contradicted by much empirical work which, by contrast, reveals that large organizations are usually honeycombed with different and contrasting cultures, many of which are deeply embedded in the belief systems of the staff concerned and are unlikely to be substantially altered by short-term management campaigns to promote a new 'image'. In sum, the cultural perspective can be of considerable value as a complement to more instrumental, goal- or decision-oriented approaches. It reminds managers (and academics) of the general importance of the symbolic dimension of organizational life, but it may never be able to furnish a practical 'toolkit' for producing new, 'management-designed' cultures on demand. Even if it could, there would remain a whole set of further questions concerning the nature of the links between belief systems and actual behaviours. Many studies have shown that staff are often involved in actions which do not appear to 'fit' their ostensible values and preferences. The links between culture and action are not straightforward.

Finally, I want to draw attention to a recently-emerging analysis which sets distinct limits to the practical usefulness which managers may hope to derive from *any* general theory of management. Whitley notes that 'the goal of an integrated, coherent and practical "science of managing" seems, if anything, further away than it did in the 1950s' (1988, p. 48). This apparent failure he attributes to the fact that: 'managerial skills differ considerably from other sorts of expertise in their limited standardization across industries, their susceptibility to change, their specificity to situations rather than problems and their diffuse, varied knowledge base' (Whitley, 1989a).

The implications of this for the subject matter of the present book are considerable. To the extent that we find the same, generic model of management being applied across a variety of non-standardized situations and tasks within the public services it will be appropriate to enquire how 'appropriate' or 'realistic' this appears to be to the 'locals' who actually run these services. Note that Whitley is *not* taking the extreme position that there are no common factors; rather he is arguing that these are of limited provenance, and that effective management will require a lot of local and particular knowledge besides:

there are general and political skills which are common to all managerial jobs insofar as these involve working with people, and indeed are probably required for all those jobs where tasks are interdependent. However, where judgement and discretion are involved in complex tasks which are highly context-dependent, skills are much more specific to particular situations and organizational fields. Here industry knowledge and personal networks are often crucial to effective management and skills are often not readily transferable. (Whitley, 1989b)

Again, this raises interesting questions for the present study. When, in 1982, Ronald Reagan invited more than two thousand business men and women into the federal government to improve its management, how relevant were their skills likely to be?

Summary

Even in such a compressed history as this it is plain that management thought has bequeathed to the modern manager a rich and varied armoury of theories, concepts and techniques. Various tensions are visible — for example between the desire for a hard-edged 'science' and the fascination with evidence of idiosyncratic leadership, the strength of informal processes or the existence of exotic organizational symbolry. Yet behind all these variations lies the broader, unifying set of assumptions introduced on pp. 2—3 — assumptions concerning the growing social importance of management and the special roles and responsibilities of managers. There may also be corresponding assumptions, often hidden, to the effect that other forms of social co-ordination and integration, such as political activity, voluntary co-operation or friendship are less efficient and probably of relatively diminishing social significance.

Though most of the major developments in management thought had their origins in the private sector (Taylorism, the Hawthorne experiments, PPBS, culture management) many of them also left their mark in the public sphere. Yet this was not a uniform influence. It was more noticeable in those parts of public sector organizations dominated by general administrative or clerical work, and in 'industrial' type areas such as nationalized industries or local authority direct labour forces. The specialist, professionalized welfare services were among the least affected. But from the mid 1970s, in both the US and the UK, this began to change. By the mid 1980s these same services were at the focus of a major movement for management change. The driving force behind this movement was a generic model of management, that is to say one which minimized the difference between private-sector business management and the running of public services. What is more (it will be argued) the particular species of genericism which was dominant tended to be of a neo-Taylorian character. The next chapter explores the circumstances surrounding this remarkable managerialist incursion.

2

Evolution: the Contexts for Managerialism in the USA and the UK

Introduction

Occasionally managerialism is written or spoken of as though it were a purely ideological phenomenon − at the extreme as some kind of peculiar intellectual enthusiasm on the parts of individuals like Margaret Thatcher and Ronald Reagan and a few like-minded cronies, which they proceeded to impose on their respective countries. A few moments' reflection should indicate that this is a most unlikely hypothesis. Managerialism may be (as is argued here) an ideology, but ideologies are normally firmly rooted in some very concrete socio-economic conditions, to which conditions the ideologies appear to give meaning. Thatcher and Reagan may have been true believers and effective 'bearers', but they were able to popularize 'the message' so successfully because it was already formulated and because the conditions for its widespread dissemination were ripe. In this chapter, therefore I will examine those conditions, first, the economic and demographic background and, subsequently, the political and ideological setting.

The economic and demographic background

The general economic background − a long economic boom until the early 1970s, global economic crisis in the mid 1970s and then slow and partial recovery, punctuated by further, sometimes sharp depressions − is well known. The focus here will therefore be on the more specific trajectories of public-sector spending, and of particular public services within those aggregates.

Table 2.1 shows the overall growth rates for social expenditure

Table 2.1 Social expenditure 1960–1981

Country	Expenditure share (%)		Annual growth rate of real GDP (%)		Annual growth rate of deflated social expenditure (%)	
	1960	1981	1960–1975	1975–1981	1960–1975	1975–1981
UK	13.9	23.7	2.6	1.0	5.9	1.8
USA	10.9	20.8	3.4	3.2	3.0	3.2
Germany	20.5	31.5	3.8	3.0	7.0	2.4
France	13.4**	29.5	5.0	2.8	7.3**	6.2
OECD average*	13.1	25.6	4.6	2.6	8.4	4.8

* Unweighted average.
** Excluding education.
Source: Adapted from OECD, 1985, p. 21, Table 1.

in the USA and the UK, with Germany, France and the OECD 13-country average as comparators. 'Social expenditure' here covers most of the big public services we are concerned with — health care, education, personal social services and income maintenance. It can be seen that, while the share of total public spending represented by social programmes rose impressively over the 21-year period as a whole, the average *rate* of increase in the last six years of the period was in every case markedly less than for the previous 15 years. This reflects the pervasive impact of the world economic crisis following the precipitous oil price increases of 1973. More detailed figures would show that the sharp slowing in the rate of growth of social expenditures began not with Thatcher (1979) and Reagan (1981) but under the preceding Labour and Democrat administrations.

It is also clear that the rates of change varied a good deal from country to country. The UK experienced the slowest economic growth of the four countries throughout the whole period, and likewise its aggregate social expenditures grew slowly. From 1960–75 the US increased its social expenditures more rapidly than the other three countries, though still not quite as fast as the (unweighted) OECD average. However, the '1960' column under 'Expenditure share' shows that this fast growth began from a very low (by OECD standards) base. Even at the end of the whole period the US remained at the bottom of the 'share league' (with the UK by this time also having a fairly low share) and nothing that has happened since 1981 has changed that.

Next it is necessary to examine how the composition of these social expenditure aggregates varied between countries and changed over time (table 2.2). A number of features are immediately obvious. A 'nationalized', tax-based National Health Service gives the UK a high share for health while a corresponding absence of even comprehensive health insurance places the US at the bottom of that particular ranking. Nevertheless the effect of the introduction of the partial systems of Medicare and Medicaid in the late 1960s shows up in the dramatic alteration of the health share in the US between 1960 and 1981. With education the picture is quite different. Here the US, with its long-standing tradition of using extensive state education as a culturally homogenizing device in a 'melting pot', self-improving society, shows the highest share, both in 1960 and in 1981.

Table 2.2 Social expenditure programme shares, 1960–1981

	Education share (%)		Health share (%)		Pension share (%)		Unemployment compensation share (%)	
Country	1960	1981	1960	1981	1960	1981	1960	1981
UK	26.6	24.5	24.5	22.8	29.5	31.2	1.4	5.9
USA	33.0	26.4	11.9	20.2	38.5	35.6	5.5	2.4
Germany	11.7	16.5	15.1	20.6	47.8	39.7	0.5	4.4
France	–	19.3	18.7	22.0	44.0	40.3	1.5	6.4
OECD average	27.3	22.7	19.0	22.7	32.0	33.8	2.6	4.0

Source: Adapted from OECD, 1985, p. 24 table 3.

Some broader features also emerge. In all countries except the UK (which started from a very high base share) the share of social expenditure going into health rose significantly. This was one of the growth areas of the 1960s and 1970s. Similarly, in all countries except the US, the share represented by unemployment compensation grew, reflecting the higher rates of unemployment stemming from the economic upheavals of the mid 1970s. Despite this growth, however, unemployment compensation remained in absolute terms a minnow alongside the whales of pensions, health care and education.

The reasons for expenditure growth (or decline) can be various. Three principal classes of reason are, first, that governments may raise the average real benefit of some programme (e.g. increase pension rates ahead of inflation), second, that the number of 'customers' for a service may increase (the proportion of pensioners in the population may go up) or, third, the qualifying regulations for receipt of a given service may be relaxed (e.g. pensions to start at 60 instead of 65). Only if *none* of these reasons applies may the analyst begin to feel confident that increased expenditure may stem from increased inefficiency. Table 2.3 shows the decomposition of spending growth in the main public-service programmes for both the UK and the US (in brackets).

Like the preceding tables, table 2.3 shows a sea change in the mid 1970s. The average real benefits on all programmes rose in both countries over the period 1960–75. For unemployment compensation, however, real benefits *fell* (again in both countries)

Table 2.3   Decomposition of the growth rates for social programmes in the UK and USA, 1960–1981

Programme	Annual growth rate of real expenditure	Of which		Average real benefit
		Demography	Coverage	
1960–1975				
Education	5.0 (6.1)	0.6 (1.1)	1.1 (0.9)	3.2 (4.0)
Health	3.4 (10.3)	0.4 (1.2)	0.0 (4.1)	3.0 (3.7)
Pensions	5.9 (7.2)	1.6 (2.1)	0.9 (2.9)	2.2 (2.0)
Unemployment compensation	10.3 (8.3)	6.5 (4.9)	−0.8 (1.0)	4.4 (2.2)
Total, above programmes	4.9 (7.3)	1.0 (1.8)	0.7 (2.2)	3.2 (3.1)
1975–1981				
Education	−2.0 (0.4)	−0.4*(−0.2*)	−0.5*(−1.2)*	*−1.1 (1.9)
Health	2.0 (3.8)	0.0 (1.0)	0.0 (0.0)	2.0 (2.8)
Pensions	4.5 (4.4)	1.0 (2.5)	0.8 (0.7)	2.6 (1.1)
Unemployment compensation	14.2 (−9.5)	19.1 (−0.7*)	5.3 (−4.2)*	*−8.9 (−4.9)
Total, above programmes	1.8 (2.0)	0.9 (1.1)	0.3 (0.5)	0.7 (1.3)

* = 1975–80.

Figures in parentheses refer to the US, e.g. an average annual growth rate of 1960–75 education shown as 5.0 (6.1) means UK = 5.0 and USA = 6.1.

Source: Adapted from OECD, 1985, pp. 39–40, tables 6f and 6g.

after 1975, and by large percentages. In the UK there was also a fall in the average real expenditure per head on education, and the real growth of benefits across all programmes was well under 1% (compared to 3.2% over 1960−75). The occasional very high figure in this table draws attention to issues which will be discussed further in the next section. Thus, a rapidly growing demographic component in unemployment expenditure is a prominent feature of the UK experience in both periods, but especially since 1975. In the late 1970s this appears to have been met by substantial expansion of coverage, but a notable reduction in the average real benefit paid. Since 1981 the Conservative governments have reversed the expansion of coverage, repeatedly redefining unemployment and eligibility for associated benefits in an ever-more restrictive way. In the US the most striking changes have perhaps been those associated with health care where, during the late 1960s, the advent of Medicaid and Medicare boosted both the coverage (4.1%) and the average real benefit (3.7%) offered by that programme. Real health benefits continued to rise following 1975, although coverage was not expanded further.

The tables run as far as 1981 and thus depict the circumstances in which managerialist ideas were gathering force. During the 1980s the right-wing governments of both countries have reduced the purchasing power of benefits (e.g., by uncoupling benefit levels from wages or inflation indices) and coverage (by tightening eligibility criteria). Finally it is necessary to relate these expenditure figures to some of the key demographic changes taking place in Britain and America. Briefly, the two decades from 1960 saw similar major changes in the population structures of the two countries, changes which had large implications for the growth (or, less frequently, contraction) of particular public services.

The most obvious change was the growth in the proportion of elderly people. In the UK the percentage of the population that was over 75 grew from 4.2% (1961) to 4.8% (1971) and 5.9% (1981). The forecast for 2001 was 7.4% (*Social Trends*, 1988). In the US there was similar growth, with the over 65s representing 9.2% of the total population in 1960, 9.8% in 1970, 11.2% in 1979 and (forecast) 12.7% in 2000 (Navarro, 1988, p. 228). It is a trend with large implications for two of the biggest social programmes − pensions and health care − (the latter because the average person of 75-plus consumes, on both sides of the Atlantic, more than six times the volume of health care resources consumed by the average middle-aged adult).

A second significant change has been the proportion of young people in the population, a variable with obvious implications for the pressures on the education system (and to some extent the health care system too − young children also consume more health care than middle-aged adults, though not by the same high multiple as the over 75s). Again, both countries exhibit a roughly similar pattern − a 'baby boom' in the 1960s followed by a period in which the proportion of young people in the population began to decline. In the UK under 15s accounted for 23.5% of the population in 1961, 24.0% in 1971 and 20.6% in 1981. The forecast for 2001 was 20.3%. (*Social Trends*, 1988, p. 129) In the US the percentage of under 18s declined from 35.7% in 1960 to 34.0% in 1970 and 28.4% in 1979. The forecast for 2000 was 26.1% (Navarro, 1988, p. 228).

A third social trend with significant implications for social policies has been the increasing numbers of one-parent families. Statistically, one-parent families (overwhelmingly female-headed) are often poor families. Thus the rapidly rising rates of divorce and illegitimacy which were characteristic of both British and American societies from the late 1960s increased demands on income maintenance and social work programmes. In the US, for example, the proportion of the official poor who were members of female-headed, and single-person households rose from 30% in 1959 to 60% in 1979 (Danziger and Weinberg, 1986, p. 11). There is also an ethnic dimension to this problem − during the 1970s alone there was a 41% increase in the number of black children growing up in fatherless families in the US − and in the majority of these cases the mother was never married. However unjust, it is easy to see how some neo-conservative American politicians were able to invoke the stereotype of the black 'welfare mother' to suggest that the taxpayer's money was being spent bolstering a sub-culture of dependency and immorality. In the UK, too, the conventional status 'married' became decreasingly typical of the population over 15, as table 2.4 indicates.

The 'throughput' of divorces rose even more rapidly than table 2.4 perhaps suggests. In 1961 there were 2.1 divorce decrees per

Table 2.4   Marital status of UK population aged 16 and over

| Year | Married | | Divorced | |
	Male %	Female %	Male %	Female %
1971	71.3	65.3	1.1	1.5
1976	69.7	64.1	2.1	2.7
1981	65.9	60.9	3.3	4.1
1986	62.0	57.9	4.8	5.6

For simplification the table excludes two other categories, 'single' and 'widowed'
Thus the category 'divorced' comprises *only* those who have been divorced but
have not at the time remarried.
Source: Adapted from Office of Population Census and Surveys (1988) no. 53,
table 7, p. 50.

Table 2.5   Illegitimate live births per 1,000 live births

Year	Number of illegitimate births per 1,000 births
1961	57
1971	82
1981	125
1987	229

Source: Adapted from Office of Population Census and Surveys (1988) no. 53,
table 8, p. 52.

1000 of the married population. By 1971 the figure had risen to
5.9, by 1981 it was 11.9 and in 1986 it reached 12.9. At the same
time the proportion of live births that were classified as illegitimate
more than quadrupled (table 2.5).

Institutions and ideologies

The summary picture is therefore one in which, until the mid
1980s, the UK remained a chronically low-growth economy with
a correspondingly modest rise in its social expenditures. The
US grew faster and until the early 1970s was still putting in

place basic social programmes (especially in health care) that were already present in the UK and other western European democracies.

In addition to these differences in economic context there are also vast differences in the institutional patterns of the two countries, and in the types of policy which it is politically feasible to launch through these organizational networks. It is commonly said that the UK is a unitary state with a strong executive and the capacity for rapid and effective central policy formulation and implementation. By contrast the usual picture of the US is of an exception to most of the Western European norms. It is a federal state in which overt political power is constitutionally fragmented in such a way as to make it very difficult for the central executive surrounding the president to carry through major national domestic policies without endless modifications and concessions to special-interest groups. The opportunities for challenging pre-sidentially-formulated programmes are legion — in Congress and its highly professionalized lobbies, in the courts, and at state and local level. Potential opponents have to be bought off with special concessions which frequently dilute the original policy almost beyond recognition. As two commentators put it in respect of some of the policies which most interest us: 'only when anti-poverty programmes are disguised within the "protective colora-tion" of a large social agenda can the programmes obtain the political support necessary for passage in any effective form' (Danziger and Weinberg, 1986, p. 14).

The resulting patterns of public services and agencies to sustain them are consequently very different on the two sides of the Atlantic. The UK has developed a heavily 'statist' network, in which senior civil servants have usually enjoyed high status and policies have been implemented in ways which embody high levels of public ownership and direct, state provision of public services (Dunleavy, 1989). The UK 'welfare state' has been by and large, not only financed by government, but also organized and staffed by public officials and state-employed professionals. Providing services has taken precedence to handing over cash. From the 1950s to the 1980s UK public expenditure showed a strong skew in favour of domestic non-transfer spending and against transfers. In the mid 1970s every country in Western

Europe devoted a larger share of its GDP to domestic transfers than did Britain (Dunleavy, 1989). An important part of Margaret Thatcher's radicalism has been her challenge to this long-standing and hitherto largely bi-partisan tradition. Her government privatized a long list of nationalized public utilities and, as we shall see in subsequent chapters, began to undermine the dominant assumption that the state itself should directly provide most public services.

In both the UK and the US the central civil service has borne a large share of political and popular discontent with 'bureaucracy'. The official statistics do not, however, bear out the oft-trumpeted charge of a rapidly-growing central government goliath, at least not in terms of numbers of staff. In the UK the number of non-industrial civil servants grew from 637,000 in 1960 to 698,000 in 1970. When Margaret Thatcher took office in 1979 the total stood at 738,000 − a significant growth, but not of the same proportions as in local authorities (including education) or the NHS. Nevertheless, by 1988 the Conservative government had reduced this number to 590,000, proportionately a far larger cut than was achieved in local authorities or the NHS.

In the US federal civilian employment has actually been declining as a percentage of the labour force since at least the early 1970s. The relevant figues are shown in table 2.6. The real growth has come elsewhere, especially in the two largest public services (education and health care). These services are both expensive, in crude financial terms, and labour intensive. As table 2.7 indicates, they have enjoyed enormous staff expansion since the 1950s.

Despite the growth in staff, however, the development of publicly delivered social programmes has been both patchy and fragile, and in many instances the US government has resorted to paying the private sector to act as provider. 'This postwar private welfare

Table 2.6 Federal civilian employment as a percentage of total employment

1960	1965	1970	1975	1980	1984
3.66	3.64	3.72	3.42	3.33	2.78

Source: Adapted from Guy Peters, 1986, p. 35, table 2.

Table 2.7 Percentage changes in employment in public education and health care services, 1951–1980

Programme	US	UK	Germany
Education	270	161	225
Health	209	167	217

Source: Adapted from Rose, 1984, p. 136, table 5.3.

state now accounts for most consumer spending on health and about one quarter of all welfare spending' (Amenta and Skocpol, 1989). The existence of a myriad of private providers poses enormous administrative problems of monitoring and regulation. Furthermore, even where programmes are run by public authorities, nothing like the centralized uniformity and equity of the UK system has been achieved. For example, since the 1960s the Aid to Families with Dependent Children (AFDC) programme has been one of the main means-tested anti-poverty programmes. Yet, labelled 'welfare', AFDC has very uneven standards of eligibility, coverage and benefits across the states, generally providing the least to the poorest people in the poorest states, and leaving many impoverished men and husband-wife families without any coverage at all (Skocpol, 1988, p. 351). Indeed, some commentators have pictured the US as a 'warfare' rather than a 'welfare' state, a country where military spending is used as the prime means of stimulating growth and averting high levels of unemployment, (Amenta and Skocpol, 1989; Navarro, 1988). Appropriately, perhaps, the military establishment has its own, large, social programmes, including the Veterans' Administration's hospitals and clinics and a system of often generous military pensions.

Two services stand rather apart from this somewhat messy set of American social programmes. Education and pensions are, in different ways, institutionally quite distinctive. Education was an early exception to the traditional American reluctance to countenance comprehensive and directly-provided social programmes (see table 2.2 above). This exceptionalism is usually attributed to the unique cultural and social problems of the US. Early democratization (at least for white males) combined with the spirit of self-improvement and new frontierism to produce widespread belief in giving people 'chances not cheques'. Even more important was the perceived role of the public-school system in integrating the vast numbers of nineteenth— and early-twentieth-century immigrants, coming as they did from very diverse linguistic and cultural backgrounds. For a long time, only a few families sent their children to private schools, and public school teachers still remain the largest single category of US public employees. As in the UK, the education service grew up as an arm of sub-national governments, but, unlike the UK, American education soon developed a high degree of parental involvement and control (through the school board system — there were nearly 15,000 of these in the mid 1980s).

The pension system is a second — if less striking — exception. It is an exception in that it is a relatively uniform, federally-run system which delivers a level of benefits roughly comparable with many of its western European equivalents. Enacted by the 1935 Social Security legislation, old age insurance was the only national system of social insurance (as distinct from non-contributory or means-tested benefits) with which the US entered the 1950s (Amenta and Skocpol, 1989). During the 1960s and 1970s expenditure grew fast, with demographic changes, coverage extensions and improvements in the real value of benefits all contributing (table 2.3 above). In constant 1980 dollars the cost of the pension system rose from $29.2 billion in 1960 to $60.7 billion in 1970 and $104.7 billion in 1980. Unlike means-tested programmes the *rate* of growth of real outlays continued to rise after the economic shocks of the mid 1970s. If one adds the other social insurance programmes (mainly Medicare and unemployment insurance) to pensions the aggregate showed a rise from 3.3% of GNP in 1966 to 7.1% in 1984 (Burtless, 1986, p. 30).

Ideologically these 'social security' programmes, together with education, have come to be regarded much more favourably by the American public than 'welfare' programmes such as AFDC (Heclo, 1986). This is a similar order of preferences (though set within a more suspicious overall stance towards social programmes in general) to that found among the British public. In the UK:

Within the overall pattern of strong (and growing) support for the welfare state, there are substantial variations in support for particular policies and services. Some services seem highly popular, pre-eminently the NHS, pensions and education .... Other services are less well-supported. In particular, the various studies indicate much lower levels of support (one fifth of the sample or less) for increased spending on child benefits, or on benefits for the unemployed, low paid or single parents, or on local authority housing. (Taylor-Gooby, 1985, p. 78)

As this climate of opinion settled in during the 1970s, the re-emerging forces of 'new right', neo-liberal and neo-conservative thought worked hard to emphasize the resonances between their own analyses and popular sentiment. In particular they asserted that many of the major expansions of social programmes which had taken place during the 1960s and 1970s had turned out to be expensive failures. In the US the 'new right' characterized the policy innovations of the Johnson era as ambitious attempts at 'social engineering' which had failed to eradicate poverty, integrate ethnic minorities, raise educational standards or lessen the upward spiral of inner-city crime and decay. In the UK the new right attacked excessive bureaucracy in central and local government and the NHS, and left-wing bias in teaching and social work. In both countries, but particularly in Britain, new right thinkers and politicians poured scorn on those who still adhered to the belief that social problems would be solved by better government planning. More planning, they argued, always produced more bureaucrats, but seldom better results. Planning was a remote, even an undemocratic process which was unresponsive to citizen preferences and which typified the 'nanny-knows best' state. Markets, not government plans, were the answer to the perceived inefficiencies and ineffectiveness of programmes devised by the bureaucrats. What is more, competitive markets would curb 'provider power', the indifference, unresponsiveness or downright arrogance of the clerks, teachers, doctors (etc.) who actually dealt with the public.

During the mid and late 1970s there were plenty of easy targets for this line of argument. 'Provider power' was a reality clearly inscribed in the experience of most public-service users. Too often public servants failed to serve. Nor did planners seem much better. For 15 years or more Britain had tried to govern itself by planning. The Labour government's National Plan of 1965 may not have survived for long, but that had not dimmed the enthusiasm of many for only marginally less synoptic forms of planning. The Public Expenditure Survey (PES or PESC, after its key committee), which had been introduced in 1961, was steadily modified and improved until it became, in the view of two leading American academics, the most sophisticated and thorough such exercise in the world (see Pollitt, 1977, p. 127). By the mid 1970s, however, PESC was in crisis (Wright, 1977). First the Labour government of 1976–9 and then the Conservatives reduced its long-term planning role and substituted an emphasis on short-term control of cash expenditures. There were many other examples. The 1968 Fulton Committee report on the civil service had recommended that each central government department should have a planning unit with a high-status head who would report direct to the minister. Some were set up, though none with the full powers envisaged by Fulton, but by the mid 1970s most of these were disappearing or suffering role redefinition (Macdonald and Fry, 1980). Meanwhile, in local government corporate planning became the officially-approved fashion, (Bains Report, 1972). Many local authorities made genuine efforts to understand and implement corporate ways of working but by the early 1980s it was hard to sustain either political or professional interest in comprehensive planning. Cutback management and 'creative accountancy' became the order of the day for local authorities that were fighting to survive in an increasingly adverse climate of central–local relations (Stoker, 1988). Again, in 1977 the DHSS introduced an ambitious system of ten-year plans for local authority social service departments, but by the end of the decade the system had been virtually abandoned, with little (apart from the plans themselves) to show for it. Finally, from 1974 the NHS adopted elaborate new planning arrangements requiring each health authority to produce both strategic and operational plans. The relevant government white paper identified this system as 'the single most important influence for better resource allocation within the service'. By the early 1980s, however, studies indicated that this vision had only rarely been achieved: 'A lack of planners, techniques or methodologies was not the main problem: a lack of incentives and in some cases considerable opposition to any new approach were far more serious factors' (Lee and Mills, 1982, p. 184).

The US had never embraced 'planning' as enthusiastically as Britain. The more fragmented and participatory character of its political institutions offers a less-favourable context for such attempts. Nevertheless, within these structural limitations, there were certainly a number of notable attempts to enlarge the sphere of planning. Probably the most (in)famous was the introduction of Planning, Programming and Budgeting Systems (PPBS) to the federal government. Originally installed at the Department of Defense in 1961, President Johnson, in 1965, decided to extend its application to the rest of the federal government. He was doing this, he said, so that 'through the tools of modern management the full promise of a finer life can be brought to every American at the lowest possible cost' (Presidential statement, 25 August 1965). In fact PPBS became *the* classic case study of over-ambitious planning (Wildavsky, 1969) and within less than a decade had withered away in most federal agencies.

Moving outside Washington, another notable example of attempted planning occurred in the health-care field. The National Health Planning and Resources Development Act of 1974 (PL 93—641) created state planning agencies (SHPDAs) and intrastate planning councils (HSAs). These bodies were given responsibility for reviewing proposals for new health care facilities and issuing (or witholding) certificates-of-need. The latter were to be related to regional health plans, also developed by the HSAs. Unfortunately these bodies soon ran into a host of problems. Chief among these were their lack of control over the resource-allocation process, their shortage of incentives which could be offered to health care providers to encourage appropriate behaviour and their great difficulties (often manifested in the courts) in defining and assembling a 'representative' membership. By the time Ronald Reagan assumed the presidency there was little to indicate that most SHPDAs and HSAs had had much success in restraining the dynamic towards concentration into high-cost, high-technology suburban, hospital-based medicine. The new Republican regime succeeded in sweeping away this never-more-than-embryonic planning system, (Mueller, 1988).

By the late 1970s, therefore, the new right had plenty of apparent 'failures' to call on as supporting evidence in their arguments for a new approach to the public services. Moreover, the radical right (neo-liberals rather than the neo-conservatives) supported its castigations of the public-sector status quo with extensive academic theorizing (e.g. Institute of Economic Affairs, 1979). Their main theoretical sources were monetarism, (Jackson, 1985), Austrian school economics (Parsons, 1988), public-choice theory and libertarian philosophy (Dunleavy, 1989; King, 1987). Most of the best-known academic exponents of these theories were American (e.g. Buchanan, 1968; Downs, 1967; Friedman, 1980; Niskanen, 1973; though in the UK the most influential figure of all was probably the Austrian, Hayek, 1986). In the hands of its interpreters (including politicians) this body of scholarship and polemic was transformed into an apparently simple (but radical) programme for addressing the major perceived contemporary problems.

The prescriptive dimension of this programme was based on a diagnosis of the governance of western liberal democracies which focused on at least seven key issues. The first was an identification of pluralism (and still more 'corporatism') as likely to lead to state/interest group bargains involving greater public spending than the median individual voter would have supported. Second, the new right developed an extremely unfavourable account of the normal role of public bureaucracies (e.g. Niskanen, 1973). Public officials were seen as being principally concerned with maximizing their own budgets and status. Typically they were in league with those special-interest groups pressing for public subsidies or welfare benefits, and enjoyed the protection of politicians who were anxious to satisfy these ever-more vocal but ultimately unrepresentative organizations. Because of the lack of competition it was also suggested that many public bureaucracies were extremely inefficient and wasteful. Third, the professions came in for special criticism. For the new right their most salient features were their claims to monopolize the provision of particular services. From the standpoint of liberal economics this 'restraint of trade' was bound to produce an undersupply of services which would also be unnecessarily expensive. Thus a public service bureaucracy dominated by a profession or set of professions was a double evil — a budget-maximizing monopolist that was likely to be both unnecessarily costly and deeply inadequate. The reverse side of the visibly rapid growth of government (table 2.1) was (fourth) a

threat to the freedom of the individual and (fifth) a subtle undermining of enterprise and self-reliance, as more and more citizens
were tempted to take the easy way out, and either become tenured,
salaried bureaucrats themselves or accept the over-generous
public handouts which those bureaucrats provided. This problem
of 'dependency' was linked to allegedly socialist notions of equality and uniformity. Most members of the new right (though not
the extreme libertarians) accepted that the government had a
responsibility to provide a minimum standard of welfare, but
(sixth) they did *not* see it as a legitimate function of government to
seek some egalitarian concept of social justice (Hoover and Plant,
1989, pp. 42–52). Such a crusade would both undermine freedoms and result in open-ended public expenditure. Finally, the
overall growth of the public sector, and especially of government
borrowing to finance its programmes, was held to 'crowd out'
private-sector growth (Bacon and Eltis, 1978; Friedman, 1980).
In the USA tax cuts were a high priority for the incoming
Reagan administration, whose intense belief in the economically
burdensome nature of welfare spending was in no way diminished
by the curious lack of empirical evidence to support it (King,
1987, p. 150).

Such an unrelentingly critical analysis could only lead its believers towards policies for cutting the size of the public sector
and increasing the efficiency of what was left. These are precisely
the policies that the new-right-influenced administrations of
Reagan and Thatcher pursued. In the 1979 Conservative manifesto Thatcher wrote that: 'No-one who has lived in this country
during the last five years can fail to be aware of how the balance
of our society has been increasingly tilted in favour of the State at
the expense of individual freedom. This election may be the last
chance we have to reverse that process.'

The manifesto went on to say that, in order to master inflation
and reduce enterprise-discouraging tax levels: 'a gradual reduction
of the government's borrowing requirement is also vital. . . . The
state takes too much of the nation's income; its share must be
steadily reduced. . . . The reduction of waste, bureaucracy and
over-government will yield substantial savings'.

In the US too, 'supply side economics' and the casting of
aspersions on the efficiency and effectiveness of government

became a popular political sport. Jimmy Carter had made criticism of federal waste and inefficiency an important feature of his successful 1976 presidential campaign. This part, at least, of Carter's manifesto was appropriated — and amplified — by Ronald Reagan during his 1980 campaign. The new President was heard to speak of 'tons of bureaucracy' and 'the government goliath'. In 1982 he set up a President's Private Sector Survey on Cost Control (PPSSCC or the 'Grace Commission', after its chairman) which, the President said: 'will give us an objective outsider's view on improving management and reducing federal costs. Special emphasis will be placed on eliminating overlap, red tape and duplication, identifying non-essential administrative activities and increasing management effectiveness' (House Subcommittee on Investigations, Post Office and Civil Service Subcommittee, 1982, p. 94).

The work of the Grace Commission (itself rather goliath-scale) will be the subject of detailed analysis in chapter 4. The points to note at this stage are the assumption that there will be plenty of red tape and non-essential activity to be found, and the further assumption that the 'objective' way to find them is to inject private-sector management expertise. These assumptions were equally prominent in the early 1980s on both sides of the Atlantic, and were derived from the constellation of market-favouring political and economic theories referred to above.

To quote from Reagan and Thatcher is not meant to imply that these two individuals, influential though they were, single-handedly popularized these views in their respective countries. On the contrary, the process seems to have been one in which Reagan, Thatcher and a number of other right-wing politicians saw the opportunity of linking particular trends in public opinion with a *pot pourri* of academic theorizing, drawn fairly selectively from the works of monetarist and Austrian economists, public-choice theorists and others. As one political journalist scathingly put it: 'most of what is currently described as Thatcherism was picked up at various ideological jumble sales over the past 13 years, often more by accident than design. Devastating though it has been for the left, a coherent philosophy it certainly isn't' (Aitken, 1988; for a more measured statement of a similar argument see Jackson, 1985, pp. 11–31 and 36).

In the US too, Reagan was as much a willing passenger on the currents of opinion as a force that drove them. By the time he came to office one experienced commentator was already describing anti-bureaucratic sentiment as 'a raging pandemic' that had gone well beyond the bounds of reasoned criticism (Kaufman, 1981). In the social policy field there was the widespread belief that President Johnson's 'war on poverty' and 'great society' programmes of the 1960s had been expensive failures, and that 'welfare' (and particularly AFDC) encouraged illegitimacy, marital dissolution and economic dependency (Danziger and Weinberg, 1986, p. 6). Even the much more popular public education system was suffering a crisis of confidence: 'One clear message Americans have given to all of the pollsters is that they believe the schools of today are in worse shape than they were five years ago and that the quality of education their children are receiving is poorer than that which they received' (Bunzel, 1985, p. 6).

As Aitken suggests, a *pot pourri* may not be coherent, but it does contain a wide variety of ingredients which, skilfully blended, can be made to appeal to a range of tastes. There were elements in the Thatcher and Reagan packages which, suitably accentuated, proved attractive to groups who were not necessarily in sympathy with some of the more extreme attacks on 'planning' or 'the bureaucracy' or 'permissive education' or 'lefty social workers'. For example, senior managers in big corporations, though they might have reservations about the anti-planning rhetoric (they themselves ran large 'bureaucracies') could sympathize with ideas of reducing public expenditure and introducing more business methods to government. In the UK, for example, a corporate executive with unparalleled experience of working to improve management in Whitehall praised the 'real and substantial strengths' of the civil service but went on to deliver a characteristic new-right anti-pluralist analysis:

'Bureaucracy' in the abstract has no friends at all. But in practice, because 'the State' is in fact a multiplicity of services for particular client groups and because to the degree that each Department is the apex, and representative of its client groups, 'bureaucracy' has many friends.... The fact is that many of the external responses to the scrutiny reports [investigations into particular government activities, supervised by this same corporate executive] showed a strong preference for inefficiency, a disregard of cost and a readiness to distort what had been recommended. (Rayner, 1984, pp. 8–9)

The number of public utterances taking roughly this line are legion. One further example may suffice. The Director General of the Confederation of British Industry, making a major speech in mid 1988, first offered the almost ritual genuflection towards the public services on the grounds that 'The excellence of the people is not in doubt', but quickly moved on to the main theme that 'what is in doubt is the capability of the system to manage'. From here he developed the assertion that 'the scale of value improvement opportunities in the public service is immense' and soon concluded that 'many public services could be better provided at lower costs and greater flexibility by the private sector' (Banham, 1988). To complete the picture, Banham made a general reference to how 'special interests' made 'a fuss' if the *status quo* was challenged, and even suggested that most of the inflationary pressures in the UK economy stemmed from the public sector. Note that all this came *after* nine years of public expenditure and staffing reductions, widening disparities in public- v. private-sector salaries, and extensive moves towards contracting out and privatization.

Even some civil servants, though no doubt offended by the generally anti-civil servant tone of the new political tide, could see advantage in some of its ingredients. For example middle managers might well be attracted by suggestions that they should be granted some of the private-sector manager's freedom to operate more flexible pay, staffing and budgetary systems instead of being rigidly tied by centrally-determined rates and regulations (e.g. Carey, 1984, p. 84; Rayner, 1984, p. 12). Similarly, many health service managers and headteachers have responded positively to proposals that they should have more budgetary autonomy and greater line-management authority over staff. Lack of management control over professional service deliverers was a long-standing problem in many public services, and the new mood might just afford managers opportunities to tighten their grip on the more independent-minded doctors, lecturers, teachers and social workers. As will be seen later in the more detailed examinations of specific measures, a dash of managerialism has not

infrequently sugared the pill of new-right public-service reductions by apparently holding out greater rewards, or authority,
or both, to elite groups within those services.

Summary: the logic of managerialism

As time has gone by, managerialism has become a steadily more
prominent component in the policies adopted by right-wing
governments towards their public services. The logic of this increasing ideological and programmatic salience runs roughly as
follows. The Reagan and Thatcher administrations both came to
power expounding the idea that government had grown too big,
too expensive and too inhibiting of individual enterprise. The
most obvious outcome of this belief would be cuts in government
functions, and some of these have certainly taken place. In particular, nationalized industries and some of the more capital
intensive/less 'face-to-face' public services (such as British
Telecom) have been sold off to the private sector. With fewer
nationalized industries, this strategy is less available to the US
federal government but privatization has nevertheless occurred,
albeit in a wide variety of forms (see Hennig et al., 1988). With
the passage of time, however, the easier privatizations have been
accomplished, or at least announced, and the salience of the core,
labour-intensive public services (education, health care and the
civil service itself) within the remaining state sector has increased.
To privatize these seems full of practical difficulties (though
partial privatization is still being pursued for selected portions).
To cut these services outright also turns out to be difficult because,
despite specific grievances about this or that, the general notion
of properly financed and run public school and health services
remains very popular with the British and American electorates
(Rose, 1984, pp. 209–10; Navarro, 1988, p. 229). The only
remaining political option, therefore, is to improve the *productivity*
of these services, so that their quality can be maintained or even
increased while the total resources devoted to them is held down.
Hence the popularity of management solutions to what were
previously conceived of as political problems. Here, then, is the

link between managerialism and the political difficulties which the major public services pose for right-wing governments.

Managerialism is thus distinct from simply better 'administration':

Managerialism, in contrast to the traditional bureaucratic ideal of 'administration', has developed in the public sector for the same reasons it has emerged in the private sector, namely an increased concern with 'results', 'performance' and 'outcomes'. Hence higher priority is given to the 'management' of people, resources and programmes compared to the 'administration' of activities, procedures and regulations'. (Aucoin, 1988, p. 152)

Managerialism is the 'acceptable face' of new-right thinking concerning the state. It is an ingredient in the *pot pourri* which can attract support beyond the new right itself. For that wider constituency 'better management' sounds sober, neutral, as unopposable as virtue itself. Given the recent history of public-service expansion the productivity logic has a power of its own which stands independently of the political programme of the new right. Yet simultaneously, for new right believers, better management provides a label under which private-sector disciplines can be introduced to the public services, political control can be strengthened, budgets trimmed, professional autonomy reduced, public service unions weakened and a quasi-competitive framework erected to flush out the 'natural' inefficiencies of bureaucracy. Given the diversity of management theories and approaches (chapter 1) the crucial question thus becomes that of *which* strands of managerialism are actually to be adopted and implemented. This can only be established by a detailed examination of what has happened to particular public services, an examination which will occupy the next two chapters.

3

First Steps: the Initial Impact in the UK

Introduction

Chapter 1 introduced a set of mutually related basic assumptions and beliefs which were said to constitute an ideology of managerialism. Management thought was shown to have provided an extensive repertoire of more specific approaches and techniques, but this superstructure of variety was founded on common basic tenets concerning the distinctiveness, importance and scope of the management function.

Chapter 2 discussed the broad political, social and economic environment of the welfare state during the turbulent 1970s. This environment presented two sets of filters to the transformation of management ideas into the specific management practices which is the subject of this chapter. First, it generated structural constraints which excluded certain possibilities on grounds of straightforward infeasibility. Second, in both Britain and the USA the political environment was one which − as the forces of the new right gained ground − increasingly favoured certain notions of management over others.

An example of the first kind of filter would have been the feasibility of governments imposing a full-blown authoritarian Taylorism on, say, health care or education because of the strong structural positions which had been won by the medical and teaching professions. These professions had constitutional, legal and other safeguards which meant that governments simply could not − at least not at first − move in like a Taylorian manager to control, measure and reorganize their work. Evidence for the second kind of filter exists (as we shall see in this and the next chapter) to the extent that the Thatcher and Reagan administrations gave much higher priority, in their treatment of civil service and welfare agencies, to narrowly construed measures of efficiency and economy than to, say, human-relations concepts of job enrichment or self-actualization for public officials. New-right doctrines led many leading politicians in both countries to the view that on the whole public officials had a soft time of it already, and that what they needed was not further 'privileges' but rather to feel the sharpness of private-sector disciplines or the nearest parallels that could be devised.

By the 1980s − in the words of a prominent architect and supporter of the UK Conservative administration's strategy − a point had been reached at which 'good management of resources put into administration must be counted as a higher policy in its own right' (Rayner, 1984, p. 2). As the details of this 'higher policy' are described in the next few pages it may be helpful to focus attention on some of the key issues raised in the two preceding chapters. One issue, as indicated in the earlier discussion of Taylorism, is how far the changes in practice may be seen as attempts to bureaucratize the fixing and re-fixing of effort levels − of what would be accepted (for individuals, units and entire organizations) as 'normal' throughput. A second issue is the extent to which, for all the fine talk about effectiveness and quality of service, the basic dynamic of reform was actually input-minimization which was in turn a response to a perceived overriding need to restrain public expenditure. The third issue concerns the variations between different services and policy sectors. How can these be best explained? Several possible reasons have already been mentioned: the relative defensive strengths of the occupational groups within a given service (especially the professions); the public esteem in which the service was held; the demographic and other trends determining demand for the service and the technical susceptibility of the relevant activities to measurement, routinization and 'de-skilling'. Each of these could modify the impact of attempts to implement neo-Taylorism.

What will *not* be attempted here is any comprehensive listing of significant management reforms. The task would be too large for the confines of the present book, and would in any case be inappropriate for a text whose prime purposes are interpretive and analytical rather than documentary. Instead I shall take three substantial parts of the state apparatus, list the major management changes which affected them from the mid 1970s on, and then offer an interpretation of these changes in the light of the relevant structural and ideological constraints. The three selected services will be the non-industrial civil service, the health service and the education service.

The civil service

The main management changes are set out below.

Selected major management changes in the civil service 1976−1989
1976 Introduction of cash limits over most public expenditure. This meant that it became much more difficult to maintain the planned volume of public-service activities in the face of high rates of inflation.

1979 Conservative government announced (and subsequently achieved) a 14 per cent cut in civil service numbers in the five years up to April 1984.

1979 Margaret Thatcher introduced Sir Derek (later Lord) Rayner to advise on promoting efficiency and eliminating waste. An Efficiency Unit was set up as Rayner's base. A programme of 'Rayner scrutinies' began (see Fry 1988a, pp. 6−7 and Warner, 1984).

1979 Michael Heseltine introduced MINIS (Management Information System for Ministers) to the Department of the Environment (DoE), (see Heseltine, 1987, pp. 16−32; Likierman, 1982). This comprised a systematic annual review of the objectives, achievements and resources used by every main division or 'command' within the department.

1980 (October) Government declined to implement the findings of Civil Service Pay Research Unit. This led to a 21-week civil service strike (March − July 1981) which the government successfully resisted. Ministers disliked the previous 'comparability' approach which they felt left civil service pay − a major item of public expenditure − too insulated from political considerations.

1981 (May) Government appointed Megaw Committee to inquire into civil service pay. Reported in June 1982, recommending a new system which brought civil service pay more closely under ministerial control.

1981 (November) Government abolished the Civil Service Department. Its pay and manpower functions were transferred to the Treasury, which was thus strengthened. The efficiency, recruitment and selection functions went to a new Management and Personnel Office (MPO) within the Cabinet Office.

1982 (May) Government announced Financial Management Initiative (FMI) to cover all departments (see Cmnd 9058, 1983).

1983 Central Policy Review Staff (CPRS or 'think tank') abolished. The conception of a relatively independent strategy unit was not to the Prime Minister's liking.

1983 Further 6 per cent cuts in civil service numbers (beyond the 14 per cent) announced. To be accomplished by 1988, bringing total numbers from 732,000 down to 590,000.

1984 Government banned union membership at the Government Communications Headquarters (GCHQ) claiming that the existence of unions there was detrimental to security. This led to a number of protest stoppages and legal actions, but the government held to its decision.

1984–85 The annual staff appraisal system (long used for most civil servants) was modified so that personal objectives were set for each individual. The achievement (or otherwise) of these was to form a subject for discussion with that individual's superior at the following year's appraisal.

1985 Government commenced experiments with performance-bonuses for grades 3–7 (Under-Secretary to Principal in the old terminology). In 1987 it was extended to grade 2. A formal evaluation after the first year showed that the scheme had not been successful, but the Treasury responded by beginning to develop proposals for 'discretionary pay' at all levels. At the same time, Permanent Secretaries were reported as being unhappy at the suggestion that they should become responsible for making merit awards to senior colleagues (Norton-Taylor, 1985).

1985 The Civil Service College introduced two new courses, the Top Management Programme (for mid-career officials about to move up to grade 3) and the Senior Management Development Programme (for grades 3 and 4).

1986 FMI reviewed and extended, with the intention of further devolving budgetary responsibilities to line managers (Treasury, 1986a).

1986 Government published review of opportunities for competitive tendering and contracting out within (formerly) civil service activities: *Using private enterprise in government* (Treasury, 1986b).

1987 The Treasury concluded negotiations with the Institution of Professional Civil Servants (IPCS: the engineers, scientists and other 'specialists') providing for 'a radical change in civil service pay' (Treasury, 1987, p. 1). This agreement — which evoked strong criticism from some other civil service unions — included the establishment of a common pay spine for a number of grades, with extra merit pay available to about one quarter of the staff concerned.

1987 Management and Personnel Office (MPO) abolished, most of its functions transferred to the Treasury.

1987 The 1987 annual white paper on public expenditure contained 1800 'performance indicators' of departments' work; there had been 1200 in 1986. This represented a major growth in such indicators since the introduction of FMI in 1982, (see Beeton, 1988, pp. 99–101).

1988 (February) The Efficiency Unit published a major report: *Improving management in government: the next steps*. This proposed the establishment of separate 'agencies' for executive work, leaving small core-departments dealing with strategic control and policy-making. It was predicted that within ten years three-quarters of the civil service could have been given agency status. Each agency would be headed by a chief executive responsible for its perform-ance, and would conduct its activities within a 'framework agree-ment' with its parent department (Efficiency Unit, 1988; for commentary see Treasury and Civil Service Committee, 1988; Royal Institute of Public Administration and Arthur Young, 1989).

1989 (January) Some departments begin to publish their own annual volumes of resource and planning information, replacing and expanding on the departmental chapters in the annual public expenditure white paper, (Peat Marwick McLintock, 1989).

Certain themes are clearly visible in this chronology, although that is not to say that the changes since 1979 have necessarily been part of a carefully laid long-term plan. Thematic consistency may result from a stream of largely reactive, ad hoc decision making so long as the decisions are shaped by a reasonably explicit and coherent philosophy. To put it more cynically, in Britain the achievement of a superficially consistent set of de-cisions concerning civil service management requires little more than a strong executive with a consistent set of prejudices.

The main themes which appear to emerge from the above list are the following:

1 A strong emphasis on the tighter control of civil service spending, both at the macro and middle levels (cash limits, cash planning and tighter ministerial control over civil service pay) and at the level of detail (FMI, cuts in civil service numbers, competitive tendering).

2 Under the Conservatives, from the early 1980s, a growing emphasis on decentralizing management responsibilities once financial targets and other performance norms have been (centrally) fixed. Whilst this tendency has not yet gone as far as (1), some evidence for it can be found in the multiplication, under FMI, of 'cost centres', in the favouring

of contracting out, in the government's evident wish to move away from fixed national rates of pay — both by spreading merit pay and by the Treasury's expressed interest in regional pay variations (Fry, 1988a, pp. 12–15) — and in the 1988 Efficiency Unit report's preference for hived-off executive agencies. There is a question mark, however, about how far this strand of policy is actually being implemented. Treasury pressures for central control remain strong (Efficiency Unit, 1988, Annex B; Treasury and Civil Service Committee, 1988, vol. 2, p. 68; Royal Institute of Public Administration and Arthur Young, 1989, pp. 8–9 and 41–43). The retiring Permanent Secretary at the Department of Industry wrote in his departing essay that 'I . . . look forward to a future in which delegation from the centre becomes a reality. There has been much lip-service to this concept, little genuine delegation' (Carey, 1984, p. 84).

3   A management philosophy which, in terms of chapter 1, might be termed 'neo-Taylorian'. The central thrust, endlessly reiterated in official documents, is to set clear targets, to develop performance indicators to measure the achievement of those targets, and to single out, by means of merit awards, promotion or other rewards, those individuals who get 'results'. The strengthening and incentivizing of line management is a constant theme. There is far less (if any) official acknowledgement of the complexities of workplace norms, beliefs and aspirations ('human relations' or 'culture') or of the equally complex issues of cognitive and motivational biases in decision making (decision making approach) and inter-institutional interdependencies (systems perspective). In so far as the 'culture' of the civil service has, from the mid 1980s, become a focus for limited discussion, the official line remains narrow. In official terms what seems to be required is a culture shift of a kind that will facilitate a more thoroughgoing functional/neo-Taylorian management process.

These three themes are, of course, interrelated, and the interrelationship will bear further discussion. The first and second themes may be seen as closely connected with the broader economic circumstances described in the previous chapter. The desire to reduce public expenditure, and to make what expenditure remains go as far as possible (value for money, or 'VFM') is obviously part of a wider policy response to the economic instabilities of the mid 1970s onwards. So also is the appetite for decentralization. Politically this promises at least four, analytically separate, advantages. First, it simply sounds good — encouraging visions of local diversity, flexibility and experiment. Second, decentralization eases the circumvention of 'rigidities' in the management of staff. In neo-Taylorian terms it can facilitate a de-bureaucratization of the employment relationship (Littler, 1978, p. 185). National agreements on wages, working conditions and work procedures may be more easily diluted if the attack on them can be conducted in a dispersed, multi-site and perhaps experimental manner rather than through a direct and usually highly visible attack at the national level. As one senior Conservative minister put it: 'The thrust of my proposals challenges the assumptions that we should have a unified civil service' (Heseltine, 1987, p. 50). Third, when decentralization takes places (as it has done) within the framework of centrally determined cash limits and other formal performance norms much of the responsibility for maintaining services within reduced circumstances or, alternatively, deciding where to impose unpopular cuts, can be loaded onto local management. A buffer is created between those who set the conditions (increasingly, since the mid 1970s, the ever-more powerful Treasury) and those who suffer criticism because they are seen, publicly, to be implementing the cuts (local managers, local and district health authorities etc.). Finally, decentralization may help prepare further candidates for the government's privatization programme (another way of cutting apparent public spending) by breaking institutions down into their component parts and clarifying the direct and overhead costs attributable to each part. As will be seen later in this chapter, these political advantages are by no means confined to operations hitherto conducted within central government departments. They also apply to decentralization attempts in public services such as health and education.

The third theme is likewise interconnected. 'Better management' is usually presented as if it were a politically neutral 'good', a set of more-or-less scientific techniques which, when properly applied, will produce large benefits without distorting normal constitutional and political relationships. This is strongly reminiscent of the way in which the new 'science' of management was supposed, in US public administration theory between the wars, to occupy a separate and complementary sphere to that of political bargaining, horse-trading and coalition-construction. Michael Heseltine was again a barometer of Conservative sentiment: 'When the literacies of the Civil Service and the generalities of their intentions are turned into targets which can be monitored and costed, when information is conveyed in columns instead of screeds, then objectives become clear and progress towards them becomes measurable and far more likely' (Heseltine, 1987, p. 21). Similarly Lord Rayner was unmistakably suspicious of the tendency of civil servants 'to manage affairs by private, and indeed, by unspoken rules' (Rayner, 1984, p. 4).

Unfortunately it seems unlikely that, even with the benefits of modern information technology, this neat division between politicians setting objectives and budgets and civil servants making closely measured efforts to implement them can be realized. The measurement devices of neo-Taylorism — microcomputers — can no more insulate policy from execution than could Taylor's own measurement devices of the 1890s. It is almost the old policy/ administration dichotomy writ new: this time the terminological division is between strategic objective-setting on the one hand and 'management' — the politically neutral business of efficient implementation — on the other. In most of their public statements Conservative ministers have simply ignored the wealth of literature — now nearly three-quarters of a century's worth, on both sides of the Atlantic — warning that such a hygienic dichotomy is unattainable. This literature speaks of a multiplicity of problems — of politicians' unwillingness or inability to define the objectives of policy precisely; of the sometimes positive value of ambiguities (March, 1978; Klein, 1983, chapter 6); of the fact that means of implementation as well as policy ends are value-laden; of politicians' need and appetite for 'interfering' in how policies are carried out and of the ways in which implementation details have to be anticipated during policy formulation while objectives and policy standards frequently have to be adjusted by 'street-level bureaucrats' and others during implementation (see, e.g., Dunsire, 1973, pp. 99–100 and 153–5; Sabatier, 1986). Case study after case study suggests that the policy process is not the rational, sequential affair implied in the FMI white papers or even the 1988 Efficiency Unit report. At the level of rhetoric, at least, the Conservative governments of the 1980s seem trapped in a strenuously simple neo-Taylorian world where politicians deliver clear policies and public officials get on with managing them.

The civil service reforms of the 1980s also appear neo-Taylorian in at least two other major respects. First there is their emphasis on economy and efficiency, to the relative neglect of other values. Second, there is the scantiness of attention they afforded to staff as people to be encouraged and developed rather than as work units to be incentivized and measured.

The Whitehall vocabulary of the 1980s soon incorporated the 'virtuous three Es': economy, efficiency and effectiveness. The 1982 white paper announcing the FMI was titled *Efficiency and effectiveness in the civil service*. In practice, however, the focus seems to have been far more on economy and efficiency than on effectiveness. (I am here following the usual convention by defining *economy* as the minimization of programme inputs, *efficiency* as the ratio between inputs and outputs and *effectiveness* as the degree to which programme *outcomes* match the original programme *objectives*). This is significant because the three Es do not always march together. Greater economy, for example, may obviously damage effectiveness (e.g. when staff are reduced to the point where not all a programme's clients can be dealt with within a reasonable time). It may also handicap efficiency, as when economizing delays the purchase of a computer and thereby prolongs the life of a relatively inefficient manual record-keeping system. Similarly, a determined pursuit of efficiency may eat into effectiveness. This could happen, for example, if increasing class sizes (more students taught per teacher) led to less effective teaching and learning as teachers became increasingly harassed by the sheer number of petty, non-educational incidents they had to deal with. Finally, increased efficiency may militate against economy. In many NHS hospitals the 1980s saw rising surgical efficiency (greater throughput of patients, lower unit costs) but also rising *total* costs, as more and more cases were treated.

The significance of these divergencies becomes apparent in the context of an overview of the various performance indicator systems which departments have introduced in line with the managerialism of the 1980s. For these systems contain many more measures of efficiency than they do of effectiveness (Pollitt, 1986). Similarly, most of the 'Rayner scrutinies' (fast, 90-day investigations of existing policies — see Collins, 1987; Fry, 1988a, pp. 6–7) emphasized efficiency savings rather than root-and-branch reconsiderations of policy effectiveness. It would appear that if civil servants have indeed responded to these new systems and scrutinies, then their energies will have been far more engaged with money and time and staff-saving revisions to internal procedures than with the larger (and admittedly more elusive) questions of the ultimate impacts of programmes on the public, and how far these outcomes are consonant with expressed policy aims. Again, this is in line with the 'time and motion' spirit of Taylorism — a concentration on the immediate, concrete, controllable things which go on within one's own organization and an avoidance of entanglement with wider-value questions of the fairness, equity or social usefulness of the product. It is also consonant with the neo-liberal scepticism concerning concepts of social justice or any collective values beyond the subjective experiences of individuals (King, 1987, pp. 11–12).

Finally, there is the overall emphasis of the Conservatives' management changes on control of staff rather than their development, on measurement rather than encouragement, on money rather than leadership or morale. Exley puts it thus: 'The creation of the Management and Personnel Office and the disappearance of the Civil Service Department, were, in themselves, changes in the organizational structure, which initially shifted the focus at the centre away from the developmental aspects of management to resource control' (Exley, 1987, p. 43). Shortly after this was written even the MPO was swallowed — into the Treasury. Exley goes on:

It is not at all clear that departments are willing to make the investment of time and effort to really change the way in which managers work, and deal with their staff. Changing management style — for that is the challenge — requires a longer term perspective and a lot of effort on the ground. Neither of these requirements fits well with the prevailing political and managerial climate. (Exley, 1987, p. 49)

Exley is far from the only observer to hold this view. Richards describes the same events as follows: 'Somewhat belatedly, it was realized how one-dimensional is the financial management initiative, and the personnel management action programme was devised to fill the gap. Unfortunately, all the clout was behind the initiative, which has tended to absorb most of the attention Departments have for change' (Richards, 1987, p. 39). Finally, Rayner himself drew attention to the need for better recognition of talent at junior levels: 'I cannot claim that this part of my programme had much success' (Rayner, 1984, p. 13).

This relative neglect of staff development may be interpreted as a product of the operation of the two sets of filters identified at the beginning of this chapter. Serious staff development is likely to be an expensive and time-consuming process. Thus in a period when economic constraints are putting great pressures on public spending, and when cuts in civil service numbers mean that fewer staff are struggling to maintain more or less the same set of services, the odds against money and time being found for staff development (other than in financial control skills) become heavy. Add to this the second, ideological filter (why should civil servants, already featherbedded in the view of many on the new right, be yet more mollycoddled?) and it should not be surprising that staff development came low down the government's list of priorities.

This has been a critical summary of management changes in central government. My prime purpose has not been to assess the spectrum of consequences attributable to these changes (for which it is too soon for reliable judgement) but rather to trace out their connections with managerialist thought, and to relate both to the specific contexts in which this ideology became so dominant. I could, for example, have dwelt on the very real impacts the FMI has had on many civil service middle managers in obliging them, often for the first time, to identify the costs of the activities they were responsible for, and to take active steps to control these (Richards, 1987, p. 27). (Taylorism may be narrow but, as Perrow pointed out (chapter 1, p. 14), within those limits it can be a powerful force). Or I could have stressed continuity — that at the time of writing the concept of a unified career service is still just about in place (Fry, 1988a) and that some experienced observers have yet to be convinced that real cultural change is being achieved (Metcalfe and Richards, 1984; Richards, 1987).

Yet these are surely the *unsurprising* elements in the story. Changing the culture and basic working conditions of large and entrenched bureaucracies is well known to be a formidable, long-term task (Metcalfe and Richards, 1987, p. 69). The historical record offers several recent examples of the derailing and absorption of attempts at grand reform. The Fulton reforms of 1968 had largely run out of steam by 1974. The great Heath redesign of central government, announced with a confident flourish in October 1970, was already beginning to be dismantled by the beginning of 1974 (Pollitt, 1984). What is striking about the reforms of the Thatcher years is how, for all their neo-Taylorian crudeness, their momentum has been sustained for a decade. The political clout behind them has not dwindled, and the political vision informing them has, if anything, become more confident and synoptic with the passing of time.

The civil service, however, is only one part of the state apparatus. What of other major state agencies, such as the NHS or the education service? Since 1982 the first of these has been delivered through 14 appointed regional health authorities (RHAs) and 192 district health authorities (DHAs). Primary, secondary and some tertiary education, by contrast, has been delivered by more than 100 democratically elected local education authorities (LEAs) with a special agency – the Inner London Education Authority (ILEA) – for the capital. In both the NHS and education, but especially the NHS, professional groups have established autonomy for themselves to a degree that has no parallel within the civil service. In both health care and education real expenditure, although faltering significantly in 1977–8, was growing again when the Conservatives came to power in 1979. How far, therefore, has managerialism manifested itself in the running of these two very different bastions of 'welfarism'? Has the civil service, perhaps, been a special case?

The National Health Service

The key management changes which have affected the NHS are listed below.

Key management changes in the NHS 1974—1989

1974 Major reorganization of the structure of the NHS, introducing four tiers (DHSS-regions-areas-districts) and the absorption of most local authority health services (under the old Medical Officers of Health) into the NHS.

1976 Publication by the DHSS of *Priorities for health and personal social services* (DHSS, 1976a). This document outlined a scheme for preferential growth in the 'cinderella services' (geriatrics, mental handicap and mental illness) and set quantified guidelines for provision.

1976 Publication and adoption of the Resource Allocation Working Party's (RAWP) report *Sharing resources for health in England* (DHSS, 1976b). RAWP set out a mathematical formula for allocating resources between the 14 RHAs according to need (mainly measured through standardized mortality rates) rather than on historical/incrementalist criteria.

1979 Incoming Conservative government publishes *Patients first: consultative paper on the structure and management of the National Health Service in England and Wales* (DHSS, 1979). Advocates a simplification of structure (abolition of area tier) and the decentralization of as many decisions as possible. 'The closer decisions are taken to the local community and to those who work directly with patients, the more likely it is that patients' needs will be their prime objective.'

1982 Area Health Authorities abolished. RHAs now supervise a larger number of smaller authorities, the DHAs.

1982 Rayner scrutinies (see p. 52) introduced to the NHS.

1983 Introduction of annual ministerial reviews of RHAs, and RHA reviews of DHAs.

1983 Publication of the Griffiths report, *NHS management inquiry* (Griffiths, 1983). Government announced that, in line with the report's recommendations, it would introduce general managers at regional, district and unit levels. These supplanted the previous arrangements (dating from the 1974 reorganization) for 'consensus management' by multi-disciplinary teams of officers. Government also implemented the Griffiths recommendations for a national NHS Management Board (located in the DHSS) and a ministerially-chaired Supervisory Board. Griffiths also advocated the introduction of a system of management budgets, and pilots for these were begun straight away (Pollitt et al., 1988).

1983 DHSS produced the first set of national NHS performance indicators, which enabled RHAs and DHAs to compare their performances on certain measures with national and regional norms (Pollitt, 1985).

1983 Competitive tendering for cleaning, laundry and catering services became mandatory for English and Welsh health authorities (see Ascher, 1987, chapter 6).

1984 Annual DHA reviews of units introduced (extending the 1982 arrangements for RHA and DHA reviews).

1984 DHSS required every DHA to include a cost-improvement programme within its short-term plan. Typically a proportion of these 'improvements' (cost savings) were taken by the RHA and redistributed in favour of priority services. By 1987–8 cost improvements accounted for 1.3 per cent of the national Hospital and Community Health Services (HCHS) budget.

1985 DHSS issued an improved, and more elaborate package of performance indicators.

1986 Introduction of annual performance review of RHAs by the NHS Management Board (these to be additional to the ministerial reviews introduced in 1982).

1987 Individual performance review (IPR) and performance-related pay (PRP) introduced for general managers.

1987 Government published white paper on primary care, including proposals for incentives for good practice for general practitioners (GPs) and support for experiments in peer review.

1988 (January)   After several months of very heavy and critical media attention to resource shortages in various parts of the NHS the Prime Minister announced a review of the service. This was conducted confidentially, by a small group of ministers, and chaired by the Prime Minister herself.

1989 (January)   Publication of the fruits of the review, the white paper *Working for patients* (CMM 555, 1989).

Its main proposals were:

- To allow hospitals to apply to the Secretary of State for self-governing status. If granted it would enable a hospital to set the pay and conditions of their own staff (including medical staff).
- To oblige the remaining hospitals to compete for patients by separating their 'providing' role from the 'purchasing' role of health authorities. Health authorities would let contracts for specific volumes of particular services, and hospitals would make priced bids for these.
- To encourage the larger general practices to hold their own budgets, which would be used to purchase a defined range of services for their patients from hospitals.
- That 'regional, district and family practitioner management bodies will be reduced in size and reformed on business lines, with executive and non-executive directors' (CMM 555, 1989, p. 5).
- To extend arrangements of medical audit so that every district henceforth has a medical audit committee.
- To give the Audit Commission responsibility for undertaking value-for-money audits of health authorities.
- To appoint more consultants and in other ways ensure that patients enjoy reduced waiting times and improved appointments systems.
- To give every consultant a more detailed, locally-negotiated job description than had been customary in the past. Also to modify the criteria for consultants' distinction awards so that

henceforth 'consultants must demonstrate not only their clinical skills but also a commitment to the management and development of the service'. (CMM 555, 1989, p. 44).

● To create two new bodies at the centre, a Policy Board to 'determine the strategy, objectives and finances of the NHS' and a Management Executive to deal with 'all operational matters', including monitoring, within the strategy set by the Policy Board.

Some difference in the periodicity of the changes, as compared with those in Whitehall, is immediately apparent. The mid 1970s, which saw few major management changes (though plenty of policy changes) in Whitehall, were a time of considerable upheaval for the NHS. Equally, there are some obvious parallels — the introduction of Rayner scrutinies (after their initial trials within Whitehall), the elaboration of systems of performance indicators, the announcement of new, more devolved budgetary systems (management budgeting), the insistence on competitive tendering and contracting out and the beginnings, for certain categories of staff, of merit pay (PRP).

Taking the differences first, the NHS was the last of a long line of Britain's major state institutions to undergo fundamental restructuring in the name of better, more comprehensive planning. In a sense the NHS changes of 1974, and the priorities document of 1976, were the last manifestations of the great enthusiasm for planning and institutional redesign which characterized the 1960s and early 1970s, (Pollitt, 1980). After central government (in 1964 and again in 1970), a national plan (1965), social services (Cmnd 3703, 1968) and local government generally (1972) came the NHS. In fact the reorganization had been a long drawn-out affair, involving extensive consultations with NHS groups, a substantial academic input and work by a private-sector management consultancy (McKinsey's). The complicated structures eventually prescribed stand in interesting contrast to the NHS reforms of the 1980s, reflecting the very different reform philosophies of the two periods. In the 1980s the emphasis swung away from elaborate attempts at centrally orchestrated organizational restructuring, away from the enthusiasm for long-range planning reflected in the priorities document, and away from the high concern for an equitable linking of resource inputs to demographic need which characterized the 1976 RAWP report. Instead the 1980s prescription was to avoid time-consuming statutory change, to create new types of post (general managers on short-term contracts), to reinforce their authority (and that of the DHSS) with a battery of new procedures (ministerial reviews, performance reviews, performance indicators, management budgeting, individual performance review) and, eventually, to introduce the competitive incentives of an internal market.

In examining the similarities between civil service and NHS developments it may be useful to look again at the three themes which I attributed to the former. The first of these was a strong emphasis on tighter spending controls and on a search for economies. This has certainly been true of the NHS also. Health authority expenditure has been cash limited (though not the bulk of general practitioner expenditure), 'cost improvement' programmes have been introduced, centrally determined manpower limits were introduced for the first time in 1983, and Rayner scrutinies have searched for cheaper ways of doing things. Even more significant, in financial terms, has been central government's refusal to adjust its annual allocations of funds to the RHAs (who sub-allocate to the DHAs) to take full account of inflation or of NHS national pay awards. By the end of 1987 this persistent underfunding had produced a situation of financial crisis for many DHAs. In 1987—8, for example, the shortfall in purchasing power amounted to 3 per cent, and this effect was, of course, cumulative, (Kings Fund Institute, 1988). There is evidence that, fairly or otherwise, general managers came to be quite widely perceived within the health service as the government's chosen agents in the imposition of cuts (Harrison et al., 1989a; 1990).

The second theme was that of decentralizing management responsibilities, albeit within tight financial targets. Here the picture for the NHS is less clear. Certainly the rhetoric of the 1979 *Patients first* document was strongly in favour of local decision making. Subsequently, however, this aspiration seemed to be submerged by a stream of measures whose actual effects, if not their intention, were demonstrably centralizing. One has to bear in mind that not only did the Treasury wish to control an expenditure programme which, throughout the 1970s had been one of the most rapidly growing, but that in the early 1980s the government came under spirited attack from the Public Accounts Committee and the Parliamentary Select Committee for Social Services because of its alleged failure to monitor NHS perform-ance (Public Accounts Committee, 1981 and 1982; Social Services Committee, 1982). The introduction of ministerial reviews (1982) and performance indicators (a rushed job in 1983) were partly in response to these Parliamentary criticisms (Harrison, 1988b). Other examples of attempts at central control came in the shape of the battles over competitive tendering (where there occurred a long drawn-out struggle between the DHSS and a considerable number of DHAs which were determined to retain their own in-house ancillary services) and the selection of general managers (where the DHSS intervened in a number of local appointments, often to try to improve the chances of non-NHS candidates). Finally there were a number of central initiatives (e.g., a 1986 initiative to reduce hospital waiting lists) which, on top of the various new review procedures, generated very large aggregate data demands by RHAs from DHAs and by the department from RHAs. In 1989 decentralization returned as a major theme in the white paper. Even within that document, however, centre-peri-phery tensions remained apparent. Of the new structures within the Department of Health (DoH) the white paper says that 'The overall effect of these changes will be to introduce for the first time a clear and effective chain of management command running from Districts through Regions to the Chief Executive and from there to the Secretary of State' (CMM 555, 1989, para. 2.6).

The third theme was that of a neo-Taylorian approach to management. Again, there is some evidence for this interpretation, but it is not entirely compelling. At first glance the introduction of performance indicators, IPR and PRP appear to fit well. Further-more, there is the move to limited-term contracts as the basis of employment for senior managers — it is not only merit bonuses which are at stake if a manager fails to live up to his or her agreed performance targets. Also, as in Whitehall, economy and efficiency appear to have taken predominance over effectiveness. Most of the NHS performance indicators are proxies for efficiency, only a few for effectiveness or quality (Pollitt, 1986a). The job for many general managers has been essentially to get more patients through fewer beds at lower unit costs, not to improve the quality of

medicine or to track down those in need who may not be receiving adequate treatment (Harrison et al., 1989a; 1990). Whilst
there has been much talk about quality assurance and 'getting
closer to the consumer' the early evidence is that this has been
mainly concerned with retraining receptionists, and extending
visiting hours, and has in any case taken second place to efficiency
savings and struggles to stay within financial targets (Pollitt, 1987;
and Harrison et al., 1991).

This is, of course, a very broad generalization, and across 192
DHAs there are many specific exceptions to it. There are places
in which training much closer to the 'human relations approach'
than to Taylorism has been provided, and others where the
introduction of general management has, for example, led to far
more attention than ever before being accorded to 'caring for the
carers', to staff career development and to the sharpening of
interpersonal skills. However, fieldwork research with colleagues
in a sample of English DHAs indicates that even these latter
developments are usually set within a highly constraining framework of financial pressures, government demands for information
and tensions with the medical profession, (Harrison et al., 1990).
The sense of a single hierarchy of authority remains far less
marked in the NHS than in most Whitehall departments, but that
does not mean that line management has not tightened its grip
somewhat compared with the past. Consensus management went
out with the implementation of the Griffiths report. The abilities of
the new general managers to change internal organizational structures, to redeploy non-medical staff and to appraise the performances of the next layer of managers beneath them have all
increased.

Yet it would be mistaken to suppose that thematic similarities
between changes in the civil service and the NHS means that
essentially identical processes have been taking place in each. For
there is at least one major difference, and one which has set
noticeable limits on the extent to which managerialist thought and
practices have been able to penetrate the health service. This
difference is the power and autonomy of the medical profession
and, to a markedly lesser extent, of the nurses and other professions supplementary to medicine. The vast majority of doctors
have no management training, are not particularly interested in
management, and are highly sensitive to possible trespasses on

their 'clinical freedom' (which includes freedom to commit substantial expenditures) by either politicians or general managers.
Thus doctors have repeatedly frustrated the government's hopes
that some form of management or clinical budgeting could be
quickly introduced to most health authorities (Pollitt et al., 1988).
Even resource management, the government's third major attempt
to involve consultants in budgeting — and one of the key elements
in CMM 555 — is hitting a variety of problems (Timmins,
1989b). Doctors are not subject to IPR, or PRP or any form of
regular external evaluation. Their contracts have been both vague
and permanent, giving them significant staying power should they
get involved in wrangles with general managers (Maynard, 1986,
p. 334). They can, of course, apply for general manager posts
themselves, but only a small minority found this an attractive idea
(nationally about 6 per cent of the first round of GM appointments
went to doctors). Doctors' representative bodies are thoroughly
entrenched at national level, and even Margaret Thatcher's anti-
corporatist inclinations have not led to her Secretaries of State for
Health noticeably reducing the range or intensity of the consultations they conduct with the British Medical Association, the
Royal Colleges of Medicine and other medical peak associations.
Bolstered by the continuing public popularity of a comprehensive
NHS free at the point of use the medical profession, from whatever mixture of altrusim and self-interest, has largely succeeded
in holding a frontier against the incursions of managerialism
(Harrison, 1988b).

Whether this resistance can continue to be so effective in the
future is hard to say. The provisions of the 1989 white paper add
up to a major increase in management authority, and a significant
redefinition of clinical autonomy. The government proposes to
strengthen line management from the top down; introduce detailed
consultant job descriptions; add a management element to the
criteria for consultants' merit awards; alter GP contracts so that
more of their remuneration is tied to the provision of specific
services at prescribed levels and to the number of patients they
look after; bring in indicative prescribing budgets to help control
drug costs and overprescribing in general practice and accelerate
the resource management initiative (RM) so that 260 acute units
will have RM in place by the end of the 1991—2 financial year.
Of course, there have been occasions in the past when doctors

have absorbed restrictions on their more expansive notions of clinical freedom (Harrison et al., 1989b), and they may do so again. On the other hand at the time of writing the BMA was conducting a major national campaign against the idea of an internal market, and was beginning to prise some detailed concessions from the Secretary of State. The opinion polls indicated that the public sided firmly with the doctors − the white paper reforms were deeply unpopular with the electorate, despite an unprecedentedly expensive and sophisticated public relations exercise by the DoH. Nevertheless, it was hard to see how the Prime Minister's administration could back down from the core proposals in an exercise with which she herself had been so closely associated.

Curiously, the more the government is forced to trim its aspirations for an internal market the more neo-Taylorian the residue of the white paper's proposals will appear. It is the internal market which raises the greatest uncertainties, not least because nothing quite like it has yet been tried anywhere in the world. Competitive behaviour could lead to over-provision of certain services, to providers 'preferring' certain kinds of patient, to maldistributions of facilities in respect of populations and to a variety of other consequences of doubtful desirability (Harrison et al., 1989c; Robinson, 1989). To some extent, therefore, there is a tension between the 'management' and the 'market' elements of the white paper. If the latter are tamed, the former loom larger. Line management will be strengthened, FPCs and health authorities made more managerial, value-for-money auditing extended, better resource use information made available (through RM), pay de-bureaucratized so that it can be partly determined by local managers and so on. To the extent that the internal market is diluted the remaining recipe becomes the familiar one to which the Conservative administration has resorted for public service since coming to power in 1979.

Education

In terms of its accessibility to a central government bent on managerial change most of the education service lies somewhere between the civil service (more accessible) and the NHS (less accessible). However this general judgement has to be qualified in so far as there are also a few respects in which education may be more resistant (less vulnerable?) than the NHS.

One major respect in which the education service is *less* resistant to centrally-driven change than the NHS lies in the degree to which its dominant profession (teaching) is less entrenched, less highly esteemed by the public and more divisively fragmented than is the medical profession. What is more, the threat of withdrawal of labour has much less stark consequences when threatened by school or university teachers than by doctors. Indeed, during 1986–7 the government was able and willing to sit out a long drawn-out series of teacher strikes and works-to-rule, and eventually impose a pay and conditions settlement which contained most of the essentials it had originally sought. Teachers are paid (much) less than doctors, they have had little independent authority to commit resources and their equivalents to 'clinical freedom' (the 'secret garden' of the curriculum plus extensive freedom in classroom practice) have proven quite swiftly vulnerable to determined invasions by central government.

A second political weakness of education, at least since the mid 1970s, has been demographic. Changes in birth and mortality rates produced a situation where the most obvious clients for education (children and young people) were falling in number and proportion just as the demand for health care (which accelerates markedly in the over 65 age group) was rising. Demographic change gave central government one good reason for intervention.

A further reason was supplied, as we saw in chapter 2, by the increasing vigour of the new-right critique of state education from the early 1970s. This critique was able to point to real popular discontent with state schools, to emphasize the lack of parental choice or control and to exploit 'scandals', such as the mismanagement of the William Tyndale school which was confirmed by an inquiry in 1974. In alliance with other political and bureaucratic groups the new right were able to amplify and focus public unease, so much so that it was a Labour government, in 1976, which declared that a 'great debate' was needed to decide how the education service should be reshaped in the future.

One countervailing factor, which might at first sight appear to offer ways of resisting a central government-driven programme of change, was the fact that state education was actually provided through democratically elected local education authorities. Would not the LEAs rally round 'their' professionals and their own ways of working, and do so with a democratic legitimacy which could not, for example, be summoned by the appointed members of a health authority? The answer appears to be that, while this may have happened in some cases, the democratic card was often in practice either unavailable or out-trumped. From the late 1970s many LEAs were, of course, Conservative-controlled, and many (though by no means all) of these approved and supported central government's managerialist proposals. Other LEAs may not have shared the government's philosophy but felt themselves obliged, by central government's tightening grip on local authority finance, to act in a more managerialist fashion themselves, (Cochrane, 1985, p. 49). At national level the local authority associations were seldom able to agree sufficiently to present the DES with a united front, or at least not for long. The most effective form of LEA lobby, the Association of Local Education Authorities, had disappeared in the early 1970s, a casualty of the restructuring of local government. By the beginning of the 1980s the foundations of the old 'partnership' between the DES, and LEAs, the teachers and the churches had crumbled (Price, 1986). From this time also education may have suffered to some extent simply because it *was* a local authority service, and therefore became caught up with the developing general sense of antagonism between, on the one hand, a central government which saw local government as the fount of ideological resistance and financial irresponsibility and, on the other, a set of local authorities increasingly distracted by constant changes in a complex system of financial controls plus − for the most ideologically recalcitrant − Whitehall-imposed reorganizations (the abolition of the metropolitan counties and the Greater London Council).

While the fortunes of the LEAs declined a new star was rising in the educational world. The one state institution which stood out as a glaring exception to the Conservative government's lack of enthusiasm for the public sector was the Manpower Services Commission (MSC). Armed with a soaring budget and a speed and flexibility of response virtually impossible for a Whitehall department, the MSC moved rapidly into education for the 14–19 age group. In the 1984 white paper *Training for jobs* the government envisaged its continued development into a 'national training authority' (Cmnd 9135). By 1987 it was paying for about a quarter of LEA work-related non-advanced further education, and much more besides.

Finally, mention must be made of the universities, independent bodies, each with its royal charter, and, instead of LEA control, subject to steering at arms' length by the DES via the University Grants Committee (UGC). In the mid 1970s the universities certainly seemed unlikely spontaneously to embrace managerialist solutions to their perceived problems. They were at the end of a period of very rapid expansion and looking forward to a phase of consolidation. Most of their academic staff were protected by a form of tenure which, short of legislation, prevented their removal for economic or other managerial reasons. Their public reputation, though somewhat besmirched by the student actions of the late 1960s and early 1970s, was still high. They controlled their own curricula and teaching arrangements. Universities might need better administration, but they did not, in their own minds, need a crash course in 'management'.

Education: key management changes 1975–1988

1975   Assessment of Performance Unit (APU) formed inside the DES. This was in part a response to early expressions of concern about 'standards', especially in reading, writing, maths and science.

1975   DES commenced a major 'rationalization' of teacher training colleges, consequent partly on demographic forecasts predicting a changed demand (quantity, quality and type) for teachers. Many colleges were closed, others absorbed into polytechnics or universities.

1976   DES briefed the Labour Prime Minister (Callaghan) on *School education in England: problems and initiatives* (DES, 1976). This memo proposed a more authoritative and interventionist role for the DES vis-à-vis the LEAs and the teaching profession.

1976 Callaghan made a major speech at Ruskin College, Oxford, declaring that the time was ripe for a 'great debate' over education. He stressed that: 'To the teachers I would say that you must satisfy the parents and industry that what you are doing meets their requirements and the needs of their children' (Callaghan, 1976).

1976 Manpower Services Commission embarked on a major study, *Young people and work*. Eventually resulted in Youth Opportunities Programme (YOP) – see 1978.

1977 DES published *A new partnership for our schools* (the Taylor Report: DES, 1977) recommending a larger role for parents in schools. It suggested that no less than one-quarter of governing bodies should be parents, elected by parents.

1977 DES published green (consultative) paper *Education in schools: a consultative document* (Cmnd 6869). It stated that: 'It is an essential facet of their [LEAs'] accountability for educational standards that they must be able to identify schools which consistently perform poorly, so that appropriate remedial action can be taken' (Cmnd 6869, 1977, p. 17).

1978 YOP introduced by the MSC, accompanied by the promise that all unemployed school leavers would be offered places under the scheme by the Easter following their leaving school. Two hundred thousand young people took up places in the first year.

1978 One manifestation of the increasingly prominent and public role of HM Inspectorate of Schools was the publication of a major analysis, *Primary education in England* (DES, 1978).

1979 Another major HMI report: *Aspects of secondary education in England* (DES, 1979).

1979 The incoming Conservative administration issued a white paper on public expenditure which cut the education programme as a whole by 5 per cent.

1980 A new education act gave statutory backing to parents' right to choose schools, and gave the minister power to require LEAs to publish their examination results and other basic information concerning the schools within their jurisdiction.

1981 Introduction of block grant system for central government finance of local authorities. Soon this led to local authorities being given spending targets which were based on previous spending patterns rather than local spending needs.

1981 University Grants Committee issued grant letters to universities implementing a selective cuts policy which was expected to reduce grant overall by 11 to 15 per cent between 1979–80 and 1983–4. Student numbers were expected to come down by about 5 per cent over the same period. The selectivity meant that some institutions were particularly hard hit, most notoriously the University of Salford, which faced a reduction of 44 per cent in its recurrent grant.

1981 The government issued a white paper, *A new training initiative*, which announced the introduction of an MSC-run Youth Training Scheme (YTS). YTS was to make available to unemployed school leavers one year's training, leading to a certificate. This represented a major MSC incursion into further education.

1982 The Prime Minister announced a Technical and Vocational Educational Initiative (TVEI) which would provide 4-year full-time courses of a technical and vocational character for the 14–18 age group. A number of pilot projects were to be financed and organized by the MSC, although provided through LEAs. Sixty-six LEAs submitted proposals and 14 were chosen.

1982 The National Advisory Body (NAB) was set up to oversee local authority higher education (the polytechnics and colleges). Its jurisdiction was extended in 1985 to include the voluntary colleges. NAB contained LEA representatives, but was under direct DES control. Previously the DES had resisted suggestions for a central co-ordinating body for polytechnics.

1983 YTS introduced — more than 400,000 places offered in the first round.

1983 Government published white paper *Teaching quality* (Cmnd 8836). Referred to the need for formal assessment of teacher performance and gave top training priority to teaching headteachers management skills.

1984 TVEI extended. Sixty-eight further LEAs submitted schemes.

1984 Government published *Training for jobs* (Cmnd 9135). This endorsed YTS and TVEI and provided increased funding for the MSC. It envisaged the latter in the role of a 'national training authority'.

1985 Publication of the *Report of the Steering Committee for Efficiency Studies in Universities* (the 'Jarratt report': Jarratt, 1985). It recommended a general tightening up of the internal management of universities, including an enhanced role for university councils (but not senates), the creation or strengthening of planning and resources committees, the introduction of systems of performance indicators and a variety of new formal controls, especially in relation to finance.

1985 The UGC issued guidelines in respect of its new exercise in 'research selectivity'. In this exercise it attempted to rank university departments by their excellence in research, and then allocated funds accordingly. It did not, however, reveal all its criteria, and the exercise provoked a storm of detailed criticism (see, e.g., Gillett, 1987).

1985 Government published the green paper *The development of higher education into the 1990s* (Cmnd 9524).

1985 Government published white paper *Better schools* (Cmnd 9469).

1986 Audit Commission issued report *Towards better management of secondary education* (Audit Commission, 1986). This recommended a tighter, accountancy-based approach to school budgeting.

1986   Committee of Vice Chancellors and Principals (CVCP) responded to the Jarratt report, outlining principles for the construction of a system of performance indicators. The 'key issues', they said, were 'value for money and accountability', (see Cave et al., 1988).

1986   Government announced that it intended to set up a series of inner-city technology colleges, outside LEA control, which would be financed by business and industry and which would act as models of technological secondary education.

1987   As part of salary agreement between the Association of University Teachers (AUT) and the CVCP commitment was given to the introduction of a staff-appraisal and career-development scheme.

1987   DES issued *Financial delegation to schools: consultation paper* (DES, 1987). This prefaced the introduction, from the autumn of 1989, of Local Management in Schools (LMS). Each LEA had to produce, for approval by the DES, a formula for financial delegation (Levacic, 1988).

1988   Education Reform Act. A long and comprehensive measure with provisions affecting all sectors of education. These included:

1   the introduction of a national curriculum for schools, with standard tests at ages 7, 11 and 14;
2   provisions allowing schools to opt out of LEA control if parents so vote;
3   the dissolution of the Inner London Education Authority and handing back of the education service to the London boroughs;
4   a requirement for LEAs to introduce schemes delegating budgets to the governing bodies of their schools (LMS − see 1987 above);

5 creation of a Polytechnic and Colleges Funding Council (PCFC) to oversee the finances of polytechnics, colleges and opting-out schools;
6 the creation of a University Funding Council (UFC) to replace the UGC — this new council to have a majority of business members and the power to attach such terms and conditions as it thinks fit to its funds.
7 the weakening of tenure for university academics.

How does this accelerating programme of change compare with the developments already discussed with respect to the civil service and the NHS? Certainly the same financial theme is again apparent: cuts in the overall education programme, cuts in recurrent funding for the universities, the CVCP's emphasis on value for money, the declared need for both universities and schools to be more active and 'accountancy-conscious' in their internal management (e.g. Jarratt, 1985; Audit Commission, 1986; DES, 1987). Along with this goes a policy of reiterated encouragement to educational institutions to seek more of their money from external sources, especially business and industry. Sponsored professorial chairs have proliferated across our universities, schools have been exhorted to approach local firms, the government itself has attempted to show the way by persuading firms to sponsor City Technology Colleges in inner-city areas. Financial dependence is evidently viewed, no doubt correctly, as another means of inducing the responsiveness to business needs which the government is keen to encourage.

The second theme — that of decentralization — is, as with the NHS and the civil service, present only in a somewhat attenuated form. Certainly there has been a good deal of rhetoric about giving control back to the parents, and about promoting responsiveness to the needs of industry. And there have been some measures to give these sentiments concrete form — on the issue of parental choice of schools, for example, or through the provisions in the 1988 Education Reform Act for financial delegation to schools (LMS) and for individual institutions to opt out of LEA control. On balance, however, the record of the last ten years looks more like one of extensive centralization. It is not so much decentralization which has occurred as a weakening of one of the members of the previous partnership: the LEA (Ranson and Tomlinson, 1986; Walsh, 1988). The imposition of a national curriculum; the massive expansion of the MSC; the insistence on formal staff appraisal in both schools and universities; the creation of the NAB and then the PCFC; the substitution of the UFC for the UGC; the increasing visibility of HM Inspectorate; the new selectivity in university research; the requirement on universities to implement the Jarratt proposals — these are not the actions of a government which is content to see a thousand flowers bloom.

The third civil service theme was that of neo-Taylorian management. Again, as with the NHS, this description is not a perfect fit. And again, the principal reason for this more diluted picture is not any tender-heartedness on the part of central government but rather the resistance of the professional service deliverers and their ability to articulate alternative schemes of a less hierarchical or authoritarian character. For example, the Association of University Teachers described its negotiations on appraisal as follows:

it proved more difficult to achieve agreement with the Vice Chancellors about staff appraisal than promotion procedures. They saw appraisal as an additional tool for managing the institution and wanted to associate it with a system of rewards and punishments. We wanted a scheme which focussed on supporting the professional development of individual members of staff. Given such fundamental differences in philosophy, the agreed advice is notable for its silence in one or two areas. (Cottrell, 1988, p. 6)

As with appraisal, so with performance indicators. The sets of PIs developed for British universities by the CVCP and the UGC are heavily financial in emphasis and relate to effectiveness hardly at all. Despite the availability of US examples where PIs have been closely linked to educational achievement British universities have settled for a narrow agenda of economy and efficiency (Pollitt, 1990a).

Similarly educational associations have had to fight hard to modify the government's somewhat mechanistic proposals for standardized testing of all school children at the ages of 7, 11 and 14. Some compromises have been achieved, but neo-Taylorian views still lurk close to the surface. 'We need to lay down what it is children are expected to be taught in school' said the Prime

Minister in 1987, 'but, more than that, we need to know whether they are learning it.' The 'set-clear-uniform' objectives-and-measure-the-achievement-of-them-approach, for all its difficulties in such a reflexive and exploratory process as education, remained the one with which ministers seemed most comfortable.

Overview

One cannot but be struck by the determination the Conservative governments of the 1980s have brought to the task of modernizing the public services. In some cases, such as education, the ideological and institutional directions had already been set by the Labour administration of 1976−9, but even there the Conservatives have driven much further and dealt more abruptly with most of the major public-service representative and professional groupings than it is easy to imagine a Labour government doing. Elsewhere their policies have represented not an extension but a sharp change from previous developments. Equally impressive has been the way in which the momentum, and ideological coherence of the various reforms has been maintained or even increased as the 1980s wore on. In the civil service, for example, crude early cuts and quite narrow 'Rayner scrutinies' were succeeded by the more comprehensive FMI and now the very unity of the civil service and its departmental structure are the targets for further changes. In education the role of central government has been significantly enlarged, a vastly expanded MSC has been used to circumnavigate stubborn LEAs and now both curricula and the basis and control of educational finance are undergoing rapid transformation at central government's behest. With the NHS it took a decade before the government felt strong − or frustrated − enough to extend market principles to the core clinical services, but once they committed themselves they did so with panache. The scope and speed of the programme envisaged in the 1989 white paper was without precedent.

None of this is to say that central government has been able to force through its programmes without significant, and sometimes successful resistance, or without allies within the public services themselves. Doctors have thus far managed to resist significant controls on their workloads, and have been extremely wary of both performance indicators and new budgetary systems. At the time of writing their representative associations are locked in a major campaign against most of the changes proposed in *Working for patients* (Timmins, 1989a). They will not be easy to convert to managerialist ways of thought. Universities and their allies in the House of Lords just managed to insert a formal statement of academic freedom in the 1988 Education Act. In schools and universities the cruder forms of staff appraisal have been headed off (at least for the time being) in favour of more developmentally-oriented approaches which recognize the limited extent to which individual teachers can be held responsible for, say, the exam performance of their students. More often, however, the government has had its way.

Well aware that it is engaged in a series of contests, the government has sought to divide its opponents. This has been most obvious on the trade-union front, where public-sector unions which have been 'responsible' (the Royal College of Nursing, the Association of Professional Teachers) have been praised or privileged, the others repeatedly branded as 'irresponsible'. There have also been signs of attempts to dilute the concept of a unified, career-oriented professionalism. More and more academic, medical and nursing work has been performed by short-term contract staff. At the time of writing government proposals for new categories of 'nurse helper' and 'licensed teachers' are under discussion (Gow, 1988). Equally important, however, have been the constituencies to which a more managerial approach is likely to bring enhanced career prospects and power. NHS administrators were among the groups least critical of the Griffiths report – and they duly carried off a high percentage of the highly-paid general manager posts (Harrison, 1988a). Some headteachers and heads of polytechnic and university departments may be far from averse to the prospect of having budgets of their own and the ability regularly to appraise their staff and award or withhold merit pay (see, e.g. Levacic, 1988, p. 54). Senior civil servants may be much less interested in maximizing the size of their departmental budget, as orthodox new-right theory predicts, than in increasing their own status by associating themselves with fashionable policies and increasing their control over other bodies they have to deal with (something quite different from just having a bigger budget — see Dunleavy, 1985 and 1986). Sitting on the NHS Management Board, running the FMI, building the DES into a much more forceful actor in the education world — perhaps even going off to work for the MSC — all these are likely to have offered such bureaucratic satisfactions. Yet despite the importance of these supports for the government's policies it remains the case that the main motive power has come from the Conservative party itself. Without that sustained political clout the public services would not be where they are now. Overwhelmingly, the developments surveyed in this chapter constitute things which have been done *to* them, against their initial resistance.

Furthermore the broad outline of what has been done has exhibited a striking uniformity. In each of the three services examined in this chapter the litany of managerialism has included:

- Regime of tight cash limits and cash planning.
- Staff cuts.
- The introduction of a system of performance indicators which stress economy and efficiency.
- The introduction of individual staff appraisal on a more formal and extensive basis than had existed before.
- The introduction of merit pay schemes, linked to appraisal.
- Proposals for more devolved budgetary systems, giving greater budgetary responsibility to 'line managers'.
- Proposals for more extensive management training.
- The introduction of new planning systems which emphasize the achievement of concrete, short-term targets.
- Considerable rhetorical emphasis on responsiveness to the consumer, although only in schools (and there to only a very limited extent) has the individual consumer been given a significant direct presence in the decision-making process. More frequently the consumer is envisaged as a collectivity ('business', 'industry', 'employers'). Alternatively consumers are represented *de facto* by central government (e.g. in the shape of the MSC purchasing courses from LEAs), or by professional providers (such as the GP in the proposed NHS internal market — see Harrison et al., 1989c, pp. 13–15).

Most of the items on this agenda also figured in the government's treatment of other public services. In the personal social services performance indicators have been introduced and the role of the central inspectorate enhanced. In the police force resource management techniques have been stressed and performance indicators sought. Performance indicators have also been introduced in social security, the prison service, the careers service, local authority planning departments (how quickly are planning applications processed?) and the administration of the courts. Devolved budgetary systems are also planned for many of these services.

What have been the results of all these changes? This is hard to discern. Not only is it still 'early days', but the struggles over the reforms themselves have extended to the manipulation and interpretation of such evidence as has emerged. What follows is therefore highly tentative.

First, there has obviously been a shift from public- to private-sector provision. In many public services ancillary activities have been or are about to be put out to private contractors. Furthermore, private competition in core activities has also grown. Private schools are booming, private hospitals and clinics and nursing homes are multiplying. The NHS is being urged to regard the private sector as a 'partner' in a much more extensive way than was usual in the past. Universities, health authorities and government departments routinely use private-sector auditors, accountants and management consultants instead of conducting internal analyses — all this on a scale which would have been thought remarkable even at the end of the 1970s.

Second, the emphasis on knowing what things cost has undoubtedly begun to bear fruit (Efficiency Unit, 1988, Annex B; Harrison et al., 1990). Evidence of greater 'cost consciousness' in the public services is widespread.

Third, savings have been made, and though some of the long lists of them proudly displayed in official documents may reflect quality or service reductions, some appear to be genuine efficiency improvements. It would be surprising, given the enormous effort invested in the search for efficiencies, if some new ones had not been found!

Fourth, managerialism has made a major impact at the level of rhetoric and vocabulary. Public officials now at least feel obliged to *talk* in terms of 'targets', 'action plans', 'cost improvements', 'income-generation opportunities' and so on, even if their affinity for such terminology is sometimes only superficial and opportunistic. The vocabulary in play, however, is a limited one. I would describe it as predominantly neo-Taylorian, with — since the mid 1980s — contrasting flashes of 'culture management'. Little reference is made to the cognitive and motivational processes which have engaged decision theorists, or to the synoptic visions of the systems approach. 'Human relations' are typically reduced to a few vague references to 'leadership' and 'initiative'. Everywhere the hierarchy of 'line management' is said to need strengthening — presumably against the forces of organizational pluralism and professional autonomy.

Whether this amounts to a fundamental shift in organizational culture is, however, doubtful. There is some evidence to indicate that the thrusting talk of decentralized management and of getting closer to the consumer has not penetrated very far down the hierarchies of our government departments and public services. In our study of the NHS we found such sentiments far more often on the lips of senior managers than ward sisters or rank-and-file consultants (Harrison et al., 1989a; 1990). Many of the latter, three or four years after the arrival of general managers, still displayed extremely vague notions of what was supposed to be happening. Metcalfe and Richards (1984) found the 'disbelief system' alive and well in Whitehall, and a later study found the core values of even senior civil servants little changed (Exley, 1987).

This point leads on to questions of morale and motivation. The advocates of slimmed-down, tightly-managed public services may not, as yet, have succeeded in changing cultures, but they have certainly dismayed and confused many of the existing staff. As one Chief Education Offficer put it in respect of schools:

It is hard to imagine how unloved teachers feel. Their two-year 'action' has been a kind of guerilla campaign which has progressively lost them the sympathy of the public .... The public has not appreciated how teachers have been bombarded with initiatives and, until very recently and save in a few places, have not been given the time essential for successful implementation of change. (Brighouse, 1987, pp. 269–70; see also Waterhouse, 1989a)

Similarly a 1988 official study of social security offices found staff morale at rock bottom. Parallel tales could be told of NHS nursing staff, of many university teachers and of over-burdened social and community workers, trying simultaneously to wrestle with the media's latest moral panic (child abuse, domestic violence) while taking on board changed management frameworks and novel performance indicators. The evident distaste with which some Conservative politicians — including some senior ministers — view 'the bureaucracy' and 'professional monopolies' have coloured the reception by public servants of many of the management changes cited in this chapter.

Even harder to dislodge has been the close association which has appeared to exist between management reform and financial cutbacks. The two may be analytically separable, but their simultaneous chronologies have struck many teachers, doctors, nurses and civil servants as a highly significant coincidence. The government should not be surprised if public servants view claims for 'better management' with considerable scepticism. The Efficiency Unit's report to the Prime Minister put it with commendable conciseness: 'The two measures which have had the most effect in altering the climate and the way the Civil Service works are manpower cuts and budgeting' (Efficiency Unit, 1988, p. 23).

Optimists may be able to detect, from the mid 1980s, a growing concern for improved personnel management, and even for shaping new, positive public service cultures (e.g. Metcalfe and Richards, 1987). Yet by the end of the 1980s, this had certainly not become a dominant theme in ministerial pronouncements or in official documents. As a set of concerns it was most frequently associated with senior public officials themselves, or with academic commentators. The political 'clout' was still principally exercised along neo-Taylorian lines. Productivity must be measured and then raised, value for money ceaselessly improved, 'bureaucratic' rigidities in the employment relationship dissolved. It was a species of managerialism under which those working in the public services experienced 'better management' as tighter control far more often than as any form of enhancement.

4

First Steps: the Initial Impact in the USA

Revolutions have to do with drastic, wrenching changes in an established regime. Causing such changes to happen was not Ronald Reagan's real agenda in the first place. It was mine, and that of a small cadre of supply-side intellectuals.

The Reagan revolution, as I defined it, required a frontal assault on the American welfare state .... Accordingly, forty years worth of promises, subventions, entitlements, and safety nets issued by federal government to every component and stratum of American society would have to be modified. A true economic policy revolution meant risky and mortal political combat with all the mass constituencies of Washington's largesse: Social Security, veterans, farmers, educators, state and local officials, the housing industry, and many more.

(Stockman, 1986, p.9)

Introduction

The assault on America's welfare state, so earnestly sought by President Reagan's first Director of the Office of Management and Budget, was originally conceived as budgetary surgery. Handouts were to be stopped. Over time, however, it became more and more a *managerial* onslaught. Expenditures were certainly to be held back (and even marginal cuts can be extremely damaging to the poorest recipients of support) but increasingly the message was 'increase the productivity of what you already have'. As David Stockman discovered, it is political suicide simply to try to remove social programmes altogether, but it may be possible to insist that fewer resources are made to go further. This is, quintessentially, a management task.

In this chapter I will briefly examine the major management reforms of the 1980s in three areas. First, it seems appropriate to look at the federal civil service itself, since it had been the target of so much of the new right's rhetoric. Second, Medicare and Medicaid were two of the fastest-growing expenditure programmes of the 1970s, and could therefore be seen as important tests for any new or revolutionary approach. Third, as a huge employer and big spender it would be difficult to leave education out of any broad analysis of US public services. Occasional references to other public services will be made at appropriate places in the argument.

The federal service

The belief that the federal civil service had grown too large and too slack was not the exclusive property of the new right and their presidential candidate. Reagan's predecessor, Jimmy Carter, had shared these views, at least to a degree, and had given them some prominence during his campaign for the presidency in 1976. But Carter's initial remedy was different, aimed more at reforming what was rather than cutting it away altogether. It was from this approach that the 1978 Civil Service Reform Act (CSRA) was born. CSRA aimed to free federal administrators from some of the accumulated regulatory rigidities so that they could manage more effectively and efficiently. But it also sought to preserve the 'merit principle', thus creating a tension between the goal of increased flexibility for managers and the goal of maintaining strong safeguards against the patronage which characterizes so much of the rest of the American political system (Nigro, 1982). This tension was actually three-way, because in selling the Act to Congress the Carter administration stressed its virtues in strengthening political control of the bureaucracy − an aim which is hard to reconcile with greater management freedom and delegation (Ban and Ingraham, 1984). The main elements of the Act were:

- Creation of a Senior Executive Service (SES).
- Introduction of new performance-appraisal and merit-pay systems.
- Introduction of new demotion and dismissal procedures.
- The first comprehensive statutory listing of merit principles and prohibited practices.

- Abolition of the Civil Service Commission and its replacement by an Office of Personnel Management (OPM) and an independent Merit Systems Protection Board (MSPB).

These reforms were introduced against a background of growing pressure on the federal service. Not only was its already negative general public image deteriorating further (because of the ideological trends described in chapter 2) but it was also suffering from a combination of structural change and competitive disadvantage. The proportion of specialist and technical personnel (with skills that were marketable outside the public service) was increasing. Meanwhile the pay levels of the service were deteriorating relative to those of rival private-sector employers – in approximately two-thirds of the years from 1970 to 1985 the rise given to federal workers was lower than that recommended to the President of the day by his pay agent, recommendations resulting from elaborate comparability exercises (Guy Peters, 1985, pp. 24–5; US Senate Committee on Governmental Affairs, 1984, pp. 20–21). Pay differentials appeared particularly unfavourable at the most senior levels – one reason for the creation of a Senior Executive Service which, in return for much greater flexibility in deployment, would be eligible for substantial performance-related bonuses (Goldenberg, 1985).

Even before Reagan came to office in 1981 there were signs that the CSRA formula was in difficulties. Congress soon moved to cut from 50 per cent to 20 per cent the proportion of SES positions that were eligible for bonuses. This amounted to a 'perceived breach of faith' as far as many members of the SES were concerned (Ban and Ingraham, 1984, p. 273). Inadequate resourcing handicapped the MSPB and the new Federal Labour Relations Board. These problems intensified in the early Reagan years. Public/private pay differentials for groups other than the SES did not narrow by much or for long. The introduction of merit pay led to problems as well as benefits. For example, for many federal workers performance-contingent remuneration appeared to *decrease* their confidence in their superiors – hardly an aid to retention – while failing to spark any perceived increase in agency effectiveness (Gaertner and Gaertner, 1985; Perry and Pearce, 1985; US General Accounting Office, 1984). By 1984 Congress recognized the shortcomings of merit pay by replacing it with a new set of arrangements, the Performance Management and Recognition System – PMRS (Perry et al., 1989). In its turn, PMRS proved disappointing. Whilst encountering less hostility it 'has not demonstrably achieved its ultimate objective – improving performance in the federal sector' (Perry et al., 1989, p. 35). Most fundamentally, perhaps, the whole implementation strategy of the CSRA was fairly decentralized and long-term, an admirable approach in principle but one which rendered the Act vulnerable to both political and resource instabilities of a kind that were commonplace in Washington (Ban and Ingraham, 1984).

On the other hand it would be unjustifiable to claim that CSRA had failed by the time Reagan took over. Amid the difficulties there were also some signs of positive change (greater delegation of staffing and other responsibilities for example) and in any case nowhere near enough time had elapsed for any final judgements to be determined. There were even a few indications that the new administration might carry on the good work; for example, top SES salaries were quietly raised by more than a third. However, this move proved to be the exception rather than the rule. The overall impact of the Reagan regime was such that 'even when implementation [of CSRA] has gone forward, its effects have frequently been lost in the larger turmoil' (Ban and Ingraham, 1984, p. 6).

At first the Reagan administration appeared to be adopting a new and quite fundamental approach to the problems of 'big government'. As the opening quotation from David Stockman indicated, the idea was that many bureaucratic problems would look smaller if the bureaucracy itself *was* radically smaller, that is, if major programmes were reduced or amputated altogether. In this regard the early rhetoric of the Reagan administration was broadly similar to the early rhetoric of Margaret Thatcher's Conservatives. In the event both delivered cuts in civil service numbers but neither found it politically feasible to produce an overall reduction in the public expenditure share – or even the social expenditure share – of GNP. During the eight years of the Reagan presidency the social programmes share of GNP actually rose slightly from its 16 per cent starting point. As Stockman's testimony made clear, the White House baulked at the first fence.

From as early as 1982 major cuts in the main social programmes (defence having already been scheduled for major *increases*) were tacitly abandoned. By 1985: 'Only the White House speechwriters carried on a lonely war of words, hurling a stream of presidential rhetoric at a ghostly abstraction called Big Government.

The White House's claim to be serious about cutting the budget had, in fact, become an institutionalised fantasy' (Stockman, 1986, p. 407).

This did not mean, however, that the Reagan administration had lost its pro-business, anti-government 'spin'. Rolling back public services and social security might be proving politically unsaleable, but managerializing these organizations was potentially a popular alternative. Some of the longer-term aspects of the CSRA were actively undermined. The third phase of the Federal Employee Attitude Survey was almost abandoned, and finally carried through only in a considerably reduced form. The evaluation staff in the OPM was decimated. Research grants and demonstration projects designed to explore better management methods were axed.

Meanwhile the new administration developed projects that more accurately captured its own distinctive approach to managing government. A welter of such initiatives followed. These included the Cabinet Council on Management Improvement (PCMI), the President's Council on Integrity and Efficiency (PCIE – founded in 1981), Reform 88 (begun in 1982) and the President's Productivity Program (announced in 1985 – for a summary of the major initiatives, see US Senate Committee on Governmental Affairs, 1984, pp. 31–5).

Perhaps the best-publicized and in many ways most characteristic example of this modified strategy was the President's Private Sector Survey on Cost Control (PPSSCC or the 'Grace Commission'). PPSSCC was announced in February 1982 – the date may be significant because this was just when the infeasibility of radical surgery to major programmes was becoming apparent. 'We mean business' said the President, 'and we intend to get results.' The Survey lasted until early 1984, and during this time more than 2,000 business executives, managers, consultants and others participated in its labours, supported by 859 companies and other organizations. It was a gargantuan exercise, supervised by an Executive Committee of 161, 95 per cent of whom were businessmen.

PPSSCC operated through 36 task forces, the majority of which concentrated on the work of specific agencies or groups of agencies. By the end of its investigations it had produced 47 reports containing 2,478 separate recommendations. Grace claimed that these, if implemented, would generate 'savings' of $424.4 billion over three years. It should be noted, however, that these estimates were immediately challenged from several apparently well-informed quarters (Goodsell, 1984). For example, a General Accounting Office/Congressional Budget Office analysis examined $298 billions of PPSSCC-proposed savings and came to the conclusion that $98 billion would be a more accurate estimate.

Despite the enormous length and complexity (and, it must be said, frequently congested prose) of the PPSSCC reports certain general themes and emphases may be discerned. The main deficiencies identified by the Commission included:

- Congressional 'interference' with the day-to-day management of federal agencies.
- Lack of continuity of personnel, especially at the higher levels.
- Lack of incentives to seek greater efficiency and economy.
- Inadequate system-wide accounting and management information systems.
- Failures to exert strong central management of finance and accounting.

The proposed remedies for these and other weaknesses are legion, yet exhibit certain common properties. Prominent among these are the assumptions that there is a (singular) 'best practice' which is both observable in the private sector and transferable to the realm of government. Of course, the architects of the CSRA were also frequent admirers of the world of business but: 'the Grace Commission's enchantment with private sector practice is even more intense . . . . The Grace Commission report emphasizes neither distinctions between public and private sectors nor diversity within either one. Instead, it glosses over differences between and within sectors' (Goldenberg, 1985, pp. 87 and 88).

These differences will be further explored in the next chapter.

For the moment suffice it to note that one general effect of such an approach is to confine the proper sphere of the 'political' to rather limited 'top of the shop' functions such as goal definition and strategy-setting. The rest of the governmental machine is then left to be treated like a business organization (or rather a rather idealized version of such an organization) where ends are already settled and attention can therefore be concentrated on selecting the most efficient means and monitoring their implementation. Hence the importance, in Reagan's Washington as well as Thatcher's Whitehall, of the terms 'efficiency', 'waste', 'cost' and 'productivity'. Some future, computer-based piece of discourse analysis may be able to confirm this author's subjective estimate that these terms crowd much more densely onto the face of the official documents of these two administrations than does the alternative vocabulary of civil service reform such as 'effectiveness', 'quality', 'recognition', 'responsiveness', 'fairness' and 'integrity'. Hence also the PPSSCC's central criticism of Congressional interference — elected representatives have no place in the efficient day-to-day running of a private business and the same rule should apply to government.

In other respects, however, Reagan's Washington was very different from Thatcher's Whitehall. Whereas the implementation of Rayner scrutinies and FMI benefited from continuing and close organizational links between the implementors, senior ministers and the Prime Minister herself, the same could not be said of the PPSSCC. Grace and his two thousand businessmen came and largely went, leaving a range of federal agencies to implement the lengthy Grace legacy of recommendations. Given that the President himself could not be expected to attend to such details, the opportunity was clearly there for agencies to pick and choose, re-package their own priorities and generally adapt the PPSSCC's work to suit their own perceived imperatives. Such a selective approach was aided by two other factors. One was the existence — already referred to — of other, parallel programmes of management reform. Some of these, such as the PCIE, had much firmer roots in the federal machine and could command considerable insider expertise and Congressional support in ways that Grace could not match. The second factor inhibiting the direct translation of the PPSSCC's recommendations into comprehensive action was the very different relationship which the US constitution fosters between, on the one hand, executive departments and agencies and, on the other, the legislature. Whereas in the UK ministerial departments are usually firmly under the control of their ministers, and are hardly ever heavily influenced by Parliamentary groups, the same cannot be said of US agencies. As has long been well known to students of American government, agencies are frequently able to defend themselves against Presidential or other 'external' initiatives by cultivating Congressional support for their existing programmes or practices.

Thus it would be an over-simplification to say that the Grace recommendations have been implemented – or rejected. Certainly there has been no across-the-board, down-the-line instruction to implement. That is hardly surprising, since the American political system does not usually permit such an unmediated executive response. Many of the 2,478 recommendations have been parcelled out, agency by agency and department by department, to become additional ingredients in the complex manoeuvres between the agencies, Congress and the interest groups which are so distinctively characteristic of Washington politics. Many of these recommendations have been partly or wholly implemented (sometimes as part of other, wider 'deals') while many others have not. It is hard to assemble a general scoresheet, but it might be hazarded that in realizing its overall vision the PPSSCC was little if any more successful than David Stockman at OMB.

Could it be said, however, that the PPSSCC changed the climate of thought in which the federal government pursued its day-to-day business? The extent of such a wider, background influence is notoriously hard to measure, but the PPSSCC's impact appears, in this respect, to be well short of revolutionary. To begin with, the PPSSCC's approach soon alienated not only (and predictably) many public-service leaders but also a dangerous number of senators and congressmen/women. Grace did not *have* to write that 'Congress interferes constantly with the day-to-day management of Federal agencies and departments, contrary to all rules of good management' (Grace, 1984). Furthermore, and despite earlier assurances to the contrary, Grace strayed well into political territory when, for example, he recommended modifications in the eligibility regulations governing retirement benefits, farm subsidies, food and nutrition benefits and student loans.

The PPSSCC reports were not the work of a cautious, careful reformer, anxious to streamline management but tender of both political sensitivities and the self-esteem of bureaucrats themselves.

Second, it is quite clear that the PPSSCC emphasized an already existing fashion rather than originating a new trend. Grace himself was hardly the first to write 'in a condescending tone that implies private sector managers are smart and government managers are not' (Hartle, 1985, p. 342). On the contrary, in this sense he was little more than another passenger on a crowded band-wagon (Kaufman, 1981). The belief that the federal civil service was inefficient and that private-sector practices held the key to transforming this deficiency ran both wide and deep. Congressional committees held hearings premised on these assumptions, hearings at which outstanding private-sector managers were paraded in front of attentive senators and pressed to reveal the secrets of their art (US Senate Committee on Governmental Affairs, 1984, esp. pp. 98–117; 152–66). [Incidentally, some of this testimony contrasted rather pointedly with the 'tighter accountancy/more competition' thrust of the PPSSCC. For example, one private-sector witness stressed the need to make all staff feel appreciated, to give them 'lots of flexibility' and to pay them well, while another argued against controlling staff numbers and for a heavy investment in education, training and motivation.] Several articles were written discussing how the precepts of the best-selling *In search of excellence* could be applied to the federal bureaucracy (e.g. Williams, 1986). In 1983, building on the belief that 'there exists a widespread perception among many Americans that the performance of government is low and that it is poorly managed' corporate leaders supported the creation of a 'Center for Excellence in Government' (US Senate Committee on Governmental Affairs, 1984, pp. 233–323). The PPSSCC, therefore, was anything but a surprise. Its interest is that of a prominent specimen rather than a rare or original find.

The wider picture

Before proceeding to examine the specific changes in health care and education it seems sensible to examine the tide of American anti-bureaucratic sentiment in slightly broader perspectives. Given the ideological background depicted in chapter 2, just how did this wave of popular suspicion translate into actual pressure for change from federal, state and local legislatures and executives? Most obviously, it assisted in the election of an anti-big government President and a cadre of state and city leaders committed to cutting back public expenditures and introducing 'business methods'. It did not, however, produce any real parallel to the attack by central on local government which took place in the UK (Cochrane, 1985; Hambleton, 1989). Indeed, President Reagan presented his programme as constituting a 'new federalism' – an empowerment of the states and a relinquishment by the federal government of unnecessarily detailed controls. A key milestone here was the 1981 Omnibus Budget Reconciliation Act (OBRA). This strengthened the role of federal block grants relative to categorical grants, though it also led to sharp reductions in the overall level of federal support. States were left with more discretion but fewer funds – a state of affairs which soon led to some co-ordinated and fierce complaints from state governors. After 1982 Congressional opposition appeared to stem any additional major reductions in federal assistance, but the reductions which had been made were not restored. Meanwhile a number of states took steps to constrain the spending of local governments, though none to the degree practised by the Conservative government in Britain.

Of the reasons which have been advanced for these Anglo-American differences three stand out as being particularly significant. The first is the set of constitutional and cultural differences between the two countries. Thus the autonomy of the states is constitutionally more deeply entrenched, and culturally more salient, than that of British local authorities. It is also better protected by the national legislature. The second reason is that British local authorities are responsible for a wider range of welfare state services than US state or local government – education, public housing, personal social services, public health, leisure services, planning and refuse collection. Thus they are a more inviting target for a new right government bent on curbing what it regards as an overblown public-service sector. Finally, as is often noted, the United States does not possess a major political party of the left. Thus there was no equivalent to Margaret Thatcher's particular crusade to reduce the status of Labour local authorities as part of her quest to free Britain from socialism.

None of this is to say that the public services somehow got away more lightly under Reagan than under Thatcher. While in Washington the coalitions of support for particular programmes — especially social security — retained sufficient defensive strength to blunt the radicalism of Stockman's cuts, there was nevertheless a steady tightening of eligibility rules and entitlements. 'Welfare' programmes were hit particularly hard.

Above all, there was an increasing disaffection with government *in general*. Dissensus among the parties over the appropriate role for government created 'conflicting expectations that no conceivable cadre of civil servants can meet' (Wildavsky, 1988, p. 753). Both Republican and Democratic parties came to include elements that were strongly critical of 'the bureaucracy'. By 1984 the President of the American Society for Public Administration was speaking of the 'snow-blanket of citizen suspicions of governmental institutions' and bewailing the way in which public debate of the issue 'has shrunk down to ankle-height' (US Senate Committee on Governmental Affairs, 1984, pp. 201–2). How, he asked, could the minimum consensus necessary for effective administration be engineered in a society where there were currently vivid disagreements over the proper purposes of government, its appropriate size, its inner structure and its budget?

At the time of writing no convincing answers had emerged to this question. Instead, for civil servants 'hard times are likely to continue', while for the most senior bureaucracy now is 'only for the brave' (Wildavsky, 1988). Given the continuing legislative reluctance to make drastic cuts in programme expenditures, especially transfer payments, American anti-bureaucratic feeling has continued to express itself by a mixture of meanness and mistrust towards civil servants themselves. Thus civil service pay has been held down, financial controls have been tightened (especially over credit management: US Senate Committee on Governmental Affairs, 1986), federal publications have been pruned, Office of Personnel Management (OPM) public management research has been politicized and re-focused on the short term, personnel management procedures have to a degree been re-centralized in the OPM (reversing the trend under the Carter administration: Goldenberg, 1985, pp. 79–80) and, in the upper reaches of the hierarchy, the proportion of short-term political appointees has been increased. Unsurprisingly, there is widespread evidence that all this has taken a heavy toll on civil service morale. Wildavsky (1988) writes of 'ubiquitous anomie'; the President of the American Society of Public Administration of his members feeling they are 'impaled on a two-pronged spear' (less government but better government: US Senate Committee on Governmental Affairs, 1984, p. 167); Carroll (1987) of demoralization and a failure to recruit to some senior positions. Better management has been attempted in a very cold climate.

Medicaid and Medicare

Health care was one of the fastest growing elements of American public expenditure during the 1970s (see chapter 2, tables 2.2 and 2.3). Though broadly similar in general structure the histories of the two main national programmes – Medicaid and Medicare – mirror the ideological distinction between 'social security' and 'welfare' described in chapter 2.

Both Medicaid and Medicare date from the mid 1960s boom in social legislation. Medicaid was a federal-state programme designed to make health care affordable to the poor. It soon became unpopular with the federal and state executives, not least because its expenditures quadrupled during its first ten years. By the beginning of the Reagan administration the federal government was contributing about $18 billion to Medicaid and the states $11 billion. Eligibility for Medicaid is linked to eligibility for other welfare benefits and this results in a system of considerable administrative complexity and one in which there is significant variation from state to state. By the mid 1970s this had resulted in an unsatisfactory situation in which probably only about half (13 million) those Americans below the official poverty line qualified for Medicaid while 6–9 million *above* the line also received it (Davis and Schoen, 1978). The public image of the programme has put it firmly in the 'welfare' side of the welfare/ social security divide, and politicians and the media have from time to time sought to connect it with the negative stereotype of a feckless, young, unmarried, black mother. In fact, though, the largest single category of beneficiaries has usually been children, while around a quarter are aged or disabled (Davis and Schoen, 1978, p. 54). Together with Medicare, Medicaid has — despite its limitations — made a substantial impact on the health status of many of the poor (Starr, 1986).

Medicare, by contrast, has attracted considerable popular support. It is presented as an insurance, not a welfare entitlement. It provides health benefits for those aged 65 or more who are entitled to social security or railroad retirement benefits. An exclusively federal programme (unlike Medicaid), it was costing about $49 billion (1982 dollars) at the beginning of the Reagan era. Like Medicaid, its costs rapidly exceeded the original estimates, ballooning more than three-fold in its first decade. Roughly three-quarters of this increase was attributable to general inflation of medical costs (i.e., not to expanding eligibility, coverage or more generous levels of benefit). Indeed, coverage, though subject to detailed alterations from time to time, has always displayed obvious gaps. After a period of rapid growth in the early 1970s the programme was still meeting only 38 per cent of the health care expenses of the elderly (Davis and Schoen, 1978, p. 93).

Presidents Nixon, Ford and Carter each made attempts to reform the health care system in general, and the spectacularly costly Medicaid and Medicare programmes in particular. The main aim was to halt the medical inflationary spiral (doctors, initially opposed to these programmes, soon found they were excellent sources of additional patients and income). Subsidiary themes were to reduce administrative complexity and provide more even and comprehensive eligibility. In the event complexity was increased still further as a layer of Professional Standards Review bodies were inserted into the system (from 1974) to carry out 'utilization reviews' of Medicare cases in an attempt to stem the suspected tide of unnecessarily generous or lengthy treatments by institutions and doctors seeking to maximize their Medicare incomes. These PSROs sometimes became considerable bureaucracies in their own right, and arguments raged as to whether they were effective or good value for money.

Meanwhile 'big', systemic solutions seemed to suffer a steady leakage of political support. Carter was the last of a line of Presidents who favoured a National Health Insurance scheme, but Congress was not sympathetic. Indeed, when he introduced a more modest hospital cost containment bill even that was rejected. Congressional lobbying by special interest groups again prevailed, the chief operators in this case being the American Medical Association, the American Hospital Association and Federation of American Hospitals. Yet if national insurance or major regulatory initiatives were politically unacceptable, that did not mean that full-blooded competition or the dismantling of the Medicare/ Medicaid programmes were popular either. Like his contemporary counterpart in London, President Reagan found it very hard to translate his anti-bureaucratic, anti-spending, pro-competitive rhetoric into major changes in the system for financing and delivering health care. In the early days his administration was alive with talk of radical moves to strengthen market forces in health care. Quite soon, however, this faded, and instead of any overarching liberalization there emerged a *pot pourri* of measures which in total amounted to an attempt to manage the existing system more tightly rather than replace it. The principal Reagan changes were as follows:

1　Substituting a prospective payment system (PPS) for the previous practice of (retrospectively) reimbursing Medicare providers. By limiting prospective reimbursement levels to the average cost of treatment for a particular diagnosis-related group (DRG) it was intended that this would act as a spur to efficiency among the providers, and thus contribute to the holding down of the total cost of the programme.

2　Raising patient deductibles and co-payments for Medicare in an attempt to make the ill meet a larger proportion of the total costs of their treatments.

3　Dismantling the state health planning agencies which had been set up during the 1970s.

4　Encouraging the further spread of Health Maintenance Organizations (HMOs).

5　Tackling Medicaid fraud and waste more vigorously, especially through the work of the newly-created Office of the Inspector General of Health and Human Services.

Of these measures the first, second and fifth are directed principally at saving federal dollars. The first (DRG-based PPS) was also held to increase provider efficiency, but that claim is, as we shall see in a moment, open to doubt. The third measure is in line with the new right's anti-planning stance while the fourth does encourage a private enterprise solution. This particular solution (the HMO) is, however, in no way a substitute for the Medicaid or Medicare programmes, and neither is it remotely new (President Nixon, for example, had also encouraged HMOs). None of these measures could be said to represent a new strategy for the development of the American health-care system.

Nevertheless, the first two measures do at the very least constitute large-scale trimming and tinkering, and their impact was felt by many thousands of health-care providers, and by millions of patients. PPS was introduced nationally in 1983. By paying hospitals only a predetermined national or regional-average rate for each type of case it was supposed to encourage hospitals to lower their expenses for in-patient stays. If they could treat the case for less than average, they pocketed a profit. If their costs exceeded the predetermined rate, they made a loss. For the originators of the DRG-based PPS system one desired result of such an arrangement was that it 'would result in hospital administrators holding sufficient authority to influence more directly the way physicians used resources' (Weiner et al., 1987, p. 465). In 1984 and 1985 both hospital admissions and average lengths of stay declined by more than previous trends would have led observers to expect. Hospitals generally improved their financial positions (Prospective Payment Assessment Commission, 1986). Their profit margins averaged 14.2% in 1984, 14.4% in 1985 and 9.9% in 1986 (Office of Inspector General, 1988, p. 32). Was PPS therefore a success?

Whilst it remains too early to attempt any definitive answer, certain additional consequences of the change (which were either not foreseen or not admitted by PPS's proponents) are already becoming apparent. These make it seem that, even if PPS is eventually adjudged a success in terms of reducing the rate of increase in the Medicare budget, it will have simultaneously created a new set of problems. First, there is the question of the quality and effectiveness of care. Falling lengths of stay may lead to reduced total in-patient costs, but they may also mean that patients are simply discharged 'quicker and sicker'. Certainly in the mid 1980s there were no shortage of reports that this was exactly what was happening. A national study indicated that although 'premature' discharge represented only just over 1% of total discharges, these appeared to be a measure taken to minimize losses on patients whose hospital costs were nearing or exceeding the DRG payment' (Office of Inspector General, 1988, p. 38). Demand for post-discharge services, whether in nursing homes, at home or in other facilities, increased. The Prospective Payments Assessment Commission admitted that 'at some level, further reductions in the length of stay will reduce quality, but that minimum level is not yet known' (Prospective Payment Assessment Commission, 1986, p. 5; see also Pollitt, 1987). Not for the first time (on either side of the Atlantic) an expenditure-saving measure was applied to a major publicly-financed service without there being any adequate system in place to measure whether that saving was purchased at the expense of a poorer-quality service.

A second troublesome consequence of PPS was that early discharge transferred patients to settings (nursing homes, homes) where Medicare payments were more tightly controlled than in hospital, or were simply not available. PPAC summarizes the point thus: 'At the time the Congress enacted PPS, the public did not perceive that beneficiaries and their families would become responsible for a larger portion of their health care costs' (Prospective Payment Assessment Commission, 1986, p. 5).

Finally, studies of the longest-operating state DRG/PPS (New Jersey, from 1980) casts doubt on whether the looked-for gain in managerial authority over doctors has in fact been achieved: 'Only the prospect of persistent deficits will compel administrators to challenge the clinical authority of physicians. DRG incentives in themselves do not force either the achievement of operational efficiency or a realignment of authority within hospitals' (Weiner et al., 1987, p. 467). In New Jersey, at least, administrators had sought and found less difficult ways of coping with the pressures of PPS. Through the political system they had pursued detailed amendments to give them more regulatory breathing space. They had sought to expand revenues, both by increasing admissions and by encouraging their doctors to choose the applicable diagnosis with the highest level of payment. A later, national study found that in a fifth of the cases reviewed an inappropriate DRG was assigned. Sixty-one per cent of these 'errors' were of the type that would have resulted in the hospital being paid more than they would have been if the coding had been correct (Office of Inspector General, 1988, p. 39).

The case of PPS has been worth spending time on because it shows rather clearly the limitations of the narrow, 'tighter-cost-accounting-forces-efficiency' approach to better management. Not only does it marginalize issues of quality and effectiveness (which may well diverge from efficiency) but it also grievously underestimates the strength and influence of organizational and political factors. Changing financial rewards may well change behaviours, but usually in much more diverse and sophisticated ways than the simpler popularizations of economic logic suggest.

The second Reagan measure — increasing co-payments and deductibles, and trimming eligibility rules — can be more swiftly dealt with. It was a simple transfer of cost from the public purse to the private pocket. Although occasionally dignified by claims that it discouraged unnecessary care by increasing the patient's awareness of cost, it is clear that the same increased expenditures were being imposed on individuals who desperately needed treatment as on those who, allegedly, were seeking care without good reason. It was little more than a federal belt-tightening exercise — one which made Medicare no more 'manageable' but certainly boosted the sales of commercial 'Medigap' insurance.

The third Reagan measure, repeal of the 1974 National Health Planning and Resources Act, selected for abolition a set of relatively unloved and arguably fairly ineffective planning organizations. The Health Systems Agencies created by the 1974 legislation had originally been intended as a first step along the road towards a much more planned national system which would include some form of national health insurance. As the 1970s proceeded, however, this scenario rapidly faded, and by the time the Reagan administration was formed HSAs remained as a lonely outpost of the regulatory approach to hospital cost containment. In 1981 the General Accounting Office issued an analysis casting doubt on HSA cost savings and by 1984 Stockman's OMB had assembled considerable additional evidence that the HSAs' certificate of need procedure for filtering hospital development was ineffective. By then, also, the executive could argue that the new PPS would have much more bite. The programme's remaining defenders on Capitol Hill finally submitted to a highly professional anti-planning campaign conducted by the American Medical Association (Mueller, 1988).

Promotion of HMOs will not be considered here, since they fall outside the focus on public-service management. Suffice it only to note that their appeal relies heavily on a kindred fixed-price logic to that which informed the enthusiasm for PPS. In the case of HMOs it is the fact that the patients pay these health care provider organizations a fixed annual amount which is supposed to propel them towards ever-greater efficiency. As with PPS, there is some evidence that this indeed occurs − at least at first − but (again as with PPS) there remains controversy over quality control and over possible attempts to select the most potentially profitable types of patient (and thereby inequitably exclude others).

Finally, there was the intensification of the search for fraud and waste. In political terms this is perhaps the easiest programme for which to win support − if caught, the perpetrators of fraud can expect little mercy from the politicians. This is perhaps especially true for health services, partly because of the very personal nature of medical care and partly because the guilty are usually individuals rather than big corporations. A large corporation caught out (say) defrauding the Department of Defense can be politically awkward, but an individual physician who cheats on his Medicaid returns can be safely condemned without much risk of public embarrassment. And in Britain as well as the US 'waste' has long been an accepted, bi-partisan target (witness Grace). Manifestos right across the political spectrum are constantly promising to get rid of it, and the public's belief in its widespread existence is apparently unshakeable.

In this particular case the Reagan administration found it had to hand a new, and potentially rather effective, administrative tool. The Inspector General Act of 1976 had created a number of Inspectors General charged with maintaining the integrity of the programmes of their respective departments. The IGs were given extensive investigatory powers and staffs and the duty of reporting both to their Secretaries and to Congress. They were also well protected against politically-motivated dismissal. President Reagan further strengthened these officers by extending their powers (PL97–375) and by grouping them together as key members of a new (1982) President's Council on Integrity and Efficiency (PCIE).

In terms of budgetary size the IG for Health and Human Services had one of the largest briefs. In Fiscal Year 1988 he was responsible for scrutinizing federal programmes costing nearly $400 billion – more than 35 per cent of the entire federal budget. In the six months to March 31st, 1988 his office imposed 177 sanctions (monetary fines or exclusions) on Medicare and Medicaid providers. During this same period there were also 264 prosecutions resulting in $33M of financial recoveries and savings (Office of Inspector General, 1988). In management terms this may have been little more than a cost-saving exercise, trimming the margins of a baroque bureaucratic system without much altering its basic structure, but it was vigorous cost-saving, conducted without the razzamatazz of Grace, yet in full public view and backed, where necessary, by research.

Education

In (short) historical perspective Britain's late 1970s 'great debate' on education (see chapter 3, pp. 72–5) appears a mere murmur in comparison with the 'crisis' in American schools. One sign of the depth of concern was that a national commission of a kind that would normally be expected to measure its language soberly could warn that 'the educational foundations of our society are presently being eroded by a rising tide of mediocrity that threatens our very future as a nation and as a people' (National Commission on Excellence in Education, 1983). Another was that a highly esteemed President of the American Federation of Teachers was willing to say publicly that 'Teaching does not have high standards today, nor is it perceived as having high standards' (Shanker, 1985, p. 11). There can be no doubt that statements like these reflected a very widespread public concern over the state of the schools. What is less clear, however, is where that concern was coming from. Without at all wishing to suggest that it was entirely 'manufactured' by the new-right media, there is some evidence to suggest that an element in the popular anxiety was 'top-down' — and actively encouraged by the Reagan administration — rather than based on first-hand local experience. Thus survey evidence tended to show that a majority were significantly more critical of the country's public schools in general than of the schools in their own community. Their perception was that 'out there' there was a crisis, even if their local school wasn't too bad (Schneider, 1984; Urban, 1985, pp. 206–7).

In the public mind the crisis in schools embraced failures of discipline, the use of drugs, inappropriate curricula (too 'permissive' — insufficient attention to a 'traditional' white, middle-class core), falling Standardized Attainment Test (SAT) scores (since the mid 1960s), poor teaching and inadequate financial support (Bunzel, 1985). Interestingly, by comparison with health policy, the term 'quality' seemed right at the forefront of the educational debate, while concern with cost control was much less prominent. As was suggested in chapter 2, in the dominant American political ideology state-run education has long been regarded as far more acceptable than state-run health care. By contrast Margaret Thatcher's administration found it much less difficult to reduce the public expenditure share of education than that of the NHS.

The task here is not to attempt to summarize the entire 'crisis' but to focus on the part management change was envisaged as playing in its solution. And this, at least in the eyes of state and county authorities, often seemed to be a very large part indeed. While opinion polls indicated that the public did not lay the blame for the situation solely on poor-quality teaching it was equally true that some tightening up on teacher quality commanded wide support. Moreover, there was a large and consistent majority in favour of some kind of merit pay. In the growing sense of crisis, state legislatures began to respond to these pressures: 'By 1984, only the rare state was not awash in reform proposals, as commissions and task forces bumped into each other at every intersection' (Finn, 1986, p. 109).

Among the most common proposals to emerge from these activities were:

better teacher training, higher standards of intellectual aptitude and achievement among entering teachers, various schemes for rewarding 'merit' on the part of teachers and for restructuring the teacher 'career path' into a 'career ladder', restoration of the principal's role to that of 'instructional leader', and a far greater performance accountability — to be accomplished mostly through testing — for individual students, teachers, entire schools, whole school systems, and even states.' (Finn, 1986, p. 110).

By now this should sound a familiar menu — closer personal accountability enforced through systems of measurement and appraisal, merit pay tied to some of these same systems, performance indicators for institutions and agencies — some or all these elements have already been encountered in almost every public service examined, both in this chapter and the previous one.

It may be worth looking in a little more detail at one of the more advanced systems applied to American schools, the Tennessee Career Ladder. Early in 1984 the Tennessee legislature approved a 'Better schools program' proposed by the governor at an estimated cost of $100 million over the first three years. The programme involved ten main elements including: curriculum reform (to strengthen 'basic skills'); increased student testing; fresh resources for in-school and special facility discipline procedures; a 10 per cent salary increase for teachers including bonuses for new teachers who stay on (to reduce wastage) and a career ladder. The ladder incorporated a number of features. There was to be a teacher certification process at each of the three levels on the ladder, with certificates having to be renewed every five years through written tests of reading, writing and professional skills. Annual bonuses (i.e. merit pay) are linked to an elaborate evaluation process whereby teachers are rated in each of five 'domains'. These are planning, strategies, classroom management, leadership and local evaluation. The data sources upon which the evaluations are based include classroom observation of the teacher, the written tests, work portfolios, opinion surveys of peers, supervisors and pupils, and an appraisal interview by a trained evaluator.

On paper this appears to be a most sophisticated scheme, far more complex (and better resourced) than most of the appraisal schemes which are beginning to appear in British schools. In practice, however, it soon encountered difficulties. After its first year there was evidence of gross incompatibilities between local and state rating scales. The paperwork for the evaluations was so complex that it took a substantial bite out of some teachers' timetables. A survey indicated that 87 per cent of local teachers held unfavourable opinions of the ladder, a similar percentage felt it had adversely affected their morale and only 5 per cent believed the evaluation process itself was satisfactory (Morgan, 1985). There were complaints that the system had been rushed into place and several experts disassociated themselves from the implementation.

The Tennessee story is far from unique. Many teachers resented the way in which new-right politicians − including the President himself − strove to make merit pay a prime item on the agenda for educational reform. Teachers' unions, originally opposed to merit pay in principle (not least because of its long and unhappy history in former periods), found themselves bundled along by a national ideological landslide and obliged to begin to talk terms (Urban, 1985; see also American Federation of Teachers, 1987): 'Most of the teacher career ladder proposals I've seen are merely devices to give a handful of people more money than others. Many, perhaps most, are a kind of cover-up for merit pay. I'm not opposed to career ladders in principle, if somebody can come up with a real one' (Shanker, 1985, p. 18).

The picture, then, is similar to that in UK schools in some respects but very different in others. The Reagan administration has not attempted the degree of centralization which has been visible under Thatcher's (especially in the 1988 Education Act), but then the nature of the US political system would hardly permit that anyway. Instead, Secretaries of Education have attempted to take credit for calling attention to the 'crisis', but have resisted the argument that they should back their fine sentiments with additional resources (Botstein, 1988). In both countries, central government has therefore played a very active role in trying to set the agenda. And the agendas they have attempted (with some success) to popularize have had strong similarities. The 'problems', according to this view, are lack of discipline, poor teaching (and teachers) and over-fancy curricula. The remedies are a reassertion of authority by teachers, greater concentration on a 'basic' curriculum, more standardized testing of pupils, regular appraisal of teachers, and merit bonuses for those who get 'results'. Unfortunately, when the remedies are put into practice it often seems that proper time and resources are not made available to support new working practices and aspirations – because of governments' simultaneous commitments to public expenditure restraint. Furthermore politicians and managers are frequently tempted to rush systems into place and then publicize the 'results' in highly selective or incautious fashion (this is not new: see Burstall and Kay, 1978, pp. 9–10). All this takes place against a background where it often appears that discipline problems are too firmly rooted in the childrens' home and local environment to make them at all easy to eliminate in the classroom. *Containing* such behaviours, given increasing diversion of resources into special correctional units of one kind or another, may prove slightly less difficult, but this is containment, not solution. Finally, it increasingly seems that, in addition to the many practical problems with merit pay, the motivational assumptions on which its advocates posit their case are seriously flawed. As a resolution to an American teachers' union convention put it as long ago as 1947: 'We, in the profession know how destructive to morale so-called merit ratings can be and how easily these devices lead to favouritism and violation of professional ethics' (National Education Association, 1947, p. 61).

Overview

In conclusion, it is important to appreciate that the impact of neo-Taylorist policies on the American public services from the early 1980s probably seemed less radical than the parallel changes in the UK. To begin with, the managerialist ideology had long occupied a more prominent and accepted place in American than in British life. Correspondingly, acceptance of the need for a comprehensive framework of public services – a 'welfare state' – was much less deeply rooted in the USA. Indeed for many people 'welfare' had become a heavily stigmatized term. Already, under a Democratic President (Carter), the government itself had begun to cast aspersions on the competence of the federal service and calls for 'better management' were increasing in volume and frequency.

Nevertheless, the onslaught of the early 1980s represented not only an intensification of budget-tightening but also a further, downward lurch in the self-esteem of many public servants. Experienced officials could be found testifying that: 'The predominant culture in the federal bureaucracy has a bias against action and for delay' and 'The responsibilities of management have been handed over to a professional managerial class within the bureaucracy, who have no power to install a value system that can inspire an organization' (Williams, 1986, pp.16 and 18).

The reforms of Grace and the President's Productivity Program, whatever their other achievements may have been, quite failed to tackle this malaise. In true Taylorist fashion, they addressed the issues of inputs and outputs, the measurement of effort levels and the refinement of accounting procedures. Perhaps it was their new-right beliefs which made the leading national politicians reluctant to admit that public services could be attractive and well-run, and that those who worked in them needed self-confidence and political acknowledgement. Or perhaps it was simply that, immersed in the labyrinthine complexities of Washington DC, no one knew *how* to move towards a more wholesome state of affairs. Whatever the mixture of reasons the federal government during the 1980s seemed to represent a condensation of all the larger self-doubts Americans entertained about their competence, cohesiveness and international standing. Managerialism flourished, but, paradoxically, the sense of public competence declined.

5

Stunted Growth: a Critique of Managerialism

Introduction

There are a number of different grounds on which a critique of neo-Taylorian managerialism can be constructed. First, one can engage in logical and conceptual analysis, and thereby identify points of vagueness, ambiguity, internal contradiction and/or omission within this particular corpus of managerialist thought. This would be a critique of the *coherence* of neo-Taylorism.

Second, whatever the coherence of neo-Taylorism, there may be evidence that it simply does not fit the empirical realities of many of the situations in which it is applied. It could be internally consistent as a logical schema, yet still incompletely model the reality of those public services which it is supposed to transform. Put more crudely, it simply wouldn't work, or at least not in the ways it was intended to. I will term this a critique of the *realism* of managerialism. Clearly, there is likely to be some overlap between a realism critique and a discussion of coherence. Conceptual vagueness and logical contradictions may well translate into very 'real' problems of implementation.

Third, social theorists commonly seek to understand bodies of thought and practice by relating them to the motives and interests of their proponents. That is, one can attempt to construct a critical explanation of the phenomenon of neo-Taylorism by showing how the spread of its associated ideas and practices benefited (in terms of power, status, income etc.) those who 'invented' or backed them. Such an analysis would be unlikely to provide a *complete* explanation of what has happened in our public services (technically, interests would be found to 'underdetermine' outcomes). Nevertheless it could substantially enhance our understanding of what was going on. This third approach might be described as a *political critique*, though that would not be to imply any necessary connection with political parties (British or American) or their programmes.

Finally, a fourth type of critique may be constructed through value analysis. A value analysis of managerialism should reveal which values it prizes and accentuates (both in theory and practice) and which it downgrades or ignores. It ought to be possible to reach some rough agreement on what this 'value map' looks like, although, of course, different individuals may come to very different conclusions as to whether or not the particular topography of values associated with managerialism is a 'good thing'. This would be a *value critique*.

Throughout this chapter the focus will be on the neo-Taylorian variant of managerialism. Some of the criticisms expressed also apply to other variants of managerialism, especially to those which adopt a 'generic' approach — i.e. those which assume the essential similarity of management wherever it is practised. I have tried to word each critique carefully so as to indicate, in each case, what I believe to be the scope of that portion of the discussion.

Coherence

Introduction

At first sight the neo-Taylorism which has been applied to most British and American public services since the late 1970s appears quite coherent. Target-setting, performance indicators, various forms of activity budgeting, staff appraisal, merit pay — all seem to hang together as complementary elements in a single vision of more tightly focused, financially disciplined, performance-conscious management. Inevitably, closer inspection reveals some tensions and contradictions. First, though, it is important to realize that even this surface appearance of unity and complementarity has frequently been achieved only by keeping the focus of reform very narrow. Many issues which are widely regarded as highly significant for public-service performance have been regularly ignored or underplayed. Among these near or total omissions are consideration of the distinctive ethical and legal bases of public services, of the issues of fairness and the possible redistributive goals of public services, of the scope for democratic participation in their operations and of the motivations of the staff who run them. The remainder of this section will consider these omissions in more detail.

Managerialism's model of the public servant

Certain omissions have a direct and unmistakable bearing on the coherence of the managerialist 'package' itself. Thus the relative neglect of motivational aspects of management in favour of control aspects generates (largely unacknowledged) contradictions. Those who proselytize on behalf of, say, (in the USA) the Grace Commission or (in the UK) FMI seldom seem willing to acknowledge the paradox that: 'managerial interventions in support of more disciplined bureaucratic control directly reinforce the perceived problem of commitment and collaboration which they were originally meant to solve' (Reed, 1988, pp. 35–6).

To put it in a slightly different way, managerialism has lacked an explicit or consistent model of the individual's commitment to and engagement with their work. *Implicitly* the model seems to have a rather old-fashioned, Taylorian flavour, with personal targetry linked to merit pay featuring as a regular ingredient – despite the empirical evidence that for many of the staff concerned this is an ineffective motivator (acknowledged in Mueller, 1986). Yet this mechanistic approach is uneasily combined with rhetorical appeals to dedication and the distinctive traditions of public service: a distinctiveness which elsewhere the genericism of managerialism effectively undermines.

Examples are not hard to find. In her foreword to the 1989 white paper on the NHS Margaret Thatcher waxed lyrical about the 'skilled and dedicated staff' who 'have coped superbly with the growing demands of modern medicine' but the white paper itself is full of proposals for more intensive control and discrimination among those staff – by the introduction of local variations in pay and conditions, the extension of 'performance pay', the alteration of the criteria for consultants' merit awards, the rapid introduction of comprehensive medical audit and so on (CM555, 1989). More discriminatory or performance-related pay arrangements were also a focus of discontent in the civil service and teaching (see, for example, Norton Taylor, 1985, p. 2; Brighouse, 1987, pp. 269–70).

Furthermore, the specific tensions occasioned by the introduction of tighter reward, disciplinary and appraisal procedures were set in a broader climate of doubt over the efficiency and appropriateness of public services. Politicians and others who owned or had borrowed the new-right, anti-bureaucratic, anti-public-sector rhetoric could hardly expect to be welcomed into government with a surge of enthusiasm and self-confidence on the part of most public servants. The latter saw very well that it was they themselves who had been the targets for the ideological onslaught. The 1980s were a decade during which reports of declining morale came from many parts of the UK public services, but public-sector managerialism appeared to offer further aggravation rather than amelioration. Reflecting on the main currents in British public administration between 1975 and 1986 an editor of the premier academic journal in the field wrote that, 'Perhaps more than anything else the period encompasses the demoralization of the participants in public administration' (Lee, 1986, p. 256).

The inadequate analysis of motivation and commitment was also a feature of management reform in the USA. Here − to an even greater degree than in the UK − the specific disruptions and anxieties of performance pay, contracting out (and so on) were overlain by a more general malaise. It was widely acknowledged that the public held a low opinion of government, and that, partly in consequence, morale in the public service was often extremely low (Wildavsky, 1988). Yet it was left largely to business leaders rather than politicians to make the argument that public-service morale was desperately in need of support (Center for Excellence in Government, 1989). In the midst of its efforts to convince the American public that public service excellence already existed and could be replicated throughout government the Center was obliged to acknowledge the power of the negative stereotype which had been fuelled by years of criticism from both right and left: 'While the current pro-business, anti-government attitudes may be faddish, the persistence of such attitudes could become a major problem for government if it is unable to recruit a new generation of public servants' (Center for Excellence in Government, 1989).

Or as another businessman more simply put it: 'Our last two Presidents, Reagan and Carter, came into office running "against the government". It should be obvious that we cannot constantly criticize government employees and expect to attract good people' (Moskow, 1987, p. 6).

This generally adverse public view interacted with many specific features which might be expected to dismay and demotivate public officials. Merit (performance) pay schemes led to widespread perceptions of unfairness in both the federal service and in teaching (Perry and Pearce, 1985, p. 158; Perry et al., 1989; Finn, 1985, pp. 111–17). Teachers also suffered from regular public vilification, from the imposition of recertification procedures and career ladders, and from tighter controls over curricula. It is not surprising that: 'many teachers are discontented with their lot. An overwhelming majority of them respond to polls by saying that if they had to live their lives over again they probably would not choose teaching as a career' (Finn, 1986, p. 117). A few years later surveys of British teachers came up with very similar results (Waterhouse, 1989a).

Meanwhile, for the federal government, the 1982 *Leuvano* consent decree demolished the already shaky foundations of the previous civil service hiring system. The 1980s were a period in which recruitment became 'a source of bitter political contention, endless, complex lawsuits, and considerable confusion about first principles' (Horner, 1989, p. 115). Security of civil service tenure was weakened. The number of temporary political appointees to high positions increased. After one brief surge in senior executive salaries pay levels continued to lag behind comparable jobs elsewhere. The managerialism of Grace, the President's Council on Management Improvement and the President's Productivity Program had little to say on these issues. The new right's vision of efficient management lacked a coherent model of the highly-motivated, productive public servant. If it had one at all it was a clockwork model that ran on targets and bonus pay, not a flesh-and-blood figure that needed public recognition and self-respect.

Centralization and delegation

A second problem with the coherence of public-service managerialism lies in its promises of, on the one hand, greater delegation to and autonomy for local units and, on the other, strengthened political and senior management control from the centre. Again, the 1989 white paper on the NHS provides a particularly clear example. In the early part of the document considerable stress is laid upon 'delegating responsibility as closely as possible to where health care is delivered to the patient' (CMM 555, 1989, p. 3). Later on, however, we learn that restructuring at the centre will 'introduce for the first time a clear and effective chain of management command running from Districts through Regions to the Chief Executive and from there to the Secretary of State' (p. 13). A similar tension was visible in the post—1983 Griffiths changes (Harrison et al., 1989a, p. 8), and in the Efficiency Unit's own 1988 appraisal of FMI (Efficiency Unit, 1988; see also commentaries by Fry, 1988b; and Flynn et al., 1988). In education, schools have been given significant new freedoms from the LEA (under LMS), but at the same time the DES has vastly increased its own central powers. The National Curriculum and the DES's new direct control of 'opted-out' schools are major increments of central control which are very hard to reconcile — other than rhetorically — with a philosophy of diversity and local autonomy.

In the US the same basic tension has been visible, though its manifestations have been rendered more diffuse by the less-centralized form of the American state. At the level of rhetoric the emphasis on decentralization has certainly been strong. President Reagan's 'New Federalism' was supposed to free states from the shackles of Washington. In practice, however, the new freedoms were often more apparent than real (King, 1987, pp. 127—31). Social and moral conservatism, rather than economic liberalism, was sometimes to the fore. Even more frequent were situations where the nominal decentralization of authority turned out to be fairly hollow because of an absence of resources. In February 1986 state governors appealed to Washington for federal tax increases and defence cuts so as to offset a situation in which there was 'responsibility flowing to the states unaccompanied by dollars' (King, 1987, p. 129). There are parallels here with both health care and education in the UK, where from the late 1980s the Thatcher administration sought to implement considerable decentralization, but within global budgets which seemed unlikely to be sufficient to maintain past levels of service in the face of rising demands.

Within the federal government itself many agencies have long enjoyed a higher degree of autonomy from central direction than would be usual for a Whitehall department. Management decentralization therefore did not enjoy the same degree of prominence, rhetorical or otherwise, as it did in, say, the FMI or the *Next steps* report (Efficiency Unit, 1988) in the UK. Indeed, if anything, the Reagan presidency sought to enforce tighter White House control over the agencies, not least through the OMB. Furthermore, both Washington *and* Whitehall witnessed one particularly subtle form of attempted centralization, namely that of financial reporting and control. In both countries new budgetary and accounting systems were introduced by central agencies with the aim of making the measurement of the cost of agency activities more standardized and reliable, and the allocation of those costs more transparent. Thus, during the 1980s the Office of Management and Budget (OMB) considerably expanded its concept of 'financial management'. It began to require all agencies to upgrade their accounting systems, obliging them to submit five-year plans for bringing their systems into line with a federal standard system (US Senate, 1986, p. 64). Standardized regulations were also introduced for the federal government's huge credit and cash management operations (Office of Management and Budget, 1986). In similar vein Executive Order 12552 of 1986 called for each agency to establish a productivity improvement programme, the plans for which were to be reviewed by OMB.

On one level, of course, such efforts were both laudable and readily understandable. Who could argue for unstandardized, obscure or ambiguous methods of recording the use of the taxpayers' monies? On another, however, a push by central agencies for comprehensive new accounting methods amounted to a bid for power, for control of what were to count as salient facts and what was to remain in shadow. The scope of such bids was greatly enhanced by the availability of increasingly sophisticated information technologies. In the public services, as in manufacturing, these technological aids engendered visions of an 'information panopticon' in which top management could instantly access up-to-date information about whatever was going on anywhere within their fiefdoms (Zuboff, 1988). Standardization, however, carried implications extending far beyond access:

Discretion often exists as to what inputs are deemed to be relevant, the costs that are assigned to the resources used, the outputs that flow from them, and their assignment in both financial and other terms. Issues of organizational interdependency will invariably arise, questions of presumed patterns of causal relationships will need to be debated, and proposals of specific valuations, weightings and assignments of priority will rarely be straightforward and unproblematic. Indeed, the difficulties of accounting in practice are such that it is often easy to arive at a whole array of costs, efficiencies and value-for-money assessments. (Hopwood, 1984, p. 177)

The empirical research necessary to establish how far and how successfully central agencies like the OMB and the Treasury did indeed use the standardization of financial and other information systems to diminish the discretion of departments and agencies has yet to be carried out. What is already clear, however, is that against the official Anglo-American rhetoric of decentralization must be set increasingly intense top-down attempts to control information.

In sum, then, the public-sector managerialism of the 1980s and late 1970s lacked coherence in a number of important respects. It was characterized by several omissions and contradictions. Its motivational model of the public servant was crude and incomplete; its stance on wider social inequalities (which the public services themselves often exemplified) was evasive and its position on decentralization was riven with contradictions.

Realism

Introduction

For at least seven reasons the neo-Taylorian model of management purveyed by Grace, FMI and the like does not accord with the reality of public service management. Few, if any, of these 'factors for difference' are new. Most have featured in the specific literatures of particular services for decades. From the mid 1970s, however, the growing ideological dominance of private-sector models of management (as charted in chapter 2) was such that these distinctive and salient features were effectively submerged. Some of the public utterances of Peter J. Grace, for example, clearly assume the widespread appropriateness (and superiority) of undiluted private-sector management. In the UK a famous passage in Sir Roy Griffiths' report on NHS management echoed the same sentiment.

We have been told that the NHS is different from business in management terms, not least because the NHS is not concerned with the profit motive and must be judged by social standards which cannot be measured. These differences can be greatly overstated. The clear similarities between NHS management and business management are much more important. (Department of Health and Social Security, 1983)

Significantly, perhaps, neither Grace nor Griffiths argued through the factors of difference and similarity point by point. Had they done so they might have been obliged to concede much more to those who argued that public services really were different. The pursuit of profit may or may not be a crucial element in these differences: it is certainly far from being the only one.

Accountability to elected representatives

The elected representative has no direct counterpart in the structure of an ordinary business firm. Analogies with boards of directors or, alternatively, shareholders, are both weak (though that has not prevented the genericists from repeatedly using them). Directors are usually appointed, rather than elected. They do not (normally) campaign on the basis of manifestos. They seldom have to work against the background of a permanently constituted alternative board of directors (how else would one conceive of a rival political party?) which is constantly seeking to use the mass media and all other available channels to discredit their efforts and put forward alternative programmes of action of their own. Furthermore, whereas directors may often assume a rough uniformity of interests among the shareholders they represent, it would be an extremely naive politician who made that assumption in respect of his or her public constituency.

Shareholders seem an even weaker analogy for the elected representative. Individual shareholders seldom spend more than a fraction of their lives actively pursuing their interests *qua* shareholders whereas many elected representatives are obliged to devote a large part of their waking hours to their public role. And it is a *public* role, not a private one. Elected representatives are generally organized into political parties whereas individual shareholders are not. Institutional shareholders, by contrast, do have an obvious organizational dimension, but their functions are still essentially private and it is only occasionally that they have to conduct their affairs in the light of the full glare of the national or local media, not to speak of an organized opposition.

Elected representatives are, then, *sui generis*. Relations between them and managers are crucial to the running of many public services, yet generic management models offer little advice on how such relationships should be conducted. In so far as models of private sector/business parentage deal with 'politics' at all they tend to treat it as some kind of regrettably unavoidable extra:

The political process can be seen as an incidental feature of management in the public domain or more seriously it can be considered as a constraint when the phrase 'the costs of democracy' is used, as though it is a special difficulty to be overcome, rather than a basic condition expressing the purpose of the public domain .... Such an approach leads one either to ignoring the political process or raising issues as to how problems it presents can be overcome. (Local Government Training Board, 1988, p. 5)

By contrast, relating to politicians can be seen as a key skill for many public-service managers (Baddeley, 1989).

Multiple and conflicting goals and priorities

Much of the managerialism examined in the first four chapters was, as we saw, rationalistic in a fairly unsophisticated, neo-Taylorian fashion. Success depended on an initial process of defining a set of clear, mutually compatible objectives. In theory these were then translated into limited sets of operational targets and finally management skills and information were harnessed to the selection, implementation and monitoring of the most cost-effective means of achieving those targets.

One may question whether this is an adequate representation of the management process in the business world. At least some recent organization theorists argue that 'problematic goals, unclear technologies, fluid participation, shifting and contradictory performance criteria, and conflicting 'stakeholders' characterize *all* complex organisations' (Reed, 1988, p. 43). What is absolutely clear, however, is that clear and limited objectives, stable and explicit priorities (etc.) are very seldom the experienced reality of public-service organizations. This has been repeatedly documented in the public-administration literature on both sides of the Atlantic, for at least the last thirty years, (Gunn, 1987, pp. 38–9).

The reasons for policy 'irrationality' and instability are often rooted in alternative forms of reasoning – political rather than economic 'rationality'; emotional or psychological logic rather than the textbook utilitarian kind. Aaron Wildavsky has been one of the most eloquent observers of these dimensions to the public-policy process:

But why, you ask, do governments set objectives they cannot achieve? For one thing, society's capacity for measuring results has outstripped its ability to cause consequences. We know that programs have failed but we have been unable to bring about the changes in behaviour that would have labelled them successful . . . . For another, these objectives (improve health, reduce crime, increase cognitive capacity) seem terribly attractive and politically seductive. (Wildavsky, 1979, p. 47)

Such objectives are so seductive, in fact, that once a party has emblazoned them upon its escutcheon it is, first, very hard for them subsequently to abandon these noble aims and, second, equally hard for rival parties to resist proclaiming matching aspirations.

Thus politicians frequently find themselves wedded (sometimes unwillingly) to unattainable objectives. Furthermore, the way in which these objectives are characteristically *expressed* adds another layer of complexity for managers. At least three pressures tend to shape the formulation of objectives in the direction of vagueness and ambiguity. First, there is the political need to build and maintain coalitions of support. Broadly expressed objectives may help in this, whereas those which are tightly defined are liable to reveal all too clearly which groups are likely to be satisfied and which are not – with the result that the latter desert the coalition or move from passive acceptance to raucous opposition. The significance of this kind of coalition-maintenance is substantial in most political systems but probably greater in the USA (because of the more extensive powers of the legislature) than in the UK. Chapter 2 indicated how, in order to construct a programme to help the poor, US legislators have more than once had to build a coalition by broadening a programme's eligibility criteria and objectives. Second, a broadly-stated objective is less likely to give immediate hostages to fortune. If the aims of a programme are fairly general, then it is easier to argue that it has been, at least in part, successful. The NHS proved a very popular institution for its first forty years, but during that time it was never given a clear set of objectives and therefore, in a sense, could not 'fail'. Third, vague wording of objectives gives politicians room for manoeuvre in another sense. It means that at election time, or at other junctures when public opinion seems to demand some novel initiative, a new set of words can be manufactured which *sound* like a new policy but in practical and financial terms may be little more than a slight change of emphasis in an old policy.

'Woolly wording' is thus attractive in the sense that it provides endless opportunities for defence, evasion and apparent innovation during the process of political debate. More positively, it may also be a true reflection of the maximum degree of agreement that can be achieved within a governing coalition at a given time or of well-calibrated uncertainty about how to resolve complex social problems. For public-service managers, however, it means that the kind of clear 'steer' from the top which is said to be charact- eristic of well-managed business corporations is comparatively rare. Much of their time may be spent in trying to determine whether an apparently changed policy emphasis does in fact have any practical implications for them, or what a grand objective of (say) greater 'consumer responsiveness' actually means, or in interpreting the broad phrases of the latest white paper to see whether 'we are already doing it'. The process of policy *inter- pretation* looms larger than managerialist models allow.

The absence, or rarity, of competing organizations

Central to the new-right analysis of public services is the idea that the absence of competition will lead to endemic inefficiency. While most public services do have *some* rivals (e.g. the guaranteed continuation of private health care was one of the planks in the political agreement that launched the NHS in 1946) it remains true that, during the period under consideration, most of the major public services retained a dominant position in their re- spective sectors. Medicaid/Medicare is something of an exception but in most cases public-service managers have indeed been able to lay their plans without having to worry too much about being undercut or 'outsold' by rival organizations. At the time of writing, this may be just beginning to change, especially in UK health care and education where (respectively) self-governing hospitals and opted-out schools may be obliged to take 'competition' more seriously. Monopoly has also been qualified by the 1980s push towards contracting-out and privatization where, for example, British local-authority direct-labour organizations or American refuse or park/recreation organizations have suddenly found themselves having to compete with private contractors.

With these (growing) qualifications, however, it remains true that many managers of core public services can afford to be 'introverted' or 'provider-oriented' to a degree that would be unusual in business. It is here that the new-right critique is at its strongest (and most popular?). As the welfare state expanded during the 1960s and 1970s the problem of 'provider power' became ever more salient. The conclusion drawn by the genericists, however, is not that their theory should be modified to fit a different cultural reality, but rather that the structural arrangements for service provision should be altered so as to inject the formerly absent element of competitive uncertainty. What these reformers tend to be much more reluctant to concede is that public-service managers facing such newly-competitive uncertainties should also enjoy remuneration packages comparable to their counterparts in business and commerce. Such a conclusion runs contrary to the deeply-held new-right belief that many public servants are already over-paid as well as over-protected.

The supply/income relationship

In price-driven markets the more goods or services a manager supplies the more the supplying organization's income grows. This is the standard business model. In most public services, however, supplying more services increases costs without any corresponding growth in income. [Notice that this proposition is *not* the same as the commonplace assertion that the public and private sectors are different because the latter is overwhelmingly profit-motivated and the former is not]. Even where charges are made (e.g. for the use of public swimming baths or for an NHS prescription) they are often symbolic or only weakly related to actual costs incurred. This is not an incidental feature of public services, alterable by some improvement in cost accountancy. Rather it is fundamental, for many public services *are* public precisely because there is little prospect of being able to finance them through direct consumer payments. This may be because the technical characteristics of the service make it non-excludable (like clear air) or because the service is specifically intended for those with insufficient income to meet market-related charges from their own pockets. In either case, the effect on the management culture may be profound. Public-service managers, instead of focusing on stimulating the public's demand for their 'products', find themselves *de facto* searching for politically acceptable ways of limiting demand and rationing what they provide.

This situation can lead to motivational problems for managers themselves and also to tensions with professional service providers (who would often like to see service expansion and development). Such difficulties are insufficiently addressed by neo-Taylorism. Moreover, (and this may add to motivational problems) managers know that their political leaders may have second thoughts about standing up for their rationing policies if they become a focus of media and public attention. Instead stop-gap solutions have sometimes been pressed on managers which, although they may relieve the immediate media pressure, create inequities elsewhere in the system and store up awkward precedents for the future. Examples include incidents where particularly heart-rending cases are apparently allowed to queue-jump in order to receive NHS treatment, and those occasions when resources are diverted to deal with local 'scandals' rather than wider problems of low standards to which they would otherwise have gone.

In brief, for many public services the relationship between the supply of the service and the resources received is ambiguous. Providing more service – even where the relevant public want and will make use of that extra service – will not necessarily increase the flow of revenue into that organization. The implications of this for public service management cultures are several. It means that one major incentive to entrepreneurialism (the 'sell-more-and-grow' line which often flavours genericist management texts) is largely absent in many public-service contexts. This, in turn, implies that some other, alternative incentives will need to be fostered – but on this as on many other points to do with the motivation of public servants, most of the 'official texts' of neo-Taylorism have been singularly lacking in suggestions. Even where, to some extent, 'extra business' *can* be won from 'competitors' – as is envisaged with open enrolment for schools and the latest ideas for hospital contracts within the NHS – this will be done in the context of a 'zero-sum' game for the service as a whole (since global authority budgets will remain cash-limited). This contrasts with much private-sector competition, where the idea is to move into expanding markets where growth can be non zero-sum and several companies can do well simultaneously (though of course some may do even better than others).

People-processing

The generic model of management tends to work with a rather narrow model of the consumer. The consumer is a bundle of preferences waiting to be satisfied. Consumers are to be researched so that the service or product can be designed so as to best meet their wants – or so that new appetites can be stimulated and supplied. In some ways this approach can have quite a refreshing influence on the more traditionally provider-dominated public services such as health care or the police force. It may encourage them to begin to ask their 'customers' what they want, and to pay more attention to 'shopfront' activities such as waiting-room procedures, receptionist training, the provision on their premises of decent food, public phone boxes and so on. On the other hand, this approach soon runs into its own limitations, which derive from substantial but unacknowledged differences between the usual 'consumer' of commercially marketed goods and services and the usual 'consumer' of public health care, education, law and other maintenance etc.

The commonplace generic model of the consumer fails to capture the distinctiveness of the public services for two main reasons. First, the provider/consumer transactions in the public services tend to be notably more complex than the classic 'purchase decision' of the consumer in a price-driven market. Second, public-service consumers are never merely 'consumers', they are always citizens too, and this has a set of unique implications for the transaction. Before proceeding further, however, it should be conceded that in practice there is wide variation in the complexity of consumption transactions in both public and private sectors. In the private sector a lawyer may give highly complex advice to a client, accomplishing this through a relationship which involves meetings, correspondence and telephone calls stretching over months or years. In the public services, by contrast, a woman may decide to go swimming and pay for her ticket at the municipal baths in exactly the same way that she would would buy a bar of chocolate from a shop − the whole thing being over in seconds and scarcely involving any great constitutional subtleties. What is being undertaken in this chapter, however, is an assessment of the adequacy of the generic model's apparent conceptualization of the consumer for the actual conditions of the public services. So to argue − as I shall − that the generic conceptualization is often inappropriate is not in any way to deny the diversity of either sector. Indeed, it may well be to argue that the generic model of the consumer is a poor guide to many *private*-sector transactions as well as most of those in the public services.

In the generic model the job of the provider is (to take the mission statement of the supermarket chain whose Deputy Chairman was called in by Margaret Thatcher to improve NHS management) that of 'making available to customers goods of high quality at competitive prices' (Griffiths, 1988, p. 197). Market research ensures that the provider knows a good deal about the habits and preferences of the customer (and prospective customer) and about the attractions of any rival providers. In the successful provider organization this information is then woven into a 'total management philosophy' (Griffiths, 1988, p. 201) which commits management to 'listening, intently and regularly' to the customer (Peters and Waterman, 1982, p. 14).

Why is the consumption of public services different? There are a number of reasons, none of them applying to *all* such transactions, but cumulatively affecting the bulk of the day-to-day work of schools, hospitals, the personal social services, the police and other major providers. First, *de jure* or *de facto*, public services are frequently compulsory − that is, the consumer cannot go (as it were) to the next supermarket, or garage, or lawyer. At the extreme, the public 'service' may be supplied directly against the will of the recipient and enforced coercively. Such extreme situations are not confined to the work of the police and prison services. During 1987 the British media were overflowing with accounts of child sex abuse in the county of Cleveland. Two NHS paediatric consultants had suddenly begun to diagnose a large number of cases of child sex abuse, many of them in children who had come in for some other complaint entirely. Once these diagnoses (established using a controversial and allegedly unreliable diagnostic technique) had been made the local Social Services Department took most of the children into local authority care, sometimes refusing to let their parents have access to them. Again, (more routinely than the spectacular events in Cleveland) individuals who are diagnosed as suffering from certain categories of mental illness are regularly confined to mental institutions against their will.

These are cases where the law permits compulsion because of the presumed seriousness of the situation. More common, in numerical terms, are those cases where public services are supplied to consumers who, *de facto*, have no real alternative. This has often been the case with primary care doctors, hospitals, schools and the personal social services. In rural areas, especially, there may be only one facility locally available – a local monopoly. Even in cities, particularly if you are poor, the *de facto* choice may be non-existent. Such circumstances – whether they be the product of monopoly or of legal compulsion – endow the 'consumption' of the public service with a new ethical basis. The ultimate defence of the supermarket manager or the car salesperson – 'They can always go somewhere else' – can no longer be played in aid. The case for some kind of consumer representation or participation thereby becomes that much stronger (Potter, 1988).

Equally, if not more frequent are those situations where a member of the public actively wants to use a particular public service, but is not permitted to (Stewart and Clarke, 1987). Council house and NHS waiting lists spring to mind as large-scale British examples. In the US, under the Reagan administration, retrenchment in social programmes typically took the form of tightening eligibility requirements (Heclo, 1986). As we have seen (p. 124), this means that public-service staff are frequently in the uncomfortable business of administering rationing procedures to disappointed clients. Where this happens in the private sector (waiting lists for the latest Mercedes) the message goes back to the production units. 'Increase output'. In the public services such messages usually fall on deaf ears, especially where they belong to the politicians of the new right. Thus the only prescription neo-Taylorism appeared to have for this uncomfortable condition of supressed consumption was that of increased efficiency. While there was often room for improvement in this department, the room was seldom on the scale of the problem. The NHS 'cost improvement programme' provided one very good illustration of this. But when the limits of efficiency savings have been reached managerialism has no more help to offer. It is a political rather than a managerial analysis which suggests a realistic way of beginning to tackle the issue:

Deciding *who* shall have access to *what* is a political responsibility . . . . [Consumerist pressure groups] call for the definition of clear and explicit criteria on which to base these vitally important decisions about how services should be rationed. They insist that criteria are brought into the open because only in this way can the decisions be understood and challenged. (Potter, 1988, p. 151)

There are other respects in which many public-service transactions are more complex than most of their private-sector counterparts. Health care, the personal social services, careers guidance, the probation service and, especially, education, usually interact with their customers discursively, face-to-face, and often over a considerable period of time. These are developmental relationships in which the establishment of trust and an appreciation, by the provider, of the unique circumstances of the individual consumer are essential to the ultimate effectiveness of the service being provided (Ellis, 1988). The case of education is particularly complex because it can plausibly be argued that one of the purposes of the provision is not to *satisfy* the consumer's current preferences so much as to encourage these preferences to change and develop. If little Claire goes into school wanting to play with dolls and comes out a couple of terms later more interested in woodwork and poetry, most observers would account that as something of a success. For all these situations the model of the consumer as someone who is given information about the product's characteristics, lines this up with his or her preferences, and then makes a point decision, seems seriously insufficient. It may be possible to argue that things would be better if more people, both providers and consumers, *did* regard the public services in this way. For the present and foreseeable future, however, the generic model is so simple as to be unrealistic. It therefore does not help the teacher, nurse or probation officer to address many of the problems which daily present themselves.

The second main reason why the generic model of the consumer seems inadequate is that the public service consumer is also (nearly always) a *citizen*. Citizenship is an awkward concept for new right neo-liberals, and an almost absent one in the managerialist literature (where 'consumer' or 'customer' are much preferred). The reasons for this shyness are not hard to discern. Liberalism 'does not really have a notion of the state' and therefore has difficulty with the concept of citizenship (King, 1987, p. 9). It is a concept with a strong connotation of *collective* rather than individual action ('Fellow citizens!'). Citizens owe duties to and possess rights of the state. All this is alien to an individualist model where the market is the chief focus of transactions and values, a market which, in principle, knows no frontiers.

Citizenship is thus a concept which has evolved in parallel with but separate from liberal economic thought. Historically, establishing the status of 'citizen' and furnishing its bearers with a full complement of rights and duties have been long-drawn-out tasks involving many struggles and much collective organizing and politicking. The rights which have been fought for have on the whole not been those of efficiency and effectiveness, but rather, justice, representation, participation and (most recently) equal opportunities. And these are, indeed, the rights which many citizens seek to inscribe in the organization of their public services. They go far beyond the agenda of managerialism but it could be argued that they address some of the distinctive issues of public services management in a more realistic manner than narrow-focus 'consumerism':

the twin values of caring and consumerism provide the rationale for [public service] consumerism. The latter can be defended on the grounds that it increases the efficiency and effectiveness of service delivery. Without minimizing the relevance of these considerations, a rationale grounded in political theory has the distinct advantage that it provides an ethic for [local] government which both enhances the standing of the institution and contains the potential to motivate all those who participate in it. (Rhodes, 1987, pp. 68–9)

Thus the reluctance of neo-Taylorians to recognize the distinctive status of citizenship in public-service transactions further handicaps the search for solutions to the problems of staff motivation (see p. 113). It also restricts the range of value concerns which the generic model can address (see below p. 138).

The management of staff

The terms and conditions of service of staff in the public services are often very different from those customarily found in the business sector. In some cases these differences may be on the wane (e.g. with the ending of tenure of British university teachers or the introduction of forms of appraisal and merit pay in many public services on both sides of the Atlantic) but they remain substantial. They include:

- Considerable constraints on the authority of line managers to hire, fire and promote.
- National, and often somewhat inflexible pay awards and grading procedures. 'The ability to offer incentives, award penalities or give rewards is negligible' (Cooper, 1983, p. 15).
- Particularly high autonomy for certain professional staff, who may be largely beyond the direct control of managers and administrators (the best-known case here being NHS doctors).

The new-right liberals are irritated by all these differences – which they see as special privileges which inhibit competition and encourage inefficiency – and would like to see them removed. Adherents of generic managerialism, whether of neo-liberal persuasion or not, are also critical of them. Each difference represents a significant limitation on the beloved manager. From this perspective the 'right to manage' includes the right to hire and fire one's staff, to move them about and to reward and sanction them. Without authority in these respects it is going to be much harder for the line manager to provide leadership and direction. National pay agreements are part of the same problem – they remove local flexibility and ensure that, given geographical variations in the cost of living, staff in some parts of the country are effectively overpaid while others are effectively underpaid, with adverse consequences for recruitment. As for professional autonomy, the managerialists conceive of management itself as the guardian of the overall purposes of the organization, and therefore it is wrong that another group of staff should be able to work to a different set of priorities and, when challenged, often successfully resist management's call for conformity. After all, in ICI or Dupont or McDonnell-Douglas there are plenty of professional experts but they are 'on tap' for management, not 'on top'.

What is unrealistic about the neo-Taylorian approach is that it assumes that these problems can be overcome and that meanwhile its other prescriptions for rationalization (merit pay, appraisal, performance indicators, delegated budgeting systems etc.) can go ahead. In practice, this assumption has contributed to declining morale and led to a good deal of conflict. In the UK, despite a general decline in the political strength of public-sector unions and professional bodies, stiff resistance to these changes has continued throughout the 1980s. At the end of the decade staff appraisal and merit pay for schoolteachers were still only at the beginning of implementation, university staff were resisting appraisal and the government had been in fierce dispute with both doctors and nurses over new contracts and grading schemes (as well as over the more general provisions of the 1989 white paper on the NHS). The actual implementation of neo-Taylorian reforms has frequently ignored all the findings of the 'culture' wing of contemporary managerialism (see chapter 1) and charged ahead in a manner likely to provoke the maximum defensiveness on the part of those whose support, however conditional, needed to be wooed. Worst treated have been the industrial, ancillary and clerical workers, who have born the brunt of job reductions and privatization (Ascher, 1987, pp. 244–6 and 264; Fry, 1988a, p. 3; Harrison, 1988a, pp. 148–51).

In the USA some of these changes have been less fraught. For example, the previously-existing management culture of US local government made contracting out a more acceptable, technical-seeming solution than in many British local authorities (where both party political and centre/local tensions were much more marked). In other cases, however, resistance and resentment have been plentiful:

To most teachers and their unions, merit pay does not suggest an incentive plan to improve knowledge and skills or to reward superior performance. It suggests instead the very antithesis of professionalism, that of untrained principals and superintendents using bogus, one-shot evaluation checklists to standardize teacher behaviour, rewarding some teachers and demoralizing others on the basis of favoritism or politics. (American Federation of Teachers, 1987, p. 9)

Resistance need not be overt in order to be effective. In changing over Medicare reimbursement to a prospective payment system based on DRGs the managerialists hoped that they were providing hospital administrators with 'the management tools needed to gain control over resource use within hospitals' (Weiner et al., 1987, p. 465). Weiner's fieldwork showed that 'The proponents, however, ignore the organizational realities' (p. 465). The doctors continued to assume responsibility for the most significant un-certainties within the health care process and to exercise the power and discretion that shouldering that burden conferred upon them. 'Rather than challenging the prerogatives of physicians, New Jersey hospital administrators sought to preserve them' (p. 479). Organizational realities proved stronger than an apparatus of managerialism founded too exclusively on economic logic.

Turning now to the federal service, the 'poor fit' of the managerialist model in matters of staff management was highlighted in the following commentary on the proposals of Grace and his fellow thinkers: 'Those who focus on the similarities of the public and private sectors tend to have an image of a civil service that is hierarchically subordinate to, and solely responsive to, the President and his priorities. That image is unrealistic given the structure and design of this country's government (Goldenberg, 1985, p. 90).

In each of these cases the bearers of the generic model underestimated the limitations of their own hierarchical or economistic conception of staff management. The distinctiveness of the public services was greater than they imagined, as was the defensive stamina of those who valued that distinctiveness.

The legal framework

Many of the distinctive features of the public services described above are reflected in the framework of administrative law which surrounds the service providers, their employing organizations and their clients. Of course, many busines companies also find their activities enmeshed in a web of regulatory requirements and legal obligations. Arguably, however, the legal framework is significantly different in the two cases, and this difference is another important feature of the public services.

To begin with, the very question of the service to be provided is framed quite differently. Sir Roy Griffiths expresses the businessman's approach: 'Most companies are constantly examining how they position themselves in a market to best meet demand or provide service within a likely level of resources. No company would ever get itself into the position of the health service of trying to be all things to all men and to be increasingly expected to meet every possible demand' (Griffiths, 1988, p. 197).

What Sir Roy did not mention was that one reason the NHS tries to be all things to all men (actually the majority of its customers are women) is that it is enjoined by public statute to provide a 'comprehensive' service. It cannot suddenly decide to move in or out of this or that particular portion of the health market just because it would make economic or managerial sense to do so. Most public services are under similar obligation to provide a service of a statutorily defined kind – they can neither relinquish such obligations (except in the rare cases where there is fresh legislation narrowing their remit) nor move into inviting new markets unrelated to their defined purposes.

Second, and at a more detailed level, many public services operate within quite complex bodies of special law – special not in the sense that it was created to govern all commercial transactions, by all companies, of a particular kind but rather in the sense that it was law written and devised exclusively for those particular organizations. In the UK, for example, the Education

Act 1981 lays some fairly intricate duties on schools with respect to children with special educational needs (Cox, 1985).

Third, the relationship between the state and the citizen or, indeed, between one administrative agency and another, is conceived in quite different legal terms from that between the business corporation and its consumer. For a long time this was clearer in the US than in the UK, for the former had a more fully developed tradition of separate administrative law (see, e.g. P. Cooper, 1983). Recently, however, there have been signs that, especially in the area of judicial review of the actions of state agencies, the British tradition of political rather than legal protections for the citizen is being modified. As the most famous post-war British law lord put it: 'In modern times we have come to recognise two separate fields of law, one of private law, the other of public law. Private law regulates the affairs of its subjects as between themselves. Public law regulates the affairs of subjects vis-à-vis public authorities' (Lord Denning, quoted in Rawlings, 1986, p. 158).

Political critique

This approach seeks to enhance understanding of managerialism by identifying those groups and organizations which stood to benefit from the spread of the kind of neo-Taylorian approaches described in chapters 2, 3 and 4. Once it is established that a particular change was in the interests of a particular group, research can be designed to explore how, if at all, that same group actually campaigned for the change and thereby increased the probability that it would actually come to pass. 'Interests' in this context should be understood as including both direct material interests (e.g. increasing monetary profit) and more subtle gains such as enhanced status within an organization, greater control over others, the pleasures of being well-known and intellectually fashionable, and so on.

The list of groups who have derived material benefits from public-service managerialism is not hard to assemble. It includes management consultants; cleaning, laundry, catering, refuse collection, leisure and other firms who have gained contracts for hitherto 'in-house' public-service work; business schools and other parts of the education and training world which have offered generic management training; accountancy firms which have moved into the expanding business of auditing the accounts of public agencies, and, last but not least, those public servants and private-sector business people who have assumed the many new senior public-service management positions created during the various restructurings. So far, so good. The next steps should be to measure the overall scale of the benefits accruing to each of these groups, and then try to trace whether and how they participated in the promotion of the managerialism to its position of ideological dominance. Unfortunately, however, it seems that not much of this research has yet been done. One is left with only a little systematic evidence plus a generous helping of anecdote.

The area in which existing research is least patchy is that of contracting out and privatization. Ascher (1987), for example, provides a useful analysis of the 'new public sector market' in Britain (pp. 54–96). She shows that contractors have conducted effective but low-key campaigns directed at key national decision makers and backed up by direct contributions to Conservative Party funds. One of the lobbyists identified in her account – Michael Forsyth – went on, after Ascher's book was written, to become the minister with responsibility for the NHS in Scotland. Ascher also indicates that the prizes are considerable – by the late 1980s the Conservative government's compulsory competitive tendering requirement had affected two thousand NHS hospitals and over five hundred local authorities. One of the larger cleaning contracts may serve as an example: in 1986 Lincolnshire County Council awarded to a private company a £3.3 million contract for cleaning its buildings. The firm saved Lincolnshire £400,000 per annum, and it was able to do this partly because it reduced hourly wages for cleaners by nearly 25% (King, 1987, pp. 125–6). A close economic analysis of six NHS catering, domestic services and laundry contracts showed that savings of 33%–66% were achieved and that the opportunity was frequently taken to rationalize the services concerned (Milne, 1987). It also demonstrated that wage reductions and redundancies were common.

The activities of management consultants and of educational and training institutions have been more opaque. There is no doubt that the Thatcher administration has had repeated recourse to the major consultancies such as Peat, Marwick, McLintock,

Coopers & Lybrand, Touche Ross and Arthur Young. Local and health authorities have also increased their use of this kind of advice, partly because they sometimes lacked internal expertise and partly because the ideological dominance of private-sector management was such that central departments were less likely to question recommendations from a consultancy than from an internal analysis.

In the educational world schools of business and management tended to be protected from the worst of the economies that were heaped upon their less-favoured colleagues in the arts and the humanities. At the Open University, for example, a new School of Management was set up (in the middle of a financial crisis at that university) and was soon providing generic management courses for the NHS among other customers. Pure 'public administration' courses were in some places absorbed into BA Business Studies or MBA courses. The Economic and Social Research Council launched a research initiative on 'Management in government'. At sub-degree level most public administration courses came under the auspices of the Business and Technical Education Council (BTEC) which put a considerable emphasis on the acquisition of technical skills and much less on matters of 'mission' and political context. Throughout higher and further education it was made clear, from the top down, that money and opportunities lay with management subjects (not with policy analysis, public administration or politics) and particularly with the generic approach.

In the United States the inter-penetration of government and business had long been more extensive than in Britain. Businessmen regularly took political positions in Washington and generic approaches to management had been around for decades. At university level generic schools of management were already fashionable in the late 1970s, and the contracting out of services was a topic of bi-partisan interest in local government well before Reagan assumed the presidency. What was witnessed during the 1980s was therefore an intensification of an existing situation. The two thousand plus businessmen and women of the Grace Commission were nevertheless a noteworthy and symbolic incursion. And in the view of at least one knowledgeable commentator: 'despite disclaimers to the contrary, substantial issues of privilege and conflict of interest are raised by how the Grace Commission worked' (Goodsell, 1984, p. 202). It was, after all, a commission of businessmen which ended up by recommending that many things done by government would be better done by business. In the absence of further research one can only note this as a general concern − questions of exactly which companies benefited and how, and of whether the total flow of such benefits were significantly greater under the Reagan administration than its immediate predecessors, remain open.

While much of interest may yet emerge from investigation of the play of interests around managerialism, one final cautionary word may be in order. Although a given constellation of interests may well be a useful explanatory factor in the sense that it provides one source of 'motor power' for the changes, it would be a mistake to conceive of these interests as static − existing like some bedrock under the shifting sands of political and management fashion. For new institutions and practices themselves help to remould old interests and stimulate the construction of new ones. Indeed, this has been one of the most subtle features of managerialism's impact on the public services. When a senior public official moves to a private-sector management consultancy firm his or her stakes and interests in alternative solutions to particular public-service problems begin to change. When enough such officials have made similar moves those who remain in the public services can see that this was not a 'one-off', but the emergence of a possible new career path for themselves too. This process is seen at its most stark in the case of privatization (but it is certainly not exclusive to that technique). Head teachers, senior social workers, nursing officers, police chief inspectors/captains and many others have been taught to think of themselves as managers, and career rewards have begun to favour those who emphasize this dimension. Even more significant have been the effects on 'consumers'. Once council tenants buy the freeholds of their houses their status, obligations and reference groups all change (Hennig et al., 1988). Some, at least, of the architects of public service managerialism realized this very well. Far from being a purely technical exercise, the articulation of what I have termed neo-Taylorism was in part an attempt at shaping a new set of organizational and political constituencies.

Value critique

As chapters 2 to 4 demonstrated, the neo-Taylorism of the late
1970s and early 1980s was dominated by the values of efficiency
and economy, with effectiveness a poor third (Cmnd 8616; Cmnd
9058; Committee of Vice Chancellors and Principals, 1985; Department of Health and Social Security, 1983; Goodsell, 1984;
Grace, 1985; Hopwood, 1984; Metcalfe and Richards, 1984;
Pollitt, 1986a; President's Private-Sector Survey on Cost Control,
1984 and many others). Other values — for example, fairness,
justice, representation, or participation — were either off the
agenda or were treated as constraints on the drive for higher
productivity. This was manifested in many ways and reflected, of
course, the public-choice economists' unremitting focus on the
theoretical inefficiency of public-sector bureaucratic 'production'.

It was also, perhaps, influenced by the wider neo-liberal view
that during the 1960s and 1970s the 'political' sphere had grown
too far and that expanded demands for 'representation', 'participation' and 'equal opportunities' were beginning to sap both
the freedom of the individual and the dynamism of economic
markets. In the UK, to take one example, the 1989 white paper
on the NHS proposed to sweep away those trade-union and local
government members of health authorities who 'usually regard
themselves as representatives' (CMM 555, 1989, p. 64). This
representation was certainly not going to be re-provided anywhere else in the system. On the contrary, the hand of management was to be strengthened throughout the health service: 'If
health authorities are to discharge their new responsibilities in a
business-like way, they need to be smaller and to bring together
executive and non-executive members to provide a single focus
for effective decision-making' (CMM 555, 1989, p. 65).

Beneath both the public choice economist's view of the market
and the neo-liberal's hostility to pluralism and the expansion of
most forms of collective political action lay a common denominator
— individualism:

[t]he basis of evaluation of anyone should be what other people are prepared to pay
for their goods and services. In this sense moral merit or desert does not
matter. What matters is the result of a person's endeavours and whether

others are prepared to pay for it. This is the only criterion of value in a free society. (Hoover and Plant, 1989, p. 51)

It is entirely in keeping with this philosophical approach that the concept of 'consumer' should be preferred to that of 'citizen' (see p. 125 above). After all, the 'consumer' is a rational, individual chooser whereas the connotations of citizenry are emphatically those of a collectivity, with rights and duties owed to or derived from the body politic as a whole (King, 1987, pp. 9 and 17–18).

Efficiency and individualism were therefore the root values which informed many of the key public-service reforms from the late 1970s on. Along with them, however, travelled certain subsidiary values, not all of which sat very comfortably together. Two in particular were economy and entrepreneurship. The specific reforms analysed in chapters 3 and 4 yielded many examples of drives for 'efficiency' and 'value-for-money', which, in practice, became exercises in input-pruning rather than output improvement. Eliminating 'waste' was the crusade on both sides of the Atlantic (Grace, 1984; Banham, 1988). Yet economizing is conceptually by no means the same thing as raising efficiency, and may even conflict with it. Since efficiency is defined as the optimal ratio between inputs and outputs, lowering inputs will only increase efficiency if it does not trigger a proportionate fall in outputs. Whether it does or doesn't is an empirical question, and one which is often difficult to determine with any certainty (because of the frequent problems of measuring public-service outputs). Thus the subsidiary value of economy, made salient by the new right's predilection for cutting public expenditure, gave a particular and one-sided twist to the drive for efficiency. 'Efficiency gains' so often became a matter of trying to get the same service from a smaller resource base rather than investing a few extra resources in order to procure a disproportionate increase in outputs.

The other fellow-traveller with efficiency – entrepreneurship – was a very different character. Whereas the economizing public manager was a tidy, prudent figure (already well-known to nineteenth-century liberals) the entrepreneur was a risk-taker and innovator. The second was as colourful as the first was grey. As the 1980s progressed some commentators, especially businessmen, began to argue for a new model of government in which hitherto core public services would actually be provided, on contract, by risk-taking, entrepreneurial private-sector organizations. The much-diminished civil service would then become an enabler rather than a provider, its role reduced to one of specifying and monitoring of contracts (Banham, 1988; Mather, 1988). Similar arguments had fuelled the rather earlier wave of contracting out of local government services in the US (Hennig et al., 1988, p. 451). Those civil servants who could not be replaced by private-sector providers would themselves be given fresh decentralized authority and encouraged to take more personal responsibility — and more risks (Efficiency Unit, 1988; US Senate, 1984, pp. 303—4).

As Parsons (1988) has noted, there are value problems with the notion of entrepreneurial activity in respect of public services. This is because of what the official documents do *not* say. They do not mention that it is intrinsic to the neo-liberal concept of the entrepreneur that s/he not merely takes risks but: 'exploits informational discrepancies between individual sellers and buyers. In other words, the entrepreneur makes profits through exploiting the ignorance of other traders' (Parsons, 1988, p. 36).

Whether or not this is an appropriate ethic for public-service provision is obviously controversial. Certainly there seems to be some value confusion, if not contradiction, between the various fellow-travellers, with efficiency. Perhaps, though, there is not — despite Parson's warnings — too much to fear from entrepreneurialism *within* the public sector. There it seems a very muted theme, with the values of economy, efficiency and subordination to political control dominant. It is in the context of privatized and contracted-out services that it may be a value to be reckoned with.

Unequal opportunities

If the values of economy and efficiency were 'in', neo-Taylorian approaches were largely silent on the issue of equal opportunities. Practically all the official documents and initiatives reviewed in earlier chapters are gender-blind. They fail to acknowledge that the public services operate in a highly gender-discriminatory society, and sometimes embody proposals or assumptions which, unwittingly or otherwise, are likely to reinforce the difficulties which women face in securing for themselves successful public service careers (Pollitt, 1989). This blindness (or 'obtuseness' as it might be better put) extends beyond gender issues to embrace questions of equal opportunities for disabled persons and ethnic minorities. The most prominent management reforms of the 1980s − on both sides of the Atlantic − have simply not concerned themselves with these matters. The value of equal opportunities has thus, implicitly, been set low.

The 'political clout' which has supported Grace, Griffiths, FMI (etc.) had been conspicuously absent from equal opportunities policies. In the US the Reagan administration's antipathy to the Equal Rights Amendment was obvious. In the UK: 'The conclusion can only be that the implementation of equal opportunities in Britain is being actively frustrated . . . the rhetoric of the British government advances the view that women belong in the family while its actions produce a mass of changes prejudicial to the interests of women' (Forbes, 1989, p. 32).

What are these actions − or at least that subset which relate particularly to the public services – which are prejudicial to the interests of women? They tend to be passively rather than actively discriminatory, but their impacts are none the less real for that. For example, there is the assumption that only a full-time work record really counts in the competition for more senior posts, and the (increasing) emphasis on job mobility in the first half of one's career, both of which disadvantage women who are involved in child-bearing (Harding, 1989). Or again, in British local authorities there is a:

workaholic 'macho' ethos . . . . Many a senior management post now has stress and long working hours written into the job description. Rather than seeing more women move into management with a greater variety of possible management styles and role models, we are witnessing a creeping 'hard' managerialism in the public sector which increasingly associates managerial competence with masculinity. (Coyle, 1989, pp. 47−8)

Nor are these assumptions exclusive to the UK. Though the federal civil service, in particular, has made considerable progress in introducing equal-opportunities hiring policies, the more subtle cultural and behavioural expectations still tend to militate against a representative proportion of women reaching the higher echelons (and take a heavy toll on those who do – Hennig and Jardim, 1978). As sociologists have frequently observed: '[M]anagerial work offers an especially compelling illustration of the relations between male socialization and the rationalization of work' (Winter and Robert, 1980, p. 257).

Before leaving this topic it is perhaps worth emphasizing that the kind of wilful neglect of equal opportunities issues referred to above is itself not equally distributed either in time or by country (Forbes, 1989). In so far as this book is heavily focused on the UK and the US during the 1980s it is concerning itself with two governmental regimes characterized by ideologies which were particularly hostile to formalizing equal rights. Both regimes espoused ideologies which combined economic liberalism with strong elements of social and moral conservatism: 'Both the Thatcher and Reagan administrations . . . have sought to halt the post–1945 trend of increased state activty in the sphere of social citizenship rights. Attacking feminism, and reimposing traditional female roles within the family, is at the core of New Right conservatism' (King, 1987, pp. 17 and 21).

As King points out, this combination of economic liberalism with social conservatism is, at root, a major contradiction within the new-right position – the same position from which many of the major neo-Taylorian public-service reforms have also flowed. During the 1980s, however, this uncomfortable mixture, contradictory though it may have been in philosophical terms, seemingly proved more of an electoral advantage than a handicap.

Value analysis can go further. It can explore the 'meta values' underpinning efficiency and it can also point to possible dynamic effects on other values if efficiency assumes a dominant role for very long. Analysis of the foundations of the concept soon indicates that: 'Its meaning is contextually determined. And this contextualism, in turn, allows a variety of potentially conflicting principles to travel together under the name of efficiency' (Goodin and Wilenski, 1984, p. 513).

According to these authors efficiency is valued because it is derived from the principle of want-satisfaction. It is good to do things as efficiently as possible because that will 'leave over' the maximum quantity of resources for use in further want-satisfaction projects. However, pursuing this trail leads to some conclusions which run counter to the dominance efficiency is usually accorded in administrative affairs. For example, since some wants are more intense than others, it may be logical to pursue a 'big' want inefficiently rather than a lesser one efficiently. The pattern of wants may well vary from context to context and group to group, so the pursuit of just plain efficiency, without an examination of the values people accord to different ends *and* means, could frequently contradict the want-satisfaction principle which gave birth to efficiency as a guideline in the first place. One 'contradiction' which this line of argument reveals – and which has clear implications for the neo-liberal hostility to the welfare state – is that: 'To feign concern for the wants served by efficiency but indifference to the wants served by distributional constraints amounts to simple inconsistency' (Goodin and Wilenski, 1984, p. 515).

Goodin and Wilenski go on to ask why want satisfaction is itself considered such a worthwhile goal. They suggest that this is because 'it is our respect for persons which underlies the desire to satisfy people's wants' (p. 515). Finally they hint that, if this is indeed a more fundamental principle than both efficiency and (even) want-satisfaction, then governments may have a primary duty to eliminate poverty, unemployment and the denial of human rights. But one does not need to accept this final step in their argument to see that the exploration of the want-satisfying foundations of efficiency throws up all sorts of philosophical conundrums for public service managerialism. If efficiency is, in some sense, only a 'surface value' then what more fundamental values are its enthusiasts actually pursuing? Whatever they may be it appears unlikely that simple input/output efficiency measures will always be an adequate yardstick of an appropriate performance.

My last point concerns the dangers attendant upon the long term dominance of efficiency as a criterion of performance in the public services. I cannot better Langdon Winner's encapsulation of the threat:

Efficiency, speed, precise measurement, rationality, productivity, and technical improvement become ends in themselves, applied obsessively to areas in life in which they would previously have been rejected as inappropriate. Efficiency —the quest for maximum output per unit — is, no one would question, of paramount importance in technical systems. But now efficiency takes on a more general value and becomes a universal maxim for all intelligent conduct. (Winner, 1977, p. 299)

There is a sense in which this is a reformulation of Goodin and Wilenski's anxieties about a 'surface value' being universalized to the point where it begins to contradict some of its own foundations. It is yet another manifestation of the narrowness of the neo-Taylorian agenda.

Conclusions

It has been shown that, from at least four separate standpoints, the kind of managerialism that was popular with the Reagan and Thatcher governments is open to serious criticism. Furthermore, perhaps the most obvious and severe of these criticisms (those here presented under the heading of 'realism') had long been well known in both the practitioner and the academic public administration literature. The attempt to impose a largely generic and neo-Taylorian model of management on the public services seems to have been either an act of culpable ignorance on the part of those concerned or an exercise in (possibly unwitting) ideological imperialism, or some mixture of the two.

The major official reports which, on both sides of the Atlantic, provided the milestones for the advance of public-service managerialism engaged little if at all with these issues of strategic or philosophical appropriateness. In conclusion, therefore, it may be useful briefly to return to some of the earlier literature in which the debate between the 'genericists' and the 'distinctivists' was given a better airing.

The literature of the 1960s and 1970s already contains many of the points made earlier in this chapter. It may be useful to begin with a 1975 essay by Michael Murray, an American academic, who, after noting that 'entire new schools are being founded on the generic model' went on to conclude that: 'The large issue, the central question, is whether public and private management are inherently different. Based on this exploratory survey of the issues, the answer is a cautious no' (Murray, 1975, pp. 364 and 370).

In defence of his position Murray could well have cited (but did not) an influential earlier essay by the management authority Peter Drucker. Drucker (1973) had discounted most of the alleged differences between profit and non-profit organizations, although he did lay considerable weight on the distinction between organizations financed by budgetary appropriations and those financed by market-derived revenues. The former (which include most public services) were said to be less efficient. This is, of course, identical to then-emerging conclusions of the public-choice economists such as Niskanen (1973). What is striking about both Murray's and Drucker's contributions is how patchy were their reviews of the relevant literature, and how slight their references to systematic empirical research. Much of the argument was either very general/conceptual or rather anecdotal.

A more systematic attempt was made by Rainey et al. in 1976, responding to the Murray article of a year earlier. Going over the same ground, but in considerably greater depth, they came to a cautious but strikingly different conclusion:

[O]ur inquiry into this comparative question points to the conclusion that it is premature to discount the significance of public − private differences [p. 233] .... It is difficult to see how a core curriculum in 'generic management' could extend beyond a handful of joint courses, such as organization theory and basic quantitative skills. Even in those courses, difficulties as to the mix of readings, cases and examples may arise. (Rainey et al., 1976, p. 242)

Their analysis indicated that the literature repeatedly referred to the salience of the role of political considerations, the objectives problem, the differing legal context, the issue of consumer 'coercion' and the lack of market competition − all issues identified and discussed above. There were also references to value differences such as: 'Greater public expectations that public officials act with more fairness, responsiveness, accountability and honesty' (Rainey, et al., 1976, p. 237).

Five years later Fottler returned to the question 'Is management really generic?' (Fottler, 1981). Again the literature, both theoretical and empirical, was surveyed. This time the author came up with a four-fold classification of 'prototype' organizations: private for-profit; private non-profit; private quasi-public (primarily public utilities created by legislative authority) and public. His overall conclusion echoed that of Rainey et al.: 'Dependence on different individuals, groups and organizations in the external environment creates different values, incentives, and constraints for management. The resulting differences in how the basic managerial processes are implemented may be more significant than the generic theory of management has acknowledged' (Fottler, 1981, p. 1).

Empirical research during the 1980s has done at least as much to reinforce as to undermine these propositions of distinctiveness. To take just one example – this time a very detailed analysis of a group of 240 senior personnel – Soloman (1986) discovered substantial differences between public- and private-sector managers, differences which were actually wider as between private- and public-service organizations than between private- and public-production organizations. Soloman observed that:

> Policy makers in the public sector are faced with special organisational imperatives. They confront political and often value-laden issues very specific to their society. The size of many governmental organizations, the pluralism in policy implementation networks, and the inadequately developed performance criteria, render the task of channeling sanctioned goal-directed activities more difficult. (Soloman, 1986, p. 256)

Findings of substantial differences between public- and private-sector managers reappeared in an even more recent survey of British managers (Alban-Metcalfe, 1989).

It is perhaps paradoxical that during the 1980s, while some management theorists in the business schools were enthusing about the spectacular variations between different organizational 'cultures', politicians and senior officials were energetically imposing on British and American public services a model of management which largely ignored their distinctiveness. In so far as uniquely public service cultures *were* acknowledged, they were treated as problems, unfortunate legacies of the past which were to be re-shaped as quickly as possible. This crude and curiously old-fashioned approach was, for the time being, dominant. As always however, there were alternative strategies lurking in the wings. It is to these that the next chapter turns.

6

Some Alternatives

Introduction

It is one thing to criticize an existing approach, but quite another to come up with a viable alternative. Criticisms of neo-Taylorism have been plentiful, but few of the critics have gone on to propose alternative strategies for the reform of the public services. The implicit alternative — particularly when service providers themselves have been the critics — has often seemed to be the *status quo ante* plus more resources. Each of us will have our own view of the feasibility of such an approach, but for two main reasons it is not one which I find either attractive or convincing. More of the kind of public-service growth which took place during the 1960s and early 1970s is unattractive because it fails to acknowledge the problem (well evidenced, and not only by the new right) of effectively unaccountable 'provider power'. It is unconvincing in so far as its proponents have been unable to offer an achievable economic scenario which would permit the spending trends of that earlier period to continue. To show that the welfare state is not an insupportable burden is one thing, but to suggest that there is plenty of room for it to continue to grow as a proportion of GDP has — at least in the case of the UK — little basis in most politico-economic analyses — even those friendly to the public services (Levitt and Joyce, 1987, pp. 157–64; Gillion and Hemming, 1985, pp. 34–6). In sum: 'The outlook is such that without substantial increases in tax revenues it will be difficult to maintain or improve effectiveness of public services unless productivity is improved, given the existing structure of services provided by the state' (Levitt and Joyce, 1987, p. 123). For these and other reasons, therefore, the 'base case' of returning to the halcyon spending days of 1960–75 will be considered no further here. Significantly, in the late 1980s it is not being proposed by the mainstream of any major political party on either side of the Atlantic. In the USA, while increased spending on education may be a possibility, welfare programmes are unlikely to grow more than marginally, and the drive to control Medicare costs seems certain to continue (Burtless, 1986). What, then, are the other alternatives to neo-Taylorism?

Before going into detail it is important to note that all the alternatives examined hereafter envisage extensive further reform of the public services. The aim is not only to increase productivity as proposed by Levitt and Joyce, but also to enhance control of professional providers and to oblige services to become more responsive to the wants and needs of their users. In these broad terms, though not at levels of greater detail, there is a striking consensus − at least rhetorically − about what needs to be done. A second general observation is that most of the 'alternatives' considered here also share a commitment to restoring a distinctive *public* dimension to public services management (see, e.g. Corrigan et al., 1988; Dilulio, 1989; Moscow, 1987; Pollitt, 1988b; Stewart and Ranson, 1988; Ventriss, 1989). Pure genericism ('management is the same anywhere') seems to be losing ground. Caution is appropriate, however, since the nature of this public dimension is usually indicated in only the most general terms, and it may be that the different commentators are not referring to quite the same thing.

A final preliminary point is that, while the 'alternatives' may be gaining ground, none of them has yet managed the kind of ideological dominance which neo-Taylorism achieved under the administrations of Ronald Reagan and Margaret Thatcher. They have yet to be − and may never be − popularized and taken up by major political parties or the mass media. Yet they have begun to attract interest in academic and management circles, and are likely to increase their appeal as the 'hype' wears off neo-Taylorian initiatives and the gains accruing from the latter are realized to be both limited and heavily offset by the lowering of morale and motivation for so many public-service staff.

The public-service orientation

The 'public-service orientation' (PSO) was developed in the mid 1980s as a philosophy around which it was suggested that UK local authorities could regain: 'a sense of purpose that can drive forward management and motivate their staff' (Stewart and Clarke, 1987, p. 161).

Faced with a situation in which local government was wrestling with both extremely tight resource constraints and a frequently unsympathetic (or actively hostile) central government (Stoker, 1988), it was hoped that the PSO could provide ground on which to regroup, remotivate and redirect the activities of staff. The core PSO commitment was to high-quality services that directly reflected customer values. Thus, borrowing from *In search of excellence* (Peters and Waterman, 1982), it was a 'value-driven' approach that demanded that management get 'close to the customer'. Many management consequences were seen as flowing from this initial stance, for example, the setting of priority on issues of access (to buildings, documents), the redesign of complaints procedures and the evolution of new forms of professionalism which would conceptualize the public as partners rather than dependants.

The advocates of the PSO were insistent that this was more than just transplanted private-sector 'consumerism', explaining that: 'concern for the citizen as well as the customer distinguishes the public service orientation from the concern for the customer that should mark any service organization. For this reason issues such as participation and public accountability are raised' (Stewart and Clarke, 1987, p. 170). PSO enthusiasts further recognized that their approach carried within itself its own set of dilemmas (e.g. that between representative and direct forms of democratic participation) but suggested that it was better to open up local government and confront these openly than to remain in the closed, demoralized and defensive posture in which many authorities then found themselves.

Although originally hatched in a UK local government context the PSO was subsequently broadened into an approach to management in the public domain in general (Stewart and Ranson,

1988). Its proponents accepted that specific management ideas could be usefully transferred from the private to the public sectors but attacked the notion that 'the private sector model' could itself be the subject of a successful transplant. After putting forward a number of anti-genericist arguments Stewart and Ranson went on to specify what they saw as some of the key features of the necessary 'new approach' to managing in the public sector. These were as follows:

- The public domain should be viewed as a site for societal learning. Organizational processes should be designed in such a way as to facilitate learning *from* citizens rather than to 'contain' public debate and activity.
- The concept of 'strategy' should be understood as referring not to the organization's competitive stance (as in the private-sector model) but to a set of expressly political purposes which themselves reflect public aspirations as revealed by a process of public debate.
- Budgeting, similarly, should be regarded as an exercise in choice determined through political bargaining, not as an instrumental search for the 'right answer'.
- The rationing of public services must be based on an assessment of need, but has also to be carried out in such a way that the original purpose of the programme in question is made manifest.
- Value-laden decisions characterize both public and private sectors, but 'the achievement of collective values is the purpose of the public domain and not of other domains' (Stewart and Ranson, 1988, p. 18).
- Public management usually entails the management of interactions between different agencies and organizations – cooperation between autonomous or semi-autonomous entities.
- Performance monitoring is concerned not only with efficiency and effectiveness 'but with the unexpected impact, and with values denied' (Stewart and Ranson, 1988, p. 19).
- There is a dilemma in reconciling political control and staff potential. The public service ethic alone is inadequate as a motivator. Staff have trade-union rights, ideas, views and suggestions. They are also themselves citizens. But all this

has to be balanced against the public's interests and the need to be responsive to customer/citizens.

- 'Marketing' in the private-sector model has to be reconceptualized as influencing public behaviour, and public managers need to develop ways of balancing *between* the differing interests of different groups within the community.
- Public accountability goes beyond the idea of just holding to account. It requires the public manager to find ways of *giving* account, in many different forms and at different levels. Caution and propriety must not be allowed to stifle experiment and responsiveness to the public.

It will be appropriate to assess the PSO (and other 'alternatives') against the same criteria which were developed during the critique of neo-Taylorism in the previous chapter. Thus it may be evaluated in terms of its coherence, realism and values, and also in respect of the political interests that are served by its promulgation.

The coherence of the PSO does seem an improvement on that of neo-Taylorism, but its promulgators freely confess that it nevertheless contains dilemmas of its own. It does make some attempt to address the question of the motivation of public servants, indeed its whole thrust is to offer them a new and distinctive rationale, directly rooted in a set of close and continuous relationships with those whom the servants serve. Stewart and Clarke write of 'positive staff policies' to retrain staff and encourage them to seek out the public's views, value them and use them as major guidelines in the formulation of both major policies and detailed operations (Stewart and Clarke, 1987, p. 166). So far, so good, but this immediately leads to a dilemma: 'Neither representative democracy nor participatory democracy sits easily with industrial democracy' (Stewart and Ranson, 1988, p. 19).

Indeed, for some of the more traditional-minded local government officers real moves towards a more customer-responsive organization may seem just as morale-bruising as the imposition of neo-Taylorist controls by central governments. No one yet seems to have developed a detailed formulation — even at the level of theory — for combining industrial democracy for public-service staffs, participation by customer/citizens in the design, operation and monitoring of the services which they are going to use, and representative democracy in the shape of traditional elections to produce representatives who will then oversee these same services. Perhaps the circle cannot be squared. If so, the PSO appears to advocate a higher priority being given to citizen participation than to the other two considerations. The likelihood of this being achieved will be further discussed when I come to examine the realism of the PSO.

This first dilemma can be reformulated in more general terms. The PSO marks an advance on neo-Taylorism in so far as it recognizes the need for the public services to be value-driven, and for the driving values to reflect the unique features of collective choice in the public domain. A coherence problem arises, however, because the actual values identified (consumer participation; local flexibility; fairness and equity etc.) appear to be in some tension, one with another. Little specific is offered by way of methods for resolving these tensions. To advocate clarity and openness in value choice is certainly a start, but in the absence of some recognized approach to actually defining and weighting the relevant values the decision maker's discomfort is simply sharper and more visible. In making this point it should be acknowledged, however, that to ask for such criteria is extremely ambitious. Neo-Taylorism only *appears* to avoid this issue by dint of its refusal to admit to its calculus the range of values with which the PSO engages.

Turning now to the realism of the PSO it may be said that it incorporates elements of increased realism concerning the particular conditions of (at least) local government, but that it may also underestimate the resistance it would be likely to encounter if there were ever an attempt to introduce it on a large scale. As suggested above, a full-blown drive for heightened customer/citizen responsiveness would be likely to encounter resistance from several quarters, some of them fairly powerful. In effect the PSO proposes a major programme of cultural change, one which appears to threaten the power base of both professional service deliverers and elected councillors. It would undermine both departmentalism and professionalism by increasing the power of customers relative to providers and by moving in the general direction of 'one-stop', local service outlets. It would dilute the

[handwritten marginalia: decentralisation increases public access but may erode the elected official's contact with the public, which may be a bad thing]

authority of elected representatives by multiplying the access channels available to their constituents, thus possibly reducing the elected representatives' (already weak) claim to be the one set of actors within the organization which is really in touch with what the people want. There is an empirical question, therefore, as to whether the incentive of regaining a coherent identity, rationale and style for the public services would sufficiently compensate for the perceived threat to professional and political legitimacy. There are certainly examples of promising beginnings along PSO lines (Stoker, 1988, pp. 203−6). But the same author also gives examples of resistance within particular local authorities. This has come from senior management and from junior and middle-ranking white-collar staff. It is easier, perhaps to confine change to the 'shop front' and the cosmetic, and it seems that this is often what has actually occurred, both in local government and the NHS (Hambleton, 1988; Pollitt, 1988b; Potter, 1988). Yet this is to betray the full intent of the PSO, whose authors explicitly distinguish their project from mere 'consumerism' (Stewart and Clarke, 1987, pp. 169−70).

The other major 'realism' doubt concerns the resource requirements implied by the PSO. Just as neo-Taylorism has in some cases been undermined by being implemented in conditions of extreme financial stringency (see chapter 3), so the implementation of the Public Service Orientation would presumably depend on adequate resourcing. The training and information technology implications of the PSO seem considerable in themselves, but to these must be added the redesign and repositioning of service facilities which would be bound to emerge from giving more weight to customer preferences. The author is not aware of any cost estimates for a thoroughgoing programme of PSO-type reforms, but the total bill, especially in the early stages, would hardly be small. This could be another reason why thus far 'consumerism' appears to have won out over the wider PSO concept: in the short run it is much cheaper to redecorate the hospital reception area and retrain the receptionists than to consider relocating or decentralizing the hospital itself.

The interests represented in and by the PSO are very different from those entwined with neo-Taylorism. As indicated in chapter 5, the latter is especially associated with the new right, and also with the small and medium sized businesses which stand to benefit from contracting out. By contrast, the PSO is associated with the Labour, Social Democratic (as was) and Liberal (as was) parties. Its intellectual origins lie at the Institute of Local Government Studies at the University of Birmingham, together with the Local Government Training Board (see, e.g. Local Government Training Board, 1988). The most conspicuous (though not the only) attempts to put elements of the PSO into practice seem to have occurred in urban authorities with Labour majorities. The GLC, Manchester, Sheffield, Hackney, and Islington were among the best-known pioneer authorities of the early and mid 1980s. Given the importance of the public-service unions within the modern Labour Party it is not surprising that the drive for greater flexibility and responsiveness among staff has encountered some of the problems referred to above. This central tension is somewhat diminished, though hardly dissolved, in local authorities where the centre parties (Liberal, Social Democrats and Democrats) are in control. In sum, therefore, while Stoker (1988) tends to associate the PSO with the 'urban left', it would be more accurate to say that from the beginning it has also recruited support from the 'urban centre', not least from senior local government officers themselves.

That the PSO admits of a wider range of values than neo-Taylorism has already been pointed out. Its 'value portfolio' contrasts sharply with that of generic management models in its emphasis on collective rather than individual values. Stewart and Ranson neatly summarize the differences (see table 6.1). Different commentators have offered somewhat varying emphases within this broad portfolio. Reformers on the urban left have acknowledged the importance of merit and efficiency as well as equality in the conduct of public affairs, but have argued for giving prominence to what they term 'merit of need' (Corrigan et al., 1988, p. 8). They claim that there is a considerable social consensus that the sick and the disabled should enjoy high priority in public provision. Another priority should be the removal of 'barriers to merit', such as wealth, class, sex and race. 'A meritocratic society must be seen to be fair to all its members: it will work only if every one is actively involved' (Corrigan et al., 1988, p. 8). If these sound very much like the traditional Labour left concerns,

Table 6.1 Value differences between the PSO model of management and a 'genetic' private-sector model

Private sector model	Public sector model
1 Individual choice in the market	1 Collective choice in the polity
2 Demand and price	2 Need for resources
3 Closure for private action	3 Openness for public action
4 The equity of the market	4 The equity of need
5 The search for market satisfaction	5 The search for justice
6 Customer sovereignty	6 Citizenship
7 Competition as the instrument of the market	7 Collective action as the instrument of the polity
8 'Exit' as the stimulus	8 Voice as the condition

Source: Adapted from Stewart and Ranson, 1988, p. 15.

slightly repackaged, other elements in this approach are less familiar. Subjecting the outputs of public services to published, measurable criteria is an acknowledgement of the force of the new-right critique. But in the vision of the urban left all this is subordinate to the central task: 'the reconstruction of a civic culture: one founded securely on an extension of the citizen's rights and responsibilities' (Corrigan et al., 1988, p. 16).

Rhodes (1987) takes a somewhat different line, but arrives at a not-too-dissimilar conclusion. He pinpoints the value structure of the PSO as the key factor which distinguishes it from the kind of consumerism with which the new right themselves would be perfectly comfortable. He sees 'caring' and 'citizenship' as the values which are needed to breathe political life into the INLOGOV/LGTB approach.

Yet how value conflicts *within* the citizen body will be tackled under PSO is, as suggested earlier, a largely unresolved issue. Under the traditional, representative model of local government the formal answer would presumably have been that such conflicts would have been resolved collectively, by the elected representatives. With PSO in place, however, it would be harder to round up such conflicts so that they could be dealt with in one place (the council chamber). Rather, they would be likely to crop up at many locations and levels, and would impact directly on decisions made by officers as well as members. Whilst it might be argued that in practice this is what already happens, the PSO, instead of brushing these awkward conflicts under the carpet of formal political responsibilities, is committed to describing them clearly and openly, and inviting public debate. All that can be said with certainty is that this would indeed constitute a 'cultural revolution' as far as much local government is concerned. In the United States, where the culture of local authorities has long been more 'technicist' than in the UK, the PSO – or at least this aspect of it – would represent an even greater wrench.

Overall, therefore, it might be said that the PSO is a much more ambitious approach than neo-Taylorism. It aims at a greater variety of objectives and seeks to realize a wider range of values. It is not surprising that this greater complexity yields problems of its own. These arise precisely because the PSO sets out to identify and confront the distinctive features of the public services, whereas neo-Taylorists approach these same features with suspicion and the intent to minimize.

Public management and strategic planning

The founding text of the 'public management approach' appears to have been a 1983 edited collection by two American scholars, *Public management: public and private perspectives*, (Perry and Kraemer, 1983). Subsequently this attracted considerable attention among the public policy/public administration academic communities in the UK and Western Europe (see, e.g., Gunn, 1987). It is hard, however, to estimate how far its influence has spread beyond the academic and into practitioner communities (recognizing, especially in respect of the USA, that these two do overlap at the edges).

Perry and Kramer began with a critique of the 'generic viewpoint', of which they both had extensive direct experience. They expressed their dissatisfaction thus:

In our experience of the generic viewpoint, good management typically meant good business management. We became aware, however, that the subject matter in our colleagues' course syllabi frequently touted techniques that failed miserably when applied to government. Furthermore, our generic curriculum, until very recently, neglected to develop in students a skill highly regarded in the public sector – the ability to interact with and manage diverse, external, and mainly political interests. (Perry and Kramer, 1983, p. ix)

This observation did not lead them, however, to quite such a thoroughgoing rejection of the appropriateness of generic, business models as that pronounced by the advocates of the PSO. Instead they argued for a 'merger':

Public management is a merger of the normative orientation of traditional public administration and the instrumental orientation of generic management . . . . The public management approach emphasizes that the individual manager must be able not only to understand and analyze the unique institutional and organizational systems in which he or she is embedded, but must also be able to bring an array of techniques and skills to bear in directing the system. (ibid., p. x)

'So far, so bland', as Gunn waspishly remarks (1987, p. 35). Nor does the remainder of the Perry and Kraemer collection generate any particularly clear summary of the specific characteristics of the approach which results from the merger. Indeed the contributors to the 1983 volume seem to adopt a variety of positions on the basic issues of how and to what extent public sector management is different. The editors themselves dwell rather more on the instrumental than the normative issues. Acknowledging their debt to Woodrow Wilson's distinction between administrative and political issues (see chapter 1, p. 15), Kraemer and Perry make it clear that their chief interest is in means, not ends. Thus they define the first characteristic of the public management approach as follows: '1. Its primary purpose is to develop an understanding of how public, primarily governmental organizations may accomplish the missions charged to them' (Perry and Kraemer, 1983, p. xi).

Nevertheless, public management proved a reasonably attractive label, and others soon began to rally to it — and reinterpret its meaning. In a special 1989 issue of the American Society for Public Administration's journal several contributors wrote of the need for the further development of this approach. For example, Ventriss argued that in respect of the normative dimension a new philosophy was needed. This, he claimed: 'must be formulated, not upon the romantic and technocratic characteristics of past efforts, but instead upon a revitalized concept of the public that emphasizes public interdependency, public learning, a new public language, and a critical evaluation of the relationship between the role of the state and public administration' (Ventriss, 1989, p. 173).

There are clear echoes of the PSO here, though they are couched in 'Americanese'. All three of the emphases identified by Ventriss are connected to the PSO theme of being close to the customer. Thus 'public interdependency', for example, means that: 'the practice of public administration must be expanded to civic and voluntary associations that mediate between individuals and the state. These associations may thus be transformed into lively democratic laboratories for civic engagement and responsibility' (ibid., p. 176).

In the same journal Dilulio sought to recover the distinctive 'public management variable' (Dilulio, 1989). He conceptualized this search as one of assembling: 'a reliable stock of generalizations ... about how, whether, and to what extent different types of management practices matter to the quality of citizens' lives, and what (if anything) can be done to change the management of given public organizations in ways that are likely to achieve specified public purposes' (ibid., p. 128).

Dilulio then engaged in a preliminary examination of the literature on schools, prisons and armies. Although recognizing that this body of research was in many ways unsatisfactory for his purposes, he did claim to find, in each case, some evidence to indicate that management factors were of great importance in determining the quality of service. The article did not, however, specify with any precision what types of management practice were likely to be most effective, still less what could be done to change the management of particular organizations to improve their achievement of public purposes.

Before coming to a critique of public management it is necessary to make mention of the development of another public sector 'approach', also American in origin, which is partly distinct from but partly overlaps the stream of writing that followed on Perry and Kraemer's work. I judge the overlap to be sufficient to justify treating this approach under the same heading as public management. The approach I am referring to is 'strategic planning', probably best known from a recent book of the same title by

Bryson and Einsweiler (1988). The label itself is borrowed directly from the generic management literature, but its public-sector proponents usually claim that: 'public and third sector organizations face problems that are quite different from those faced by firms and that therefore they require their own distinctive brand of strategic planning (Backoff and Nutt, 1988, p. 120).

Strategic planning in its US, public-sector form appears to concern process more than content or output (for a discussion of this distinction see Lewis, 1988, p. 2). In practical terms various versions have been tried out at state (California, Ohio), county (Hennepin/Minnesota, Dade/Florida) and city (San Francisco, Albany, Memphis) levels (Kaufman and Jacobs, 1987, p. 35). Different academic authors advance different models of the process, pitched at different levels of detail and incorporating more or less specific recommendations concerning the actual techniques appropriate to each stage. One of the more detailed such models is that of Backoff and Nutt (1988). This specifies the six stages and then goes on to offer a variety of suitable techniques for use at each stage (see below).

Stages in the strategic management process
1 *Historical context*
   (a) Trends and events
   (b) Directions
   (c) Ideals

2 *Situational assessment*
   (a) Strengths
   (b) Weaknesses
   (c) Opportunities
   (d) Threats

3 *Strategic issue agenda*
   (To be decided upon by the strategic management group in the light of the analysis of stages 1 and 2).

4 *Strategic options*
   (a) Action sets
   (b) Strategic themes

5 *Feasibility assessment*
   (a) Stakeholder analysis (internal and external)
   (b) Resource analysis

6 *Implementation*
   (a) Resource mobilization
   (b) Stakeholder management

                    (adapted from Backoff and Nutt, 1988, p. 123)

This model may be processual, but it would be unfair to say that it was mechanistic or non-political. Indeed (to take one aspect) the advice on managing stakeholders (stage 6b) is quite Machiavellian. Two of the suggested steps are 'determining which antagonistic stakeholders must be surprised (kept in the dark) to prevent their opposition from mobilizing' and 'asking supportive stakeholders to sell the strategy to those who are indifferent' (ibid., p. 130). The authors certainly recognize that the problems of multiple stakeholders and value conflicts are commonplace in the public sector, and that managers cannot simply assume that 'politics' will be taken care of before (or after) the planners set to work. On the other hand the concept of 'stakeholder analysis' is taken straight from the generic management literature and Backoff and Nutt say little about the relative legitimacy of the different stakeholders in terms of democratic theory. Nor do they discuss the requirements of public accountability and the constraints these may place on both tactics and strategy.

How robust are the public management and strategic planning approaches set against the kind of critical criteria to which neo-Taylorism and the PSO have already been subjected? The answer has to be that neither of these overlapping bodies of literature could yet be said to perform well. Both have something of the air of rearguard actions, comprising slightly ramshackle structures hastily erected in the hope that they will provide some defence against the anti-public service, anti-planning forces of the neo-liberal new right. In terms of *coherence*, therefore, neither scores particularly highly. Public management is such a 'broad church' (Gunn, 1987, p. 43) that it is difficult to discern any distinctive pattern of key propositions against which to assess internal coherence. In so far as there were previously tensions between the 'normative' stance Perry and Kraemer attribute to traditional US public administration and the more instrumentalist approach of generic management studies, these have been papered over rather than resolved. To assert that public management needs to take account of both is obviously sensible, but it hardly constitutes a new 'paradigm'. As it stands, different writers are free to take markedly different stands on the priority to be accorded to the different elements in the package, yet apparently still qualify for the public management label. In most cases it seems that: 'the political context is recognized as a set of constraints/variables that must be dealt with, but the manager is treated as a specialist in implementation or technique and, consequently, the political nature of public administration is left out' (Nigro, 1989).

A recent collection of papers reviewing European experience with public-management approaches reflects a marginally greater willingness to address the political elements as integral to the manager's role, but lacks coherence in other respects (Kooiman and Eliassen, 1987). After presenting a confusing collection of conceptual taxonomies (and remarkably little empirical evidence) the editors conclude that there is a 'lack of scientific knowledge about public management' (ibid., p. 239).

Strategic planning appears vulnerable to the same criticism. Even at the end of a lengthy overview its core intellectual identity remains curiously vague. To be told that 'strategic planning to date comprises a number of approaches (i.e. bundles of concepts, procedures and tools) that vary in their applicability and usefulness to different situations' does not inspire much confidence (Bryson and Einsweiler, 1988, p. 216). Whilst there is certainly a reasonably consistent emphasis on the importance of citizen participation, strategic planning is if anything even less specific than the PSO about how to handle conflicts between the values that may be expressed by participating citizens and those of the elected representatives charged with running public-service organizations. In sum, the coherence of strategic planning seems limited and its novelty content very low: 'From the planning literature, we find that the critique and suggestions embodied in strategic planning are longstanding, well-developed and well-known' (Kaufman and Jacobs, 1987, p. 30).

A final point about coherence is that most of the literature reviewed in this section shares with neo-Taylorism an apparent lack of interest in developing a model of the public-service worker. With one or two recent exceptions (Lewis, 1988) issues of morale and motivation are only fleetingly alluded to. The project is couched in terms of a search for successful processes and techniques, not for loyal, committed and highly motivated persons.

The vagueness of the public management and strategic planning approaches also makes it hard to assess their *realism*. It all depends *which* strands are emphasized in practice. It may be argued that, whether coherent or not, the Bryson and Einsweiler compendium (1988) contains case studies of innovative and apparently successful planning initiatives in US state, city and county governments. On the other hand, the difficulty in establishing what is and what is not strategic planning leaves the reader wondering whether these successes can really be attributed to a coherent and distinctive approach which is sufficiently well-specified for it to be reproducable in other public-sector contexts. As far as the public management approach is concerned (at least in the Perry and Kraemer version) its realism seems flawed by its resuscitation of the old Wilsonian politics/administration dichotomy. That in practice there is usually no clear line between public 'missions' and the selection of means for their achievement has been repeatedly established in empirical studies including, indeed, some of those carried out under the public management or strategic planning labels.

In terms of *interests* both public management and strategic planning clearly reflect the recent dilemmas of the US public-services sector. Beset by neo-liberal budget-cutters and anti-planners, practising public-service managers were in desperate need of some new slogans or labels to shore up what remained of their activities. Similarly, from the late 1970s, academics with backgrounds in public administration and planning were faced with submergence beneath the swelling tide of generic management studies. To express their problem in generic terms, they needed more 'product differentiation', and these approaches promised to provide it. One practising planner put the case for strategic planning with concise forthrightness: 'Nowadays its the way to get federal bucks for planning. You have to use the right buzz words to get a share of the dwindling dollars' (quoted in

Kaufman and Jacobs, 1987, p. 29). Its academic proponents were almost equally candid: 'while more traditional public planning may have a bad name because of the recent conservative turn in American politics, strategic planning is more favoured because of its identification with private sector corporate planning practice' (Bryson and Einsweiler, 1987, p. 7).

The situation in UK local government was, of course, rather different, and this may go some way towards explaining why strategic planning has yet to catch on in Britain. Planning was probably more deeply embedded in UK local government anyway and, although undoubtedly diminished under the Thatcher administrations, was at least not threatened with extinction. Furthermore, UK local authorities had recent memories − if not current experience − of their own corporate planning processes. Whilst these were not usually full 'strategic planning' they contained sufficient elements of the latter to reduce still further its appeal on grounds of novelty. Finally, UK local authorities were in a different situation in so far as their major problem frequently appeared to be hostile intervention from central government. They saw themselves as beleaguered by Thatcherite interference rather than Reaganite neglect, and, again, this may well have reduced the perceived appropriateness of strategic planning.

A *value analysis* of public management and strategic planning is difficult because the main texts seem shy of direct statements of values. In general terms, it may be said that the chief concern of these texts is with quality. This contrasts, therefore, with the priority accorded to cost saving in the work of the Grace Commission and several other Presidential initiatives (see chapter 4). 'Quality' here is to be construed in terms of what 'matters to the actual quality of citizens' lives' (Dilulio, 1989, p. 127). Some writers go beyond this rather instrumental formulation to advocate not just the improvement of the quality of citizens' lives but also the re-modelling of relationships between the citizen and the state. Thus Ventriss (1989, p. 176) argues that: 'the administrator's public stewardship in the future involves increasing the public's understanding of policy' and that this will entail: 'increasing the capacity and knowledge of the public by facilitating politically educative interactions between the public and administrators'.

Elsewhere, however, this more developmental emphasis is not

to the fore. For example it is largely absent in the two seminal texts already referred to, *Public management* (Perry and Kraemer, 1983) and *Strategic planning* (Bryson and Einsweiler, 1988). It is probably fair to say that these approaches *are* characterized by a concern for re-establishing distinctively civic or public values, but that there is considerable vagueness as to what these values might be. In any case the proponents of both approaches frequently find it prudent to present their material with the main emphasis being laid on its instrumental virtues rather than its developmental or philosophical dimensions. What is more certain is that public management and strategic planning do not share either the dominant concern with economy and efficiency, or the anti-public service, anti-professional sentiments of neo-Taylorism.

'Cultural' approaches

An early academic assessment of the Thatcher administration's FMI concluded that: 'the accepted concept of management is too narrow and restricted to do justice to the full range of public management problems' and that: 'political clout needs supplementing by cultural changes which can sustain a broader concept of management'.

The authors warned, however, that: 'broadening the meaning of management involves overcoming some deeply entrenched attitudes which maintain the separation of management and politics' (Metcalfe and Richards, 1984, pp. 452–3). This critique was one of a growing number, on both sides of the Atlantic, that drew on the concept of organizational 'culture' – the notion that each organization embodies 'an ordered system of meaning and of symbols, in terms of which social interaction takes place' (Geertz, 1973, p. 144). An organisation's culture, it was suggested, influenced the kind of commitment employees felt towards their organisation's 'mission', how adaptable they were, the quality of service delivery they aspired to, their confidence in management, and so on. From a purely academic point of view, therefore, the concept of culture could be deployed to help explain why (in, say, the case of FMI) reforms were being held back by an existing Whitehall 'disbelief system' (Metcalfe and Richards, 1984, pp.

448−9). Used in more instrumental/prescriptive ways, however, a cultural analysis might suggest that for management: 'The problem is one of changing people's values, norms and attitudes so that they make the 'right' and necessary contribution to the healthy collective "culture"' (Lynn Meek, 1988, p. 454).

Several mentions have already been made of probably the most influential single piece of cultural analysis, Peters and Waterman's *In search of excellence* (1982). There were many others that were equally prescriptive. According to some, 'managing corporate cultures is now possible' (Kilmann et al., 1985, p. 431) and the design of a culture appropriate to the organization's mission and circumstances had become a prime task for top management.

There is one sense in which cultural analysis is a neat, mirror image of neo-Taylorism. It is concerned with the 'soft stuff' of beliefs, attitudes, rituals and symbols, not the 'hard stuff' of efficiency measures, savings targets and 'bottom lines'. It focuses on the very space which neo-Taylorism usually leaves blank − the subjective sense of engagement (or lack of it) which public servants have with their tasks and the distinctive pattern of beliefs and disbeliefs through which they give meaning to the organizational life around them. In this sense, therefore, it is very much an 'alternative'.

The next step is obviously to enquire in more detail into what are, and what should be, the actual contents of public-service organizational cultures. And it is here that one encounters the first problem. There seem to be more sermons urging reformers to take account of existing cultures, and prescriptions setting out menus for new cultures, than there are detailed studies of the components of present public-service cultures. Nevertheless there are some clues. For example, in describing the disbelief system of the British civil service Metcalfe and Richards refer to at least three elements.

- There is extreme scepticism about proposals for restructuring organizations. It is commonly expressed in phrases which refer to the futility of 'tinkering with institutions'.
- The belief that reforms normally fail. Their chief value is the indirect effect they may have in keeping people up to the mark by occasionally giving them a jolt.

- Immediate doubt about management theories of concepts which address broader or longer term issues (as opposed to narrow practical techniques of obvious and immediate applicability). Such ideas are frequently dismissed outright as mere jargon (Metcalfe and Richards, 1984, pp. 448–9).

In a later paper these same authors contrast what they see as the existing 'administrative culture' with the 'management culture' which they suggest is sorely needed to handle the heightened environmental instabilities of the 1980s and 1990s. The old and the (hoped for) new are presented as a series of pairs, viz:

- From an emphasis on procedural conformity to an emphasis on performance assessment.
- From a culture of hierarchical subservience to one emphasizing the taking of personal responsibility.
- From the valuing of continuity to the valuing of innovation.
- From a culture of propriety (correctness, equity etc.) almost regardless of cost to a culture of cost-consciousness (Metcalfe and Richards, 1987, pp. 71–2).

In the United States entire institutions emerged with the express mission of fostering a culture of 'excellence' in federal, state and local administration (Barbour et al., 1984; Center for Excellence in Government, 1989; Williams, 1986). The exact content of the proposed 'excellence' was not always very clearly specified, but its general flavour seemed to have to do with raised self-esteem among public officials, with 'quality government' and with improving the image of the public service in the eyes of business people and the general public.

In addition to those who focus specifically on the public services, there are more generic prescriptions for cultural success. Best known are Peters and Waterman's eight points (1982):

- A bias for action ('Do it, fix it, try it').
- Closeness to the customer – a commitment to listening to their wants.
- Encouragement to autonomy and entrepreneurship within the organization.
- Respect for the rank-and-file employee/resistance to 'we/they' attitudes to management/other worker relations.

- Emphasis on a few core organizational values (e.g. reliability, attention to detail).
- Concentration on activities the organization knows and understands ('Stick to the knitting').
- Simple organizational structures with lean top-level staffs.
- A combination of centralization of the core values/philosophy with maximum decentralization of operations.

Another widely-employed framework is Handy's typology of four cultural ideal-types:

- Power cultures (Zeusian).
- Role cultures (Apollonian or 'bureaucratic').
- Task cultures (Athenian).
- Person cultures (Dionysian).

Handy argued that each has a particular pattern of strengths and weaknesses. A role culture may work well for one kind of task in one kind of environment, while in different circumstances a task culture could be a much better 'fit' (Handy, 1976, chapter 7). Several commentators have seen public service cultures as being predominantly Apollonian, and the changing environment of the 1980s and 1990s as requiring a shift towards more Athenian attitudes, emphasizing performance, individual expertise and multi-disciplinary team work (Metcalfe and Richards, 1987; Pollitt, 1989b).

Advocates of a 'cultural' approach to change made a number of points in favour of their chosen perspective. Some suggested that in the contemporary conditions of high environmental turbulence an appropriate value orientation would provide a more secure foundation for the public services than any particular organizational structure. The stability of the latter would always be at risk from further environmental displacements, whereas a value-set which emphasized the positive value of communication, experimentation and flexibility stood a good chance of riding the waves of change (Metcalfe and Richards, 1987, p. 79). Others argued that greater attention had to be given to cultural factors if the wastage of talent was not to climb, and the level of public service morale to fall, still further. Most writers who adopted a cultural perspective opposed genericism, stressing the need to recognize the distinctive circumstances of the public services (Moskow, 1987). Most also pointed to the need to preserve (or in some cases reinstate) some of the positive features of what they took to be the traditional culture, particularly loyalty (Metcalfe and Richards, 1987, p. 66) and a sense of civic duty and purpose (Ventriss, 1989, p. 173). Certainly the cultural approach holds out the prospect of a more historically-aware analysis than the usually 'timeless' neo-Taylorism. A thorough historical inquiry is usually held to be a necessary precursor to grasping the intricacies of an organization's prevailing culture (Handy, 1976, pp. 185–7; Pettigrew, 1985, p. 26).

Some of the works of 'cultural' writers – perhaps especially the American ones – are strenuously 'non-political'. For example, they explicitly avoid taking any stand on questions of the proper size for the public sector (Center for Excellence in Government, 1989) or, more generally they refrain from relating their analyses to specific political interests, group tactics or economic contexts. Others, however, insist that a proper understanding of organizational change is only available when both intra-organizational politics and extra-organizational factors are combined: 'Chief among [the factors determining organizational change] will be the role of business and economic factors outside the firm, and historical, cultural and political processes inside the firm, together with the interplay between these two sets of contextual variables, as providers of both the necessary and sufficient conditions for continuity and change' (Pettigrew, 1985, p. 26). Although the above quotation is taken from a study of ICI the author advocates an essentially similar approach to public-service organizations (Pettigrew et al., 1988). The actual *content* of organizational changes needs to be understood in relation to the environmental *context* and the political *processes* within and between the organizations concerned.

The present author must confess to some affinity with this position. It is indeed my contention that a grasp of both socio-economic and ideological shifts is essential to understanding the rise of managerialism (chapter 2). It is also part of the foregoing argument that specific political interests powerfully combined to ensure that it was a neo-Taylorist variant of managerialism which was widely implemented in both the UK and the US during the early and mid 1980s (chapter 2, 3 and 4). Furthermore there appear to be good reasons for believing that the limited impact of neo-Taylorism in some areas was connected with the way in which its protagonists effectively ignored (or actively attacked) the public-service cultures which were already in place (chapters 3, 4 and 5).

Any critique of cultural approaches has to recognize the diversity alluded to above. Thus, for example, some treatments can be criticized as unrealistically apolitical but others cannot. The reader's best remedy is to follow up some of the sources first-hand — Metcalfe and Richards (1987) and Williams (1986) are probably as good places as any to start.

The *coherence* of cultural approaches is sometimes obscured by their vagueness. If only a few beliefs or values are discussed, and then in very general terms, or 'culture' itself is not clearly defined, cultural approaches may be scarcely more than exhortations to virtue. A problem with some writers is that they define culture — or imply a definition — in such a way as to include *either* the social structure *or* actual organizational behaviours (or both) within the concept. This contrasts with the usage adopted here (and elsewhere: Geertz, 1973; Handy, 1976) which confines culture to the realm of expectations, beliefs, meanings and symbols. The difficulty with these wider definitions is that their omnibus nature signals a loss of discriminatory power. If social structure and belief are both defined as part of 'culture', for example, it becomes harder to discuss any tensions, which may exist between these elements — e.g. *between* employees' expectations and the actual structure of the organization, (Lynn Meek, 1988, pp. 464—5). And if culture is defined as including actual behaviour then it becomes all too easy to assume a straightforward, transitive relation from belief to action — despite plenty of evidence that this relation is often highly complex and subtle (i.e., our actions frequently diverge from our beliefs).

A second problem with some cultural analyses is their vagueness concerning the actual tools and techniques for 'culture management'. In so far as our concern here is prescriptive (that is, with what should actually be done by or to public-service organizations) it will be necessary to know: (1) what existing cultures are like; (2) what the cultures desired for the future are like; and (3) by what techniques (1) can be remoulded into (2). In general the public service literature (at least) is extremely non-specific about what these techniques might be. Leadership by example is one frequent candidate, training usually gets a mention and symbolic change (new logos; new office layouts; appointment of new kinds of people to particular posts) is often referred to. But this author does not know of anything which amounts to a full action programme for cultural change. It may well be that the coherence of the 'cultural change' position is flawed by sheer lack of knowledge about how to do it.

Cultural analyses clearly score over neo-Taylorism (just as the 'human relations' school scored over classic Taylorism) by offering a more realistic — or at least more complex — model of the employee. Indeed, Peters and Waterman themselves acknowledge that: 'The stream today's researchers are tapping is an old one, started in the late 1930s by Elton Mayo and Chester Barnard, both at Harvard. In various ways, both challenged ideas put forward by Max Weber, who defined the bureaucratic form of organization, and Frederick Taylor, who implied that management really can be made into an exact science' (1982, p. 5).

The mechanistic, target-oriented, merit pay-chasing figure of neo-Taylorism is replaced by a meaning-seeking individual who is sensitive to informal group norms, themselves derived from a complex (and partly mythologized) history of organizational interactions. When cultural analysis is married to a micro-political treatment of internal élites (as in the work by Pettigrew referred to above) an even more elaborate framework emerges, one which is capable of generating very convincing accounts of organizational change.

In other respects, however, the *realism* of prescriptive cultural analysis must be questioned. For just as the accounts of cultural change become more complex, more political and more convincing so the apparent requirements for would-be 'cultural engineers' escalate. Seriously to envisage a planned change to the culture of a major public-service organization would necessitate both an enormous ration of management effort and an unprecedentedly generous timescale. It is hard to see political leaders (certainly not those of the neo-liberal new right) conceding either. Winning the hearts and minds of most or all of the various groups making up the organization would at the minimum require several years of

assiduous staff development work. Even if this were to be embarked upon there is, as already indicated, a distinct lack of
knowledge as to which techniques would actually prove effective.
In short, management does not 'own' the organizational culture,
and is usually in no position simply to manipulate it in the service
of their own objectives (Pollitt, 1989b). On the contrary, any
complex organization usually displays a number of contrasting
(and sometimes competing) sub-cultures and each may be deeply
rooted in the minds of the relevant groups of staff: 'culture
should be regarded as something that an organization "is", not as
something that an organization "has": it is not an independent
variable, nor can it be created, discovered or destroyed by the
whims of management' (Lynn Meek, 1988, p. 470).

At best, therefore, a sensitive management may be able to
shape its actions and messages so that they appear to 'go with the
flow' of certain aspects of an existing culture, may be able to
appeal to traditional organizational values to support innovative
developments, or may encourage and reward one set of attitudes
while discouraging another. This is a much less heroic role than
that of cultural engineer. A more appropriate analogy might be
that of a portrait painter — management can show back to the
organization a picture of itself which, though recognizably realistic,
emphasizes certain strengths and brings out a positive overall
sense of character. Blemishes may be more easily acknowledged
and attended to when seen in this larger, and fundamentally
sympathetic perspective.

In terms of *interests* cultural approaches appear to be of mainly
academic origin. Teachers, researchers and consultants in the
organization theory/business studies field borrowed from earlier
work by anthropologists. The growing fascination with organizational cultures during the 1970s was part of a broader movement within the social sciences which rejected the positivism of
the natural science model and insisted on renewed attention
being given to the social construction of meaning. It probably
came as a great surprise to most of these academics when Peters
and Waterman's *In search of excellence* — methodological warts and
all — became such an enormous popular success. Once this had
happened, however, the approach provided a useful vehicle for
others. Senior public servants, particularly, could use its apparent

respectability to bolster their own efforts to dilute the rigours of neo-Taylorism. The message seemed to be that changing cultures was necessary if the broader objectives of public service reform could be achieved and that, in practical terms, this implied more attention being given to matters of morale and staff development.

What *values* are explicit or implicit in cultural approaches? The most popular generic analyses — and their public-service applications — all seem to emphasize team work, flexibility, an orientation to performance rather than regularity, the encouragement of innovation and a commitment to listening and responding to consumers (Peters and Waterman, 1982; Handy, 1986; Metcalfe and Richards, 1987). Efficiency assumes the role of a subordinate rather than a dominant goal — its chief value lies in its contribution to the achievement of desired outputs such as adaptable, reliable, high-quality services. Cultural approaches are generally more tender to the interests of the employees/providers than neo-Taylorism, presumably because the basic commitment to such an approach involves acceptance of the importance of subjective perceptions and beliefs, whether economically 'rational' or not.

Competencies

The 'competencies' approach is a recently-emerging alternative to neo-Taylorism. It is strongly connected with the work of the Management Charter movement in the UK (Reid, 1988). The central thrust of this approach is that there is a generic set of management competencies, and that all managers need to acquire them. This should be accomplished through a mixture of study, practice and reflection on practice, with a greater emphasis on the last two than has been customary in formal education. The implications of this approach seem to be that high priority should be given to the acquisition of basic competencies by all managers because, until this is secured, the success of larger management systems is likely to be inhibited by the lack of basic skills. The underlying assumption is the usual managerialist one that organizational performance is first and foremost a function of the quality of its managers.

It is not appropriate to give the competencies approach the

same kind of treatment as the other 'alternatives' examined in this chapter. There is as yet very little literature which attempts to apply the approach to the public services. Moreover, there is a sense in which it is fundamentally different from both neo-Taylorism and the other alternatives because it is explicitly a 'micro' approach, focused on improving each individual manager, rather than one which addresses system-wide organizational issues. Nevertheless I believe it is necessary to afford it at least a brief discussion, partly because it represents yet another new species of generic managerialism, and, more practically, because it seems probable that it will henceforth play an important part in management education throughout (at least) the UK (Reid, 1988).

The competencies approach shares the messianic qualities identified in chapter 1 as one characteristic of managerialism. Here is the Chairman of the Council for Management Education and Development and Chief Executive of Shell UK:

For too long the chains of the first industrial revolution have made men subservient to machines, have led to negative and defensive attitudes in the work force, depriving us of the potential of our most valuable resource – the initiative, ingenuity and creativity of our people.

The time is ripe to prepare the managers to lead the new revolution in which these human qualities will be the dominant feature: right because organizations in the private and the public sector want it; right because the young men and women of the new generation demand to be prepared and to be involved. (Reid, 1988, p. 1)

Note that it is being suggested that 'competencies' are for public-service managers as well as those from the business and commercial sector. Clearly, also, this is intended to be a more 'worker-friendly' approach than neo-Taylorism. The accent is on continuous self-improvement and updating leading to a hierarchy of 'professional' qualifications.

Unfortunately the limitations of this kind of approach are already becoming apparent. First, it easily degenerates into the listing of discrete, measurable competencies – indeed, for some this is part of its appeal. Yet it is highly questionable whether 'good management' can be disaggregated in this way, and, even if it could, the notion of a single, objective scale of measurement is likely to continue to prove illusory (Burgoyne, 1989, pp. 57–8:

Pye, 1988, pp. 62—3). Second, the emphasis on competencies tends 'to leave out the moral and ethical' (Burgoyne, 1989, p. 59). In this, of course, it is similar to Taylorism and some other generic approaches. Third, it is always in danger of neglecting group and structural factors: 'high levels of individual member competence do not guarantee group or organizational competence and effectiveness' (Burgoyne, 1989, p. 60). Fourth, it is not surprising that the efforts to arrive at a definitive list of competencies have tended to produce a variety rather than a uniformity of elements. As Pye (1988, p. 63) puts it: 'any definition of effectiveness must also be relational: dependent on time, context and evaluating audience. In essence there can be no absolute conception of managerial competence or effectiveness'.

This is, of course, precisely the argument advanced at greater length in chapter 5. All generic models, including the competencies approach, are likely to encounter considerable difficulty when applied to the particular context and audience of a given public service at a given point in time. Competence is a social construct. Whilst there may be some micro-political or social skills which are valued across a very wide range of times and contexts there are many other aspects of successful management which are not so portable: 'managerial skills are different from other technical and professional forms of expertise in their relative low degree of standardization, their susceptability to change, their specificity to situations rather than problems and their internal relationships with the systems they are managing' (Whitley, 1989a).

Overview

While the scaffolding of concepts and assumptions varies considerably from one 'alternative' to another there is nevertheless — as indicated in the introduction — a clear overlap between their 'recommendations'. The PSO, public management and most cultural analyses all stress the importance of getting closer to the consumer. Public management and the PSO both call for the re-establishment of a distinctive public-service ethic, and this seems entirely consonant with the emphasis of most cultural analyses on developing a set of core values to guide the organization through its turbulent environment. All praise 'flexibility' (put like that, who could oppose it?). All place performance and quality (as defined by consumers) above unreflective rule-following or conformity to precedent. At this level therefore — that of broad goals and values — it might be argued that all the major alternatives point in roughly the same direction.

When it comes to means, however, significant differences are apparent. The PSO is probably the most overtly 'political' of the alternatives here considered, and explicitly recognises the need to build coalitions of political support and, indeed, to remodel relations between political representatives and career officials. Public management is less convincing on this score, its exponents usually preferring to work on the instrumental side of their generic/ public administration 'merger'. Some cultural approaches present themselves as though they were 'non-political', but others more fully acknowledge the need for the negotiation and use of power relationships if attitudes are successfully to be influenced. To some extent these variations are probably no more than simple reflections of the broader political and business cultures from within which these ideas have come. Thus the more 'technicist' culture of American local government accepts the relatively a-political, generic, process models of strategic planning while the increasingly party-conscious world of British local government gives birth to PSO. But there are other differences too. As I have indicated, some 'recipes' are considerably more concrete and precise than others. Both the PSO and public management advocates are happy to discuss particular techniques and methods by which their formulations might be carried into practice. Culture analysts seem more reticent in this respect — they are more comfortable discussing the need to pay attention to cultural variables than specifying what, in practical terms, to do about them. None of the alternatives examined appears to offer a detailed prescription for curbing provider power, although the PSO comes closest, and is certainly the most explicit in recognizing the issue and elaborating on its implications.

Finally, it may be worth acknowledging that the evaluation criteria deployed in this chapter and the preceding one are by no means necessarily those which will determine the short-term fates of either neo-Taylorism or its alternatives. The 1980s have provided many illustrations of just how far a particular approach can be pushed despite incoherences, startlingly narrow and unrealistic assumptions and the presence of obvious vested interests. Those charged with putting particular management reforms into practice seldom enjoy the luxury of prolonged reflection on these issues, and in any case are frequently acting under the twin imperatives of authoritative orders from above and tight timetables. What then matters may be getting something in place, in time, in minimal working order and in a form that bears at least superficial and rhetorical resemblance to the locally dominant managerial ideology. In a broader, longer-term perspective, however, I would argue that the criteria used here do have a real importance. If a particular approach *is* incoherent or unrealistic, or if it grossly favours some interests and values over others, then this is very likely to affect its eventual viability, and its chances of providing a foundation upon which the next changes will be based. Political clout can keep a deeply inadequate approach in being for years, but it cannot ensure that its roots will grow deep in the organizations where it is implanted. Real cultural change requires a widespread identification with and enthusiasm for the incoming model. Chapters 3 and 4 indicate that during the 1980s these were not widely forthcoming among UK and US public services. Demoralization rather than remoralization was the common response. After a decade of neo-Taylorism it was time for a new tack.

7

Beyond Taylorism?
The Coming of Quality

Introduction

From the late 1980s and particularly in the early 1990s clear signs began to emerge that neo-Taylorism was undergoing a re-evaluation by those same political parties which had so vigorously launched the ideology a decade or more previously. This watershed was coincident with, but is hardly sufficiently explained by, leadership changes on both sides of the Atlantic. In 1988 President Reagan was succeeded by a man whose whole career had been 'of government'. In 1990 John Major replaced the deposed Margaret Thatcher and very soon began to make positive statements about public services, a central plank in his prime-ministerial platform.

Two examples of the new mood will suffice to convey its flavour. First, within 8 months of taking office John Major launched a *Citizen's Charter* in the preface of which he wrote:

To make public services better answer the wishes of their users, and to raise their quality overall, have been ambitions of mine ever since I was a local councillor in Lambeth over 20 years ago...
I want the Citizen's Charter to be one of the central themes in public life in the 1990s. (Prime Minister, 1991, p. 2)

Slightly earlier, Americans had been treated to the publication of a National Commission report entitled *Leadership for America: Rebuilding the Public Service* (Volcker, 1989). This had confirmed many of the features mentioned in earlier chapters – general demoralization, low pay, increased politicization of the federal bureaucracy – and had urged reform. It was perhaps characteristic of wider features of the two political systems that in the UK the mood should quickly crystallize into a white paper and programme of centrally-driven action while in the US those concerned about the public service should be drowned in knowledgable, data-rich reports and monographs, but (at the time of writing) still lack any convincing new national policy with which to address the so extensively exposed deficiencies (see also Lane and Wolf, 1990; US Merit Systems Protection Board 1989; US General Accounting Office, 1990).

The remainder of this chapter will offer an analysis of these new developments. The main focus will be on the shift away from neo-Taylorism in the UK, since it is here that the nature of the change is clearest and the resultant policies most concrete and coherent. First, however, a brief review of developments under the Bush presidency.

Public management under Bush: recognition but no resolution

Unlike his two predecessors Bush did not make bureaucracy-bashing a prominent part of his Presidential campaign. After a lifetime of public service this would in any case have been incongruous, but no doubt his reticence was reinforced by the growing evidence of crisis in the federal service. The trends identified in chapters 2 and 4 (see pp. 40–8 and 87–95) continued to take their toll of civil service morale. In 1989 a task force reported on the state of the public service and drew attention, *inter alia*, to weaknesses in the new performance-related bonus system for the Senior Executive Service, inadequacies in career development and low levels of executive pay (Volcker, 1989, pp. 90, 100 and 200 respectively). In a seperate investigation the General Accounting office arrived at similar conclusions:

unfortunately, our work indicates that negative perceptions of federal employment, along with less than competitive pay and insufficient acknowledgement of federal careers, may make federal employment unattractive to many graduates. (US General Accounting Office, 1990, p. 5)

Indeed, during the 1980s new downward spirals began to appear, reflecting both the fragmentation of power in the US governmental system and the impatience of many policymakers with a run-down and demoralized federal bureaucracy. Wise describes a process by which expediency leads to the circumnavigation of fundamental reform, only to result in further problems for the public service:

Congress mandates governmentwide procurement, personnel and budget policies (e.g. Gramm-Rudman-Hollings). Then, Congress gets frustrated with the effects on the capacity of federal organizations to adapt to environmental imperatives that Congress (or more likely a particular committee) considers vital. The response is often a hybrid organization – government corporation, government-sponsored enterprise – that is created to facilitate escape from the inflexibility of governmentwide management policies and to accomplish goals more effectively in conjunction with the private sector...However, the structuring of such organizations . . . often does not include understanding of how the management systems that will be adopted by the new organization will affect behaviour of other organizations in the relevant organizational field or the ability of the new organization to play its new role. (Wise, 1990, pp. 151–2)

In this context the Comptroller of the General Accounting Office (and others) have raised the spectre of a 'hollow government':

It is a calculated disinvestment. We are on a downward slope in government operations. We are denying ourselves the long-term incentives needed to make government work. (quoted in Goldstein, 1989, p. 13)

At the time of writing no grand plan for dealing with these trends had emerged from either end of Constitution Avenue. The writing had been on the wall for at least a decade, but one President had been ideologically and temperamentally unsuited to positive public service reform while his successor had concentrated his energies on issues of high policy, especially internationally. Meanwhile Congress had not been able to summon, still less implement and maintain, a coherent vision of the future federal service. As one recent comparative study of higher civil services put it: 'America's flame of managerial reform seems to have died down to a glowing ember' (Hede, 1991, pp. 507–8).

The new Conservative emphasis: quality and quasi-markets

In the UK, too, the limitations of neo-Taylorism were becoming more widely recognised. Cost-cutting, staff reductions and capital starvation had not achieved popularity, either with the wider public (who favoured *more* public spending, at least on education and the NHS) or, most certainly, with public servants themselves. Somehow Conservative policies towards the public services had to be made to appear more positive and appealing, certainly to the external constituency of voter/users and, if possible, to the large internal constituency of public service workers also. In the third Thatcher term, following the decisive electoral victory of 1987, several commentators sensed that 'the pace and scale of change . . . increased dramatically' (Hoggett, 1990, p. 20). This second wave of reforms, re-packaged but essentially continued by the Major administration from 1990, comprised four main elements:

1   A much bolder and larger scale use of market-like mechanisms for those parts of the public sector that could not be transferred directly into private ownership (quasi- markets).
2   Intensified organizational and spatial decentralization of the management and production of services.
3   A constant rhetorical emphasis on the need to improve service 'quality'.
4   An equally relentless insistence that greater attention had to be given to the wishes of the individual service user/'consumer'.

In the academic literature this package has become known as the 'new public management', or NPM. Each of its four principal elements merits further discussion.

Obviously the Conservative preference for *market and quasi-market mechanisms* was not new (see p. 40 above). What was different was the confidence with which the Government was prepared to design and implement such mechanisms across huge and complex public services which had hitherto been regarded as unsuitable for the market 'treatment'. Schools, universities, polytechnics, NHS hospitals, GP practices and the whole field of community care were all to be subject to more or less market-like regimes. Schools and institutions of higher education would compete for students and be financed mainly according to their relative success or failure in doing this. By the NHS and

Community Care Act, 1990 the NHS was divided into sets of 'providers' (hospitals, clinics, community units etc.) and sets of 'purchasers' (DHAs, those general practices with practice budgets). The purchasers were to buy those services they deemed their communities to need, using formal contracts to ensure that they obtained the best 'value for money' from among the competing providers (Harrison et al., 1992; see also p. 65–6 above). Similarly, in the field of community care, local authority Social Services Departments became the purchasers of services from a multiplicity of (public and private) providers (Warner, 1992).

These reforms did not merely alter lines on organization charts: huge changes of role and skill were involved for those groups of staff concerned. DHAs had to invent the purchaser role–to become what the then Secretary of State for Health famously termed 'the people's champion'. Social Service Departments (SSDs) had to learn about contracting and needed to set up comprehensive systems for assessing individual clients' needs. Hospitals were obliged to 'market' themselves as high quality providers. Head teachers, also, had to 'sell' their schools as never before, as well as looking very carefully at the costs of employing above-average proportions of senior, experienced staff. Many professionals were thus propelled into roles they had never trained for and often did not relish.

The new quasi-markets were highly *managed* markets, in at least two senses. First, in the case of health and community care the 'purchasers' were not the final users of these services but public bodies (the DHA, the Social Services Department) which had to decide where public resources should be directed. So the contracts and service agreements were usually negotiated between one set of managers and another (which, incidentally, gave managers in the providing agencies a further source of influence over the rank-and-file professional service deliverers).

The quasi-markets were also managed in the sense that they were entirely artificial constructions which ran according to sets of rules, definitions and formulae invented largely by senior officials in Whitehall. Thus, under LMS (pp. 78–80) the formula by which an individual school received its annual budget had to be approved by the DES, while in higher education similarly elaborate formulae, worked out by the new Universities Funding Council (p. 79), determined exactly how each university was rewarded or penalised for its performance in the race to recruit more students (e.g. Universities Funding Council, 1992). In the case of the NHS it was quite clear that the government was constantly altering the rules and generally intervening in the market they had created in order to secure more politically acceptable outcomes. It was the government which insisted that the numbers of patients waiting for operations for more than two years was a key target for reduction, even if that led to increase in average waiting times for those elsewhere in the waiting list maze – or, indeed, to the temporary downgrading of local priorities (O'Sullivan, 1992). It was the government which intervened to adjust and clarify the rules over which kinds of 'queue-jumping' were permissable and which were not (O'Sullivan, 1991). It was the government which instructed managers not to shift to new referral patterns too quickly.

Decentralization was the second element in the 'new wave' of the late '80s. Like the preference for market-like mechanisms, it was not new. Rather it was a case of an intensification of an existing trend. 'It wasn't until the mid-1980s that real progress in creating more devolved managerial forms began to occur' (Hoggett, 1991, p. 248). In *theory* this appeared to have almost universal support. All political parties supported 'decentralization' and detested 'monolithic bureaucracy'. In practice, however, the Labour Party (and to a lesser extent the Liberals) opposed certain decentralizations, when they were linked to market-like mechanisms. The code word in such cases was 'fragmentation'.

In a textbook competitive market no central power exists – except for that of the state which creates and maintains the law governing contracts, ownership etc. In the public service quasi-markets of the late 1980s and 1990s, however, decentralization leaves central bodies with far more than this. Central bodies define the missions, create the appropriate supporting corporate cultures, set performance targets and then monitor, evaluate and inspect to ensure that targets are met (Hoggett, 1991, p. 252). Control through hierarchical line management is relinquished, but control through cultural manipulation, targets and contracts is substituted. The question of sanctions for poor performance is central to both the 'hands-on' (traditional, hierarchical) and the 'hands-off' modes, but becomes less avoidable in the latter because failures are much more visible (since there are explicit targets, often embodied in contracts).

The third element in the reforms of the late 80s and early 90s was the emphasis on '*quality*'. Conservatives typically linked this to the introduction of quasi-markets, claiming that the pressures of competition would oblige service providers to raise quality. But 'quality' became a buzzword right across the political spectrum, even in those sections of the Labour Party where the market mechanism was still an object of intense suspicion (see, e.g., Pfeffer and Coote, 1991; Pollitt, 1991).

The literature on public sector 'quality' has ballooned since the late 1980s (examples include Audit Commission, 1989; British Rail, 1990; Gaster, 1991; National Audit Office, 1988; Prime Minister, 1991; Treasury, 1991). My bracketing of the term in scare quotes signals that its precise definition is not at all straightforward. Indeed, its use by politicians and managers alike has become positively promiscuous (Pollitt, 1991, p. 4). In the rapidly developing private sector literature on quality (on which many of the early public service initiatives have been more or less based) most contemporary definitions stress the need continuously to meet and improve upon customer requirements. This, in turn, implies a systematic effort to ascertain what those requirements are, and then a setting of standards by those producing the services to ensure that the requirements are met. Finally, the actual services rendered must be monitored to ensure that standards are being met (Centre for the Evaluation of Public Policy and Practice, 1992).

At least two points need to be made about this approach to quality. First, quality is not some entirely new dimension of performance. On the contrary, it is likely extensively to overlap the more familiar performance criteria of economy, efficiency, effectiveness, equity etc. Service users, in other words, are likely to want fast, fair services which are effective but not wasteful. Second, most of the literature stresses that it is essential to respond to *user* (customer) requirements. Potentially, at least, this sets a sharp limit to the extent to which either public service professionals or managers or, indeed, ministers or councillors, can prescribe what the 'right' services ought to be.

Perhaps the single most ambitious exercise in raising public service quality has been the Citizen's Charter, launched by and personally identified with John Major. To some extent this was simply a round-up and repackaging of a range of existing initiatives, but it also included some genuinely new measures. Almost as soon as Mrs Thatcher departed, senior Conservative spokespersons began to argue for a more compassionate image, a marriage of efficiency and quality in the core public services (Bevins, 1991). The shift away from the bleaker mood of neo-Taylorism could hardly have been more clearly enunciated. The Charter white paper itself claimed that:

The Charter programme will be at the heart of government policy in the 1990s. Quality of service to the public, and the new pride that it will give to the public servants who provide it, will be a central theme' (Prime Minister, 1991, p. 4).

The ways in which the Charter programme sought to achieve these noble objectives were instructive. Some prominence was given to further privatization and to the extension of competitive tendering. This was quickly backed up by a further white paper, *Competing for quality*, which gave guidance on 'the role of public sector managers in buying services on behalf of citizens' (Treasury, 1991, p. ii). Alongside these confirmations of belief in the virtues of the market mechanism, however, came a veritable confetti of lesser charters – for NHS patients, for parents of state school children, for the tenants of public housing authorities and for the recipients of state financial benefits. These were portrayed as devices for 'giving more power to the citizen' (Prime Minister, 1991, p. 2) although their targets and guidelines did not usually extend citizen's *legal* rights. They did, however, spell out existing rights and, beyond the law, what citizens had a right to *expect*. Thus the Patient's Charter referred to access to information, choice of GP, respect for privacy, dignity, religious and cultural beliefs and so on. It also offered more specific guidelines on maximum waiting times, the minimum amount of time per week a full time GP must be available to see patients and sundry other items. The Parent's Charter presented a similar mixture: rights to 'five key documents', information about how to choose a school and details of how to appeal against unsatisfactory decisions.

Clearly this approach to quality heavily overlaps with the fourth and final element in NPM – the increased emphasis on *user/consumer responsiveness*. In so far as standard-setting is a central feature of quality assurance and improvement the question obviously arises of 'standards in relation to what?' Overwhelmingly, the answer of contemporary management theorists has been 'in relation to consumer wants and aspirations'. This sounds good, but in practice tends to pose major problems for several major public services. Do 'consumers' (users) understand what is on offer? Are they actually likely to know what will work best for them, in terms, say, of medical treatments or pedagogic strategies in educational institutions? Are they cognizant of resource constraints, or will they ask for the impossible? What will become of the professional service providers – will they be effectively 'deskilled', deprived of most of their discretion and made slaves of the latest public fad or fashion?

Despite these problems, and despite the reluctance of the Conservative administrations to extend the basic legal rights of public service users, widespread changes do seem to have occurred. Many public service organizations have vastly improved their complaints systems; information leaflets have multiplied and become much more user-friendly; reception staff have been initiated into the mysteries of 'customer care' and the opinions of NHS patients and local authority residents about the services they receive have been relentlessly polled (see, e.g., Dixon and Carr-Hill, 1989; Local Government Training Board, 1989).

These sorts of developments command cross-party support. Where the Conservatives begin to part company with Labour and the Liberals is over the issue of user *representation*. On the whole the Conservative administrations of the 1980s and 1990s have been more reluctant than the opposition parties to see any extension or enhancement in formal mechanisms for user representation. Thus Community Health Councils were rather cold-shouldered during the *Working for Patients* reforms, and DHAs had their local authority membership removed in order to 'clarify' their managerial role. The Conservative vision of consumer-responsiveness is more a matter of the robust individual consumer exercising informed choice and less a question of collective user representation in formal councils or boards. Yet this theoretical distinction has not been entirely clear-cut on the ground. In the schools sector the Conservatives both increased the proportion of governors who were to be parents and considerably extended the responsibilities of governing bodies. In this case, however, unlike the NHS, powers were effectively being taken *away* from another 'representative' body – the Local Education Authority.

The New Public Management: an assessment

It is far too soon to attempt a definitive evaluation of the NPM, but it is already possible to identify both real contrasts and broad continuities with the neo-Taylorism of the early and mid 1980s.

The contrasts are obvious from the immediately preceeding paragraphs. Generalized public servant–bashing has all but ceased. The drive for quality has been thrust into the headlines and the service user has been plucked from relative obscurity to serve as the rhetorical pivot upon which many new devices and initiatives are said to balance. The *presentation* of many public services is being transformed, and both paternalistic professionalism and bureaucratic immobilism are (almost) everywhere in retreat.

Equally, the continuities are considerable. The drive for efficiency has not gone away, and the overall pressure on budgets has scarcely diminished. During the 1992 election campaign the relative restraint of both Conservative and Labour promises for increased public service spending was noticeable and no doubt needed to be understood in the context of the sobering figures for the Public Sector Borrowing Requirement which emerged at the same time. Quality might be the theme of the 1990s, but it will have to be won through gains in efficiency, not large increases in spending. The increased prominence of competitive mechanisms in almost every public service appear to have at least as much to do with driving down unit costs as with promoting quality.

Where does NPM fit in among the alternative approaches outlined in chapter 6? To put it briefly, it appears to borrow most heavily from the 'cultural' approaches (pp. 164–72). Peters and Waterman's 'eight points' (pp. 166–7 above) remain central, certainly to the rhetoric of much current change and seemingly to some of the substance too. By contrast, the Public Service Orientation's emphasis on improving the mechanisms of representative and industrial democracy as well as user-responsiveness is absent, as is the broader PSO commitment to engaging with collective needs and values (pp. 150–6). An emphasis on getting closer to citizens and service users does not, of course, discriminate between these various approaches, since it is a common feature of the NPM, the PSO and most of the 'cultural' approaches coming from the private sector.

However, NPM is not simply culture management. The continuities with neo-Taylorism have already been noted. In effect NPM, as practised by the Conservative administrations of the 1990s, attempts to integrate the new 'cultural' elements with continuing threads of neo-Taylorism. Whether a coherent garment *can* be woven out of these two essentially dissimilar approaches remains to be seen. Empirical research in the field (or the pipeline) should reveal whether and where each of these two contrasting elements within NPM is gaining the upper hand. First impressions are that the recent changes in the UK are very much management-led (not user-led). The role accorded to citizens in the process is mainly one of feeding back, via questionnaires and other market research, their (dis)satisfaction levels with what managements have designed and delivered. NPM, in other words, is not so much a charter for citizen empowerment as managerialism with a human face. Even this, of course, is a significant step away from neo-Taylorism, though whether the shift is of a kind to begin to restore the bruised morale of public service staff remains an open question.

8

Reflections

It is not easy nowadays to remember anything so contrary to all appearances as that officials are servants of the public; and the official must try not to foster the illusion that it is the other way round.

(Sir Ernest Gowers, 1954)

It is important to be clear about what has been said and what has not – about the *scope* of the analysis. Since the argument has moved about from country to country, and from level to level, it may be worth remapping its intended territory. At the outset it was established that managerialism constituted an ideology, and that within that ideology there existed a variety of more specific theories and models of what constituted good management. Subsequently it was argued that, faced with real problems in the running of major public services, the Reagan and Thatcher administrations had on the whole opted to respond with one particular model, a fairly narrow and mechanistic one which I termed neo-Taylorism, because of its resemblances to the 'scientific management' school of the late nineteenth and early twentieth century.

The chief features of both classic Taylorism and its 1980s descendant were that they were, above all, concerned with *control* and that this control was to be achieved through an essentially *administrative* approach – the fixing of effort levels that were to be expressed in quantitative terms. Rewards, narrowly conceived as direct financial remuneration, were then to be geared to above-average performance in respect of the newly-established norms for effort. In parallel with this increasingly detailed control of measurable activity went a de-control of the employment relationship, at least in the sense of a move away from 'standard terms and conditions' across large groups of employees. Managers were to have greater discretion to negotiate, or impose, local terms which would more closely reflect local labour market conditions, and the particular performance achieved by the individual employee. This whole set of changes was conducted within a larger framework of ideas which upgraded the importance of 'management' and distinguished this activity from 'politics'. The latter was, on the whole, viewed as an impediment to efficiency and therefore as a process best segregated into its own particular institutions (Parliament, Congress etc.) where it would not contaminate the proper running of executive agencies.

Subsequently I argued that the actual impact of these neo-Taylorist reforms was at first as narrow as the approach itself. In both the UK and the US greater cost-consciousness was drummed home and significant staff reductions were achieved. Batteries of performance indicators were installed and much more extensive contracting out to private-sector providers was encouraged or, in some cases, imposed. On the other hand, while indicators may have shown significant improvements in economy and efficiency, there was much less information available concerning the overall effects of these changes on the effectiveness or quality of services.

A major question (no pun intended) is whether the appearance, from the late 1980s, of the New Public Management, fundamentally changes this somewhat pessimistic interpretation. To a degree I believe it must. The recent emphasis on quality and on meeting user requirements, even if much of it remains superficial, does at least acknowledge that Taylorian efficiency is an insufficient gospel, both for public service workers and for the citizens they serve. However, the value structure of NPM is indeterminate: 'quality' and 'consumer responsiveness' sit alongside a fierce and continuing concern with economy and efficiency. It is not clear which group of values will take priority when (as at some point is inevitable) a trade-off has to be made. Although some private sector quality gurus insist that 'quality is free' it is hard to see how, in the public services, this could possibly *always* be so (unless either 'quality' or 'free' are very idiosyncratically defined). Hood (1991) points out that NPM still prioritizes the 'sigma-type values' of frugality and cost reductions, and takes for granted rather than reinforces 'theta-type values' of fairness, rectitude and mutuality. If this is true then there is a danger that, within tight budgets, higher quality for some may be purchased at the price of lower quality (or no service at all) for others. The fragmentation of hierarchies and the spread of market-like mechanisms increase the chances of such 'market segmentation'.

So although NPM may sometimes succeed in squeezing higher quality and productivity out of the resources devoted to the public services, there are likely to be other times and places where it results in something much less attractive. At least two degenerative forms of NPM may be predicted. The first, segmentation and exclusion from service, has already been referred to. The second concerns the ability of service providers to disguise covert reductions in quality. If service providers continue to control the definitions of quality (Pollitt, 1991) and if information about achieved quality is not subject to independent external review, cost-driven quality reductions may be massaged and concealed. The technically 'incomplete' contracts and quasi-contracts which are increasingly characteristic of the NPM's 'markets' lend themselves to just such obfuscation (Bartlett, 1991).

To criticise neo-Taylorism and NPM is not, however, to condemn managerialism as a whole. At the level of the entire ideology, it may be that the expectations attaching to 'better management' are exaggerated. Certainly some of the more apocalyptic visions of management as *the* key to a better, future world seem remarkably free of any serious theoretical or empirical underpinnings. Within the bounds of this book, however, it has not been possible to pursue these larger questions very far. This important task remains for others to address. My focus, though still wide, has been on what managerialism *does* (or might) have to offer, rather than on alternative socio-economic analyses which allocate a radically smaller role to 'management' as an agent of change. The 'alternatives' explored in chapter 6 are therefore alternatives to neo-Taylorism *within* managerialism. Each alternative still assumes that a transformation of our public services can be achieved through deliberate political and managerial activity within those services.

At this point it may be worth addressing some possible misinterpretations. First, it is *not* claimed here that each and every public service reform in the UK and the US since the late 1970s has had a neo-Taylorist character. Second, neither is it suggested that all those responsible for implementing neo-Taylorist innovations have been neo-liberal ideologues. Third, it is no part of my argument that increased cost-consciousness and improved efficiency measurement are unimportant. Finally, it is not asserted that the UK and the US have undergone identical processes of 'Taylorization'.

The first of these possible misinterpretations mistakes the focus and level of the book. Chapters 1 to 5 are concerned with a dominant model within an equally dominant ideology. These sections of the book describe the conditions favouring its growth, the circumstances sustaining its dominance and the weaknesses and contradictions it nevertheless contains. The analysis is focused on the *generality* of what happened, on the broad tone and character of major, system-wide programmes of reform. Of course, there are other stories to be told, but they are not told here. The leadership of this particular agency may have designed, financed and implemented a far-sighted programme of staff development. That school or hospital may have succeeded in achieving wide professional involvement in management. In some colleges and universities performance measurement systems may focus on 'value added' rather than narrow, unit cost efficiency, and may involve significant inputs from a wide variety of 'stakeholders', including students themselves. Undoubtedly, a few such successes have been achieved. Indeed, the author has direct knowledge of some and has referred to them elsewhere (Pollitt, 1987, 1988b; 1990). The scale and complexity of the public-sector is such that, even if they wished, central governments could not control every corner or homogenize every reform. The kind of imaginative developments referred to here have not, however, constituted the dominant trend. Indeed, they are often achieved only with great effort, 'against the grain'.

The second possible misinterpretation is quickly dealt with. Nowhere have I suggested that neo-Taylorian reforms were carried through solely by a determined band of politically-conscious neo-liberals. On the contrary, in chapters 2, 3, 4 and 5 there are a number of references to the range of interests which have been involved in the processes of 'selling' and implementing these changes. Some implementors have had little effective choice – they have been 'under orders'. Others have been uncomfortable with the nature of the changes, but have not been able to see any realistic alternative, at least not in the short term. This is what Held (1987, p. 182) terms 'pragmatic acquiescence'. Others still may have been sceptical about the efficacy of the approach, but nevertheless gone along with it because it held out the promise of some gain in income or status. Finally, there are those who have supported neo-Taylorian reforms as 'true believers', though even they may have identified with only some elements of the overall set of ideas described in chapter 2, while distancing themselves from others. Similar distinctions may be made for the implementors of NPM. All this is to make the perhaps familiar point that ideological dominance is sustained by a combination of forces, seldom by 'purists' alone. This, in turn, implies that the rise of a new ideology, or alternative model within an existing ideology, does not necessarily entail the 'conversion' of a vast number of fervent followers of the old religion. Rather it may be a matter of gradually detaching a considerable number of individuals who previously could not 'see' another way, or could find no support in their part of the system for one, or could not see one that would be in their own interests.

Third, the argument against neo-Taylorism and the reservations over NPM are not a rejection of efficiency and cost-consciousness. These will always be important, but they only take on their full meaning within a context in which the broader purposes of a public service are discussed and defined, and a concern with effectiveness assumes greater salience. As has often been remarked, it is possible to run a concentration camp economically and efficiently but that does not make it a desirable public service. The critique in chapter 5 includes the suggestion that efficiency is a surface value, taking on significance only when it is coupled with some specification of which wants deserve to be satisfied. Such a specification lies outwith the boundaries of neo-Taylorism. In practice the Reagan and Thatcher administrations exhibited the usual political reluctance to be precise about who was to be served and (especially) who was not, so public services were left with admonitions to 'be efficient' at a set of tasks which are often poorly defined.

Finally, what is revealed by the Anglo-American comparison? It is has been suggested here that a broadly similar ideology coloured the approach of the Reagan and Thatcher administrations to their respective countries' public services. This is quite a limited claim, and one which allows for considerable variations in what was actually done – and where. Even on the level of general ideas there was some difference between the two, not least in the more prominent vein of moralizing which ran through US social policy, reflecting the greater political strength of neo-conservative (as opposed to neo-liberal) groups within the American new right. Another salient difference was the less 'political', more 'technicist' view of local service provision which was already prevalent in the Arnerican political culture. At the level of practice many more differences became visible. These were inevitable, given that the two countries started from very different positions in terms of their constitutional structures, patterns of party political activity and public-service cultures. Indeed, perhaps the more surprising phenomenon was the extent to which similarities did appear – in the assumption of public sector inefficiency, the recourse to private-sector expertise, the stubborn belief in the usefulness of merit pay, the squeeze on general public-sector pay levels, the tremendous emphasis on new accounting procedures and the push, as the 1980s wore on, to abandon national agreements and procedures in favour of 'flexibility' for particular groups of staff.

Like most books, this one has not turned out exactly as its author originally intended. As the work has gone forward my sense of the narrowness of neo-Taylorism has, if anything, sharpened. At the same time, however, my estimation of the difficulty of developing alternative modes of reform has soared. Certainly the fact that the new right is deeply sceptical of the whole organization of the welfare state – and that this same ideological grouping dominated the Reagan and Thatcher regimes – set severe limits to the kind of reforms undertaken. Ultimately, it is impossible to win the hearts and minds of those who know that you actively disapprove of them, and for much of the time this has been the perceived relationship between new-right administrations and a variety of public-service employees – social workers, teachers, doctors, and civil servants. Of course governments of all political persuasions have always fallen out with their employees from time to time, especially over matters of pay. What was new under new-right administrations was that these routine tensions were exacerbated by a political philosophy that saw civil servants and other public-service workers as predominantly self-interested and *necessarily* less efficient than their private-sector counterparts.

Since the late 1980s, in the UK, NPM has taken the edge off the sourness which existed between the government and its servants. In the US the suspicion of the federal service runs deeper, but at least the problem of demoralisation has begun to receive increased attention. But cultural change is a difficult business and there can be no guarantee that the mere cessation of overt hostilities will herald the development of a positive, new public service culture. Certainly there are those who possess such a vision and are working to realize it, yet several obstacles lie in their path. As chapter 6 made clear, each of the main alternatives to neo-Taylorism sports its own characteristic weaknesses and limitations. In so far as the promoters of NPM draw on available models of cultural change they will be employing promising but largely unproven 'technologies'. Furthermore they will be seeking deep change in a cool resource climate, so that buying off resistance will seldom be an available option.

Even if the technologies of cultural change prove effective, however, a deeper difficulty would remain. For there are obvious structural tensions between the dynamics of the political process and the requirements of a programme of broad-scope cultural and organizational change. In brief, such a programme would require the commitment of substantial resources over a period of time – say 10 years – which easily exceeds the normal span of political attention.

These resources would have to be devoted to a cause which few politicians understand in any detail and which lacks all the characteristics of being a vote-winner. Bashing the bureaucrats may sometimes be a popular political sport; giving them time and money to improve themselves sounds distinctly dull. It is to John Major' s credit that he has been willing at least to start down this road. On the other hand the lesson the new right has repeatedly drawn is that the appropriate response to a demoralized, under-resourced public service is not reform but replacement – by privatization or through fragmentation and the introduction of some form of internal market. NPM contains within itself both the reformist and the replacement tendencies. It remains to be seen which one becomes dominant.

How can this tension between the interests and time scales of politicians and those of public-service providers be resolved? From within the managerialist perspective there seem to be only two basic possibilities. The first is to assume that politicians will always be unreliable partners, and therefore to distance the services from the politicians – privatization and autonomous or decentralized agencies are different manifestations of this tendency. The second is somehow to change politicians. This option is less frequently discussed, but there are a few texts recommending more 'training' for politicians in order to equip them better for the organizational complexities of governing (e.g. Dror, 1986). How far such rational remedies would succeed in counterbalancing the 'irrational', short termism of political life is an open question.

There is at least one other approach to the problem, but it is a political rather than a managerial one. It is to alter the political incentives themselves, and to begin to do so by deliberately extending the range of actors involved in the running of the public services. I offer this as a final 'reflection', conscious of the fact that it opens up a quite new agenda, most of the discussion of which must await the next book rather than this one.

If it were possible significantly to increase the direct participation of the public in the design, delivery and assessment of public services, then politicians would have to reckon with a new, informed and highly legitimate source of opinion on 'what should be done'. So, too would the professional (and other) providers. This would not be the consumerism of the new right, but the active participation of users and taxpayers in the running of everyday services – a real cultural shift (Pollitt, 1986b). This is not a particularly new idea, but though it goes all the way back to classical Athens, it remains a somewhat idealistic concept, in the sense that complex contemporary societies offer few examples to work from. The only one of the chapter 6 'alternatives' which comes anywhere close to it is the Public Service Orientation. In theory, rising levels of general education, combined with the possibilities of modern information technology, should make a large extension of public participation less difficult, but there are still many obstacles – political, practical and ideological – in its way. Certainly it would not be an attractive strategy for neo-Taylorists or the new right. It would represent uncertainty rather than control. It would generate a distinctively public-sector form of institutionalization rather than a generic one. It would expand the 'political' sphere rather than diminishing it. Whether it would also expand the public services themselves cannot be predicted with any confidence, but it would almost certainly alter their configuration. New forms of direct democracy offer the possibility of resolving some of the most deep-rooted problems currently facing public-service mangers – and the near certainty of generating a set of new ones.

References

Aitken, I. 1988: 'Samizdat in search of a Gilmour', *Guardian*, 24 October, 2

Alban-Metcalfe, B. 1989: 'What motivates managers: an investigation by gender and sector of employment'. *Public Administration*, 67 (1), Spring, 95–108.

Allison, G. T. 1983: 'Public and private management: are they fundamentally alike in all unimportant respects?'. In J. L. Perry and K. L. Kraemer (eds), *Public management: public and private perspectives*, California: Mayfield Publishing.

Alvesson, M. 1987: *Organisation theory and technocratic consciousness: rationality, ideology and quality of work.* New York: de Gruyter.

Amenta, E. and Skocpol, T. 1989: "Taking exception" explaining the distinctiveness of American public policies in the last century'. In F. Castles, (ed.), *The comparative history of public policy*, Cambridge: Polity.

American Federation of Teachers 1987: *Resource kit: merit pay and career ladders.* Washington DC: AFT.

Argyris, C. 1960: *Understanding organizational behaviour.* London: Tavistock.

Ascher, K. 1987: *The politics of privatisation: contracting out public services.* Basingstoke: Macmillan Education.

Aucoin, P. 1988: 'Contraction, managerialism and decentralization in Canadian government'. *Governance*, 1 (2), April, 144–61.

Audit Commission 1986: *Towards better management of secondary education.* London: HMSO.

Audit Comission 1991: *Assuring quality in education: the role of local education authority inspectors and advisors.* London: HMSO.

Backoff, R. W. and Nutt, P. C. 1988: 'A process for strategic management with specific application for the nonprofit organization'. In J. M. Bryson and R. C. Einsweiler, (eds), *Strategic planning: threats and opportunities for planners*, Chicago: Planners Press.

Bacon, R. and Eltis, W. 1978: *Britain's economic problem: too few producers*, (2nd edn.). London: Macmillan.

Baddeley, S. 1989: 'Political sensitivity in public managers'. *Local Government Studies*, 15 (2), 47–66.

Bains Report 1972: *The new local authorities: management and structure.* London: HMSO.

Ban, C. and Ingraham, P. (eds) 1984: *Legislating bureaucratic change: the Civil Service Reform Act of 1978.* New York: SUNY Press.

Banham, J. 1988: *Redrawing the frontiers of the public sector*, The Redcliffe Maud Memorial Lecture, London: Royal Institute of Public Administration.

Banyard, R. 1988: 'How do UGMs perform?' *Health Service Journal*, 21 July, 824–5.

Barbour, G. P., Fletcher, T. W. and Sipel, G. A. 1984: *Excellence in local government management.* Palo Alto, California: Center for Excellence in Local Government.

Barnard, C. I. 1938: *The functions of the executive.* Cambridge, Mass: Harvard University Press.

Bartlett, W. 1991: *Quasi-markets and contracts: a market and hierarchies perspective on NHS reform.* Bristol: School for Advanced Urban Studies.

Beeton, D. 1988: 'Performance measurement: the state of the art'. *Public Money and Management*, 8 (2), Spring–Summer, 99–103.

Bevins, A. 1991: 'Tories "must present compassionate image"' *Independent*, 23 March, 6.

Botstein, L. 1988: 'Education reform in the Reagan era: false paths, broken promises'. *Social Policy*, 18 (4), Spring, 3–11.

Bourn, J. B. 1974: 'The administrative process as a decision-making and goal attaining system'. Block 2, Part 2 of *D331 Public Administration*, Milton Keynes: Open University Press.

Brighouse, T. R. P. 1987: 'Britain's schools: an end of year report' *Educational Management and Administration*, 15, 263–75.

British Rail 1990: *Quality through teamwork.* London: Quality Office, British Railways Board.

Bryson, J. M. and Einsweiler, R. C. 1987: 'Strategic planning: introduction' *Journal of the American Planning Association*, 53 (1), Winter, 6–8.

Bryson, J. M. and Einsweiler, R. C. 1988: *Strategic planning: threats and opportunities for planners.* Chicago: Planners Press.

Buchanan, J. 1968: *The demand and supply of public goods*, Chicago: Rand McNally.

Bunzel, J. H. (ed.) 1985: *Challenge to American schools: the case for standards and values.* London: Oxford University Press.

Burgoyne, J. 1989: 'Creating the managerial portfolio: building on competency approaches to management development'. *Management Education and Development*, 20 (1), 55–61.

Burnham, J. 1941: *The managerial revolution.* Bloomington: Indiana University Press.

Burrell, G. and Morgan, G. 1979: *Sociological paradigms and organizational analysis.* London: Heinemann.

Burstall, C. and Kay, B. 1978: *Assessment: the American experience.* London: Department of Education and Science.

Burtless, G. 1986: 'Public spending for the poor: trends, prospects, and economic limits', 18–49. In S. H. Danziger, and D. H. Weinberg (eds), *Fighting poverty*, Harvard: Harvard University Press.

Callaghan, J. 1976: Speech at Ruskin College, Oxford. Text printed in *The Times Educational Supplement*, 22 October.

Carey, Sir P. 1984: 'Management in the Civil Service'. *Management in Government*, 39 (2), 81–5.

Cave, M., Hanney, S., Kogan, M. and Trevett, G. 1988: *The use of performance indicators in higher education: a critical analysis of developing practice*. London: Jessica Kingsley.

Carroll, J. D. 1987: 'Public administration in the third century of the constitution: supply-side management, privatization, or public investment'. *Public Administration Review*, January–February, 106–14.

Center for Excellence in Government 1989: *The program*. Washington DC (leaflet).

Centre for the Evaluation of Public Policy and Practice 1992: *Considering Quality: an Analytical Guide to the Literature on Quality and Standards in the Public Services*. Uxbridge: CEPPP, Brunel University.

Chandler, A. D. Jun. 1977: *The visible hand: the managerial revolution in America*. Cambridge Mass: Belknap Press.

Charles, S. and Webb, A. 1986: The economic approach to social policy. Brighton: Wheatsheaf.

Child, J. 1969: *British management thought*. London: Allen and Unwin.

Clark, P. A. 1975: 'Organizational design: a review of key problems'. *Administration and Society*, 17 (2), August, 213–56.

Cd, 9230 1918: *Report of the machinery of government committee* (the Haldane Committee). London: HMSO.

CMM 555 1989: *Working for patients*. London: HMSO.

Cmnd 3703 1968: *Report of the Committee on Local Authority and Allied Personal Social Services*, (Seebohm Report). London: HMSO.

Cmnd 4506 1970: *The reorganization of central government*. London: HMSO.

Cmnd 6869 1977: *Education in schools: a consultative document*. Department of Education and Science, London: HMSO.

Cmnd 8616 1982: *Efficiency and effectiveness in the civil service*. London: HMSO.

Cmnd 8836 1983: *Teaching quality*, Department of Education and Science London: HMSO.

Cmnd 9058 1983: *Financial management in government departments*. London: HMSO.

Cmnd 9135 1984: *Training for jobs*. London: HMSO.

Cmnd 9297 1984: *Progress in financial management in government departments*. London: HMSO.

Cmnd 9469 1985: *Better Schools*. London: HMSO.

Cmnd 9524 1985: *The development of higher education into the 1990s*. London: HMSO.

Cochrane, A. 1985: 'The attack on local government: what it is and what it isn't'. *Critical Social Policy*, 4 (3), 44–61.

COHSE 1987: *The introduction of general management in the National Health Service*. Memorandum to the House of Commons Social Services Committee, Confederation of Health Service Employees.

Collins, B. 1987: 'The Rayner scrutinies'. In A. Harrison and J. Gretton (eds), *Restructuring central government*, Oxford: Policy Journals, 11–41.

Committee of Vice Chancellors and Principals 1985: *Report of the Steering Committee for Efficiency Studies in Universities*. 'Jarratt Report'.

Cooper, P. J. 1983: *Public law and public administration*. California: Mayfield Publishing.

Cooper, Sir F. 1983: *Freedom to manage in government*. London, Royal Institute of Public Administration lecture, 19 April.

Corrigan, P., Jones, T., Lloyd, J. and Young, J. 1988: *Socialism, merit and efficiency*. London, Fabian Society pamphlet no. 530.

Cottrell, P. 1988: 'Agreement on promotion and appraisal guidelines' *AUT Bulletin*, 151, January, 6–7.

Cox, B. 1985: *The law of special educational needs: a guide to the Education Act 1981*. London: Croom Helm.

Coyle, A. 1989: 'The limits of change: local government and equal opportunities for women'. *Public Administration*, 67 (1), Spring, 39–50.

Danziger, S. H. and Weinberg, D. H. (eds) 1986: *Fighting poverty*. Harvard: Harvard University Press.

Davies, P. 1988: 'More than just window dressing'. *Health Service Journal*, 14 July, 790–1.

Davis, K. and Schoen, C. 1978: *Health and the war on poverty: a ten year appraisal*. Washington DC: Brookings Institution.

Department of Education and Science 1976: 'School education in England: problems and initiatives' (a confidential memorandum, known as the 'Yellow Paper', leaked and published in *The Times Educational Supplement*, 15 October 1976).

Department of Education and Science 1977: *A new partnership for our schools* (Taylor Report). London: HMSO.

Department of Education and Science 1978: *Primary education in England: a survey by HM Inspector of Schools*. London: HMSO.

Department of Education and Science 1979: *Aspects of secondary education in England: a survey by HM Inspectors of Schools*. London: HMSO.

Department of Education and Science 1987: *Financial delegation to schools: a consultation paper*, London: HMSO.

Department of Health and Social Security 1976a: *Priorities for health and personal social services in England: the way forward*. London: HMSO.

Department of Health and Social Security 1976b: *Sharing resources for health in England: report of the Resource Allocation Working Party*. London: HMSO.

Department of Health and Social Security 1979: *Patients first: a consultative paper on the structure and management of the National Health Service in England and Wales*. London: HMSO.

Department of Health and Social Security 1983: *NHS management inquiry* (The Griffiths Report). London: DHSS.

Dilulio, J. J. jun. 1989: 'Recovering the public management variable: lessons from schools, prisons, armies. *Public Administration Review*, 49 (2), March/April, 127–33.

Dixon, P. and Carr-Hill, R. 1989: *The NHS and its customer: customer feedback surveys* (vols 2 and 3), York: Centre for Health Economics.

Dowie, J. and Elstein, A. 1988: *Professional judgement: a reader in clinical decision making* New York: Cambridge University Press.

Downs, A. 1967: *Inside bureaucracy*. Boston: Little Brown.

Dror, Y. 1986: *Policy making under adversity*. New Jersey: Transaction Books.

Drucker, P. F. 1973: 'Managing the public service institution'. *The Public Interest*, 33, 43–60.

Drucker, P. F. 1974: *Management: tasks, responsibilities, practices*. London: Heinemann.

Dunleavy, P. 1985: 'Bureaucrats, budgets and the growth of the state: reconstructing an instrumental model'. *British Journal of Political Science*, 15, 299–328.

Dunleavy, P. 1986: 'Exploring the privatization boom: public choice versus radical approaches'. *Public Administration*, 64 (1), Spring, 13–34.

Dunleavy, P. 1989: 'The United Kingdom: paradoxes of an ungrounded statism'. In F. Castles (ed.), *The comparative history of public policy*, Cambridge: Polity.

Dunsire, A. 1973: *Administration: the word and the science*. Oxford: Martin Robertson.

Edwards, M. 1984: *Back from the brink*. London: Pan.

Efficiency Unit 1988: *Improving management in government: the next steps*. (The Ibbs report). London: Cabinet Office.

Eliassen, K. A. and Kooiman, J. 1987: 'Opportunities for public management', 239–52. In K. A. Eliassen and J. Kooiman (eds), *Managing public organisations: lessons from contemporary European experience*, London: Sage.

Ellis, R. (ed.) (1988): *Professional competence and quality assurance in the caring professions*, London: Croom Helm.

English, D. 1988: 'This is my new crusade'. *Daily Mail*, 29 April, 6–7.

Exley, M. 1987: 'Organization and managerial capacity', 42–56. In A. Harrison and J. Gretton, (eds), *Reshaping central government*, Oxford: Policy Journals.

Finn, C. E. jun. 1986: 'Teacher unions and school quality: potential allies or inevitable foes?', 99–124. In J. H. Bunzel (ed.) *The challenge to American schools: the case for standards and values*, London: Oxford University Press.

Flynn, A., Gray, A., Jenkins, W. and Rutherford, B. 1988: 'Implementing "The next steps"'. *Public Administration*, 66 (4), Winter, 439–45.

Forbes, I. 1989: 'Unequal partners: the implementation of equal opportunities policies in Western Europe'. *Public Administration*, 67 (1), Spring, 19–38.

Fottler, M. 1981: 'Is management really generic?'. *Academy of Management Review*, 6, 1–12.

Friedman, M. 1975: *Unemployment or inflation?* London: Institute for Economic Affairs.

Friedman, M. and Friedman, R. 1980: *Free to choose: a personal statement*, Harmondsworth: Penguin.

Fry, G. K. 1984: 'The development of the Thatcher government's "grand strategy" for the civil service: a public policy perspective'. *Public Administration*, 62 (3), Autumn, 322–35.

Fry, G. K. 1988a: 'The Thatcher government, the Financial Management Initiative and the "New Civil Service"'. *Public Administration*, 66 (1), Spring,

1–20.

Fry, G. K. 1988b: 'Outlining "The Next Steps"'. *Public Administration*, 66 (4), Winter, 429–38.

Gaertner, K. and Gaertner, G. H. 1985: 'Performance-contingent pay for federal managers'. *Administration and Society*, 17 (1), 7–20.

Gastor, L. 1991: *Quality at the front line*. Bristol: School for Advanced Urban Studies.

Geertz, C. 1973: *The interpretation of cultures*. London: Hutchinson.

Gillett, R. 1987: 'Serious anomalies in the UGC comparative evaluation of the research performance of psychology departments'. *Bulletin of the British Psychological Society*, 40, 42–9.

Gillion, C. and Hemming, R. 1985: 'Social expenditure in the United Kingdom in a comparative context: trends, explanations and projections' 22–36. In R. Klein and M. O'Higgins, (eds), *The future of welfare*, Oxford: Blackwell.

Goldenberg, E. N. 1985: 'The Grace Commission and civil service reform: seeking a common understanding', 69–94. In C. H. Levine (ed.), *The unfinished agenda for civil service reform: implications of the Grace Commission Report*, Washington DC.: Brookings Institute.

Goldsmith, W. and Clutterbuck, D. 1984: *The winning streak: Britain's top companies reveal their formulas for success*. London: Weidenfield and Nicolson.

Goldstein, M. 1989: 'Hollow government' *Government Executive*, 21, October, p. 13.

Goodin, R. E. and Wilenski, P. 1984: 'Beyond efficiency: the logical underpinnings of administrative principles' *Public Administration Review*, 44 (6), Nov./Dec. 512–17.

Goodsell, C. T. 1984: 'The Grace Commission: seeking efficiency for the whole people?'. *Public Administration Review*, 44 (2), 196–206.

Gow, D. 1988: 'Baker plans two-tier teaching'. *Guardian*, 25 May, 1.

Gowers, Sir E. 1954: *The complete plain words*. London: HMSO.

Grace, P. J. 1984: *Burning money: the waste of your tax dollars*. New York: Macmillan.

Grace, P. J. 1985: 'Government waste: any is too much' *The Public Interest*, 79, Spring, 111–30.

Griffiths, Sir R. 1988: 'Does the public serve? The consumer dimension'. *Public Administration*, 66 (2), Summer, 195–204.

Gulick, L. and Urwick, L. F. (eds) 1937: *Papers on the science of administration*. New York: Institute of Public Administration.

Gunn, L. 1987: 'Perspectives on public management', 33–46. In J. Kooiman and K. A. Eliassen (eds), *Managing public organisations: lessons from contemporary European experience*, London: Sage.

Guy Peters, B. 1985: 'Administrative change and the Grace Commission'. In C. H. Levine (ed.) *The unfinished agenda for civil service reform: implications of the Grace Commission Report*, Washington DC: Brookings Institution.

Haber, S. 1984: *Efficiency and uplift: scientific management in the progressive era, 1990–1920*. Chicago: University of Chicago Press.

Hambleton, R. 1988: 'Consumerism, decentralization and local democracy'.

Public Administration, 66 (2), Summer, 125–47.

Hambleton, R. 1989: 'Urban government under Reagan and Thatcher' *Urban Affairs Quarterly*, 24 (3), March, 359–88.

Handy, C. B. 1976: *Understanding organizations*. Harmondsworth: Penguin.

Harding, N. 1989: 'Equal opportunities for women in the NHS: the prospects of success?' *Public Administration*, 67 (1), 51–63.

Harrison, S. 1988a: 'The workforce and the new managerialism', 141–152. In R. J. Maxwell (ed.), *Reshaping the National Health Service*, London: Policy Journals.

Harrison, S. 1988b: *Managing the National Health Service: shifting the frontier?*, London: Croom Helm.

Harrison, S., Hunter, D. J., Marnoch, G. and Pollitt, C. 1989a: *The impact of general management in the National Health Service*. Milton Keynes: Open University/Nuffield Institute for Health Services Studies.

Harrison, S., Hunter, D. J., Marnoch, G. and Pollitt, C. 1989b: 'General management and medical autonomy in the National Health Service'. *Health Services Management Research*, 2 (1), 38–46.

Harrison, S., Hunter, D. J., Johnson, I. and Wistow, G. 1989c: *Competing for health: a commentary in the NHS review*. Leeds: Nuffield Institute for Health Services Studies.

Harrison, S., Hunter, D., Marnoch, G. and Pollitt, C. 1992: *Just Managing: power and culture in the NHS*. London: Macmillan.

Harrison, S and Pollitt, C. 1992: *The Handbook of Public Services Management*. Oxford: Blackwell.

Hart, D. K. 1983: 'The honourable bureaucrat among the philistines'. *Administration and Society*, 15 (1), 43–8.

Hartle, T. W. 1985: 'Sisyphus re-visited: running the government like a business'. *Public Administration Review*, 45 (2), 341–51.

Hartley, J. 1983: 'Ideology and organizational behaviour'. *International Studies of Management and Organization*, 13 (3).

Harvey-Jones, J. 1988: *Making it happen: reflections on leadership*. London: Collins.

Hatry, H. P. 1983: *A review of private approaches for delivery of public services*. Washington DC: Urban Institute Press.

Hayek, F. 1986: *The road to serfdom*. London, Ark Paperbacks (first published 1944).

Heclo, H. 1986: 'The political foundations of anti-poverty policy' 312–40. In S. Danziger and D. H. Weinberg (eds), *Fighting poverty*, Harvard: Harvard University Press.

Hede, A. 1991: 'Trends in the higher civil services of Anglo-American systems' *Governance*, 4: 4, October, pp. 489–510

Held, D. 1987: *Models of democracy*. Cambridge: Polity.

Hennessy, P. 1989: *Whitehall*. London: Secker and Warburg.

Hennig, M. and Jardim, A. 1978: *The managerial woman*. London: Boyars.

Hennig, J. R., Hamnett, C. and Feigenbaum, H. B. 1988: 'The politics of privatization: a comparative perspective'. *Governance*, 1 (4), October, 442–68.

Heseltine, M. 1980: 'Ministers and management in Whitehall'. *Management*

Services in Government, 35.

Heseltine, M. 1987: *Where there's a will*. London: Hutchinson.

Hewton, E. 1988: 'Teacher appraisal: the present position'. *Education*, 17 (1), January, i–iv.

Hodgkinson, C. 1978: *Towards a philosophy of administration*. Oxford: Blackwell.

Hoggett, P 1990: *Modernization, political strategy and the welfare state: an organizational perspective*. Bristol: School for Advanced Urban Studies.

Hoggett, P. 1991: 'A new management in the public sector?' *Policy and Politics*, 19: 4, pp. 243–56.

Hood, C. 1991: 'A public management for all seasons?' *Public Administration*, 69: 1, Spring, pp 3–19.

Hoover, K. and Plant, R. 1989: *Conservative capitalism in Britain and the United States: a critical appraisal*. London: Routledge.

Hopwood, A. G. 1984: 'Accounting and the pursuit of efficiency' 167–87. In A. Hopwood and C. Tomkins (eds), *Issues in public sector accounting*, Oxford: Philip Allan.

Hopwood, A. G. 1988: 'Accounting and gender: an introduction'. *Accounting Organizations and Society*, 12 (1), 65–9.

Horner, C. 1989: 'Securing competence and character in the public service': *Governance*, 2 (2), April, 115–23.

Iacocca, L. 1984: *Iacocca: an autobiography*. New York: Bantam.

Iacocca, L. 1988: *Talking straight*. New York: Bantam.

Ingraham, P. W. and Rosenbloom, D. H. 1989: 'The new public personnel and the new public service'. *Public Administration Review*, 49 (2), March–April, 116–25.

Institute of Economic Affairs 1979: *The taming of government*, conference paper, London: Institute of Economic Affairs.

Jackson, P. (ed.) 1985: *Implementing government policy initiatives: the Thatcher administration 1979–83*. London: Royal Institute of Public Administration.

Jarrat, Sir A. 1985: *Report of the steering committee for efficiency studies in universities*. London: CVCP/UGC.

Johnson, N. 1987: 'The breakup of consensus: competitive politics in a declining economy', 144–60. In Martin Loney (ed.), *The state or the market: politics and welfare in contemporary Britain*, London: Sage.

Joubaert, C. 1988: 'Strategy in the public sector'. *Public Money and Management*, Autumn, 17–20.

Kaplan, R. 1984: 'The evolution of management accounting'. *Accounting Review*, July, 390–418.

Kaufman, H. 1981: 'Fear of bureaucracy; a raging pandemic'. *Public Administration Review*, 41 (1) January/February, 1–9.

Kaufman, J. L. and Jacobs, H. M. 1987: 'A public planning perspective on strategic planning'. *Journal of the American Planning Association*, 53 (1), Winter, 23–33.

Keeling, D. 1972: *Management in government*. London: Allen and Unwin.

Kelly, J. E. 1978: 'Understanding Taylorism: some comments'. *British Journal of Sociology*, 29 (2), June, 203–7.

Kelman, S. 1985: 'The Grace Commission: how much waste in government?'. *The Public Interest*, 82, Winter, 62–82.

Kilman, R. H., Saxton, M. J. and Serpa, R. 1985: *Gaining control of the corporate culture*. San Francisco: Jossey-Bass.

King, D. S. 1987: *The new right*, London: Macmillan Education.

Kingdon, J. 1986: 'Public administration: defining the discipline'. *Teaching Public Administration* 4 (1) and (2).

Kings Fund Institute 1988: *Health finance: assessing the options*, briefing Paper 4, London: King's Fund Institute.

Klein, R. 1983: *The politics of the National Health Service*. London: Longman.

Kooiman, J. and Eliassen, K. (eds) 1987: *Managing public organizations: lessons from contemporary European experience*. London: Sage.

Koontz, H. and O'Donnell, C. 1978: Essentials of Management. New York: McGraw-Hill, 2nd edn.

Kotter, J. P. 1982: *The general managers*. New York: Free Press.

Lane, J. E. 1987: 'Against administration'. *Studies in Higher Education*, 12 (3), 249–60.

Lane, L. and Wolf, J. 1990: *The human resource crisis in the public sector*. New York: Quorum Books.

Lazarsfeld, P. F. 1959: 'Sociological reflections on business: consumers and managers', 99–155. In R. A. Dahl, M. Haire and P. F. Lazarsfeld (eds), *Social science research on-business: product and potential*, New York: Columbia University Press.

Lee, J. M. 1986: 'Editorial: the next generation: a hand-over note'. *Public Administration*, 64 (3), Autumn, 251–6.

Lee, K. and Mills, A. 1982: *Policy-making and planning in the health sector*. London: Croom Helm.

Lehman, C. and Tinkler, R. 1987: 'The "real" cultural significance of accounts'. *Accounting, Organizations and Society*, 12 (5).

Levacic, R. 1988: 'Schools and the management of public money'. *Public Money and Management*, 8 (3), Autumn, 53–6.

Levine, C. H. (ed.) 1985: *The unfinished agenda for civil service reform: implications of the Grace Commission report*. Washington DC: The Brookings Institution.

Levine, C. H. 1986: 'The federal government in the year 2000: administrative legacies of the Reagan years'. *Public Administration Review*, May–June, 195–205.

Levine, C. H. 1988: 'Human resource erosion and the uncertain future of the US civil service: from policy gridlock to structural fragmentation'. *Governance*, 1 (2) April, 115–43.

Levitt, M. S. and Joyce, M. A. S. 1987: *The growth and efficiency of public spending*. Cambridge: Cambridge University Press.

Lewis, G. 1988: *Corporate strategy in action: the strategy process in British Road Services*. London: Routledge.

Likierman, A. 1982: 'Management information for ministers: the MINIS system in the Department of the Environment'. *Public Administration*, 60 (2), Summer, 127–42.

Littler, C. R. 1978: 'Understanding Taylorism'. *British Journal of Sociology*, 29 (2) June, 185–202.

Local Government Training Board 1988: *Management in the public domain: a discussion paper.* Luton: LGTB.

Local Government Training Board 1989: *Learning from the public.* Luton: LGTB.

Lukes, S. 1974: *Power: a radical view.* London: Macmillan.

Lynn Meek, V. 1988: 'Organizational culture: origins and weaknesses'. *Organization Studies*, 9 (4), 453–73.

Macdonald, J. and Fry, G. K. 1980: 'Policy planning units: ten years on'. *Public Administration*, 58 (4), Winter, 421–37.

McSweeney, B. and Sherer, M. 1988: 'Value for money auditing: some observations on its origins and theory'. In D. Cooper and T. Hopper (eds), *Critical accounting*, London: Macmillan.

March, J. G. 1978: 'Ambiguity, bounded rationality and the engineering of choice'. *Bell Journal of Economics*, 587–608.

March, J. G. and Olsen, J. P. 1984: 'The new institutionalism: organizational factors in political life'. *American Political Science Review*, 78, 734–49.

Martin, D. W. 1988: 'The fading legacy of Woodrow Wilson'. *Public Administration Review*, 48 (2), March–April, 631–6.

Martin, R. 1977: *The sociology of power.* London: Routledge and Kegan Paul.

Mather, G. 1988: *Government and the private sector: relationships, roles and responsibility: government by contract*, text of a speech to the Royal Institute of Public Administration Conference, University of Kent, 16 September.

Maynard, A. 1986: 'Financing the UK national health services'. *Health Policy*, 6, 329–40.

Mayo, Elton, 1933: *The human problems of an industrial civilization.* New York: Macmillan.

Merkle, J. 1980: *Management and ideology: the legacy of the international scientific management movement.* Berkeley: University of California Press.

Metcalfe, L. and Richards, S. 1984: 'The impact of the efficiency strategy: political clout or cultural change?' *Public Administration*, 62 (4), Winter, 439–54.

Metcalfe, L. and Richards, S. 1987: 'Evolving public management cultures' 65–86. In J. Kooiman and K. A. Eliassen (eds), *Managing public organizations: lessons from contemporary European experience*, London: Sage.

Meyer, J. W. and Rowan, B. 1977: 'Institutionalized organizations: formal structure as myth and ceremony'. *American Journal of Sociology*, 83, 340–64.

Millar, B. 1988: 'NHS managers seen in flesh and blood'. *Health Service Journal*, 21 July, 818.

Miller, P. and O'Leary F. 1987: 'Accounting and the construction of the governable person'. *Accounting, Organizations and Society*, 12 (3), 235–65.

Milne, R. G. 1987: 'Competitive tendering in the NHS: an economic analysis of the early implementation of HC (83) 18'. *Public Administration*, 65 (2), Summer, 145–60.

Minford, P. 1987: 'The role of the Social Services: a view from the new right', 70–82. In Martin Loney (ed), *The state of the market: politics and welfare in contemporary Britain*, London: Sage.

Morgan, B. 1985: 'State acted before plan fully studied for pitfalls': *Chattanooga Times*, 15 August.

Moskow, M. H. 1987: *Managing in the public sector: presidential address to the Industrial Relations Research Association*. Washington DC: Center for Excellence in Government.

Mueller, A. E. 1986: *The public sector: present and future*, speech delivered to the Institute of Personnel Management, 23 October.

Mueller, K. J. 1988: 'Federal programs to expire: the case of health planning'. *Public Administration Review*, 48 (3), May–June, 719–25.

Murray, M. 1975: 'Comparing public and private management'. *Public Administration Review*, 35, July–August, 364–71.

Nathan, R. P. 1983: *The administrative Presidency*, New York: Wiley.

National Audit Office 1988: *Quality of clinical care in National Health Service hospitals*, HC 736, London: NAO.

National Commission on Excellence in Education 1983: *A nation at risk: the imperative for educational reform*. Washington DC: US Government Printing Office.

National Education Association 1947: 3 *Journal of addresses and proceedings*, 85, Washington DC.

National Economic Development Council 1963: *Conditions favourable to faster growth*, London: HMSO.

Navarro, V. 1988: 'Welfare states and their distributive effects'. *Political Quarterly*, 59 (2), April–June, 219–35.

Nichols, T. 1980: 'Management, ideology and practice', 279–302. In G. Esland and G. Salaman (eds), *The politics of work and occupations*, Milton Keynes: Open University Press.

Nigro, F. A. 1982: 'Civil service reform in the United States'. *Public Administration*, 60 (2), Summer, 225–33.

Nigro, L. G. 1989: personal communication to the author, 20 March.

Niskanen, W. A. 1973: *Bureaucracy: servant or master? Lessons from America*. London: The Institute for Economic Affairs.

Norton-Taylor, R. 1985: 'Whitehall top brass rebel on pay plan'. *Guardian*, 29 April, 2.

OECD 1985: *Social expenditure, 1960–1990: problems of growth and control*. Paris: OECD.

Office of Management and Budget 1986: *Management of the United States government: fiscal year 1987*. Washington DC: Office of Management and Budget.

Office of Inspector General 1988: *Semiannual report to Congress, October 1st 1987–March 31st 1988:* Washington DC: Department of Health and Human Services.

Office of Population Censuses and Surveys 1988: *Population Trends*, 53, Autumn, London: HMSO.

O'Sullivan, J. 1991: 'BMA agrees to "queue jumping" at hospitals', *Independent*, 12 June, 82.

O'Sullivan, J. 1992: 'NHS operations delayed by Charter' *Independent*, 5 March, 82.

Palmer, J. L. (ed.) 1986: *Perspectives on the Reagan years*. Washington: Urban Institute Press.

Parsons, S. 1988. 'Economic principles in the public and private sectors'. *Policy and Politics*, 16 (1), 29–39.

Patten, J. and Pollitt, C. 1980: 'Power and rationality: theories of policy formulation'. Paper 8, Block 2, *D336 Policies, people and administration*, Milton Keynes: Open University Press.

Patterson, J. T. 1986: 'The health policy context', 6–12. In C.E. Hill (ed.) *Current health policy issues and alternatives*, Georgia: University of Georgia Press.

Peat, Marwick, McLintock 1989: *Departmental annual reports*, London: Klynveld Peat Marwick Goerdeler.

Peet, J. 1987: *Healthy competition: how to improve the NHS*. London: Centre for Policy Studies, Policy Study no. 86.

Perrow, C. 1979: *Complex organizations: a critical essay*, 2nd edn, London: Scott, Foresman and Co.

Perry, J. L. and Kraemer, K. L. (eds) 1983: *Public management: public and private perspectives*. California: Mayfield.

Perry, J. and Pearce, J. 1985: 'Civil service reform and the politics of performance appraisal', 140–60. In D. Rosenbloom (ed.), *Public personnel policy: the politics of civil service*, London: Associated Faculty Press.

Perry, J. L., Petrakis, B. A. and Miller, T. K. 1989: 'Federal merit pay, round 2: an analysis of the performance management and recognition system'. *Public Administration Review*, 49, Jan–Feb. 29–37.

Petchey, R. 1986: 'The Griffiths reorganisation of the National Health Service: Fowlerism by stealth?'. *Critical Social Policy*, 17, Autumn, 87–101.

Peters, J. and Waterman, R. H. 1982: *In search of excellence: lessons from America's best-run companies*. New York: Harper and Row.

Pettigrew, A. 1985: *The awakening giant: continuity and change in ICI*. Oxford: Blackwell.

Pettigrew, A. McKee, L. and Ferlie, E. 1988: 'Understanding change in the NHS'. *Public Administration*, 66 (3), Autumn, 297–317.

Pfeffer, N. and Coote, A. 1991: *Is quality good for you? A critical review of quality assurance in welfare services*. London: Institute for Public Policy Research.

Pirie, M. 1985: *Privatization*. London: Adam Smith Institute.

Pollitt, C. 1977: 'The public expenditure survey, 1961–1972'. *Public Administration*, 55 (2), Summer, 127–42.

Pollitt, C. 1980: 'The development of government in Britain', 60–119. In Open University *D336 Policies, people and administration: block 1: the administrative context*, Milton Keynes: Open University Press.

Pollitt, C. 1984: *Manipulating the machine: changing the pattern of ministerial departments, 1960–83*. London: Allen and Unwin.

Pollitt, C. 1985: 'Measuring performance: a new system for the National Health Service. *Policy and Politics*, 13:1, pp. 1–15.

Pollitt, C. 1986a: 'Beyond the managerial model: the case for broadening performance assessment in government and the public services'. *Financial Accountability and Management*, 2 (3), Autumn, 155–170.

Pollitt, C. 1986b: 'Democracy and bureaucracy', 158–191. In D. Held and C. Pollitt (eds), *New forms of democracy*, London: Sage.

Pollitt, C. 1987: 'Capturing quality? The quality issue in British and American health policies'. *journal of Public Policy*, 7 (1), 71–92.

Pollitt, C. 1988a: 'Models of staff appraisal: some political implications'. *Higher Education Review*, 20 (2), Spring, 7–16.

Pollitt, C. 1988b: 'Bringing consumers into performance measurement: concepts, consequences and constraints' *Policy and politics*, 16 (2), 1–11.

Pollitt, C. (ed.) 1989a: 'Implementing equal opportunities' *Public Administration*, 67 (1), Spring (theme issue).

Pollitt, C. 1989b: 'Organizational cultures', Book 8 of *B782 Managing health services*. Milton Keynes: Open University Press.

Pollitt, C. 1990: 'Measuring university performance: broadening or narrowing?'. *Higher Education Quarterly*, 44 (1), Winter.

Pollitt, C. 1991: *The politics of quality: managers, professionals and consumers in the public services*. Egham: Royal Holloway and Bedford New College.

Pollitt, C., Harrison, S., Hunter, D. and Marnoch, G. 1988: 'The reluctant managers: clinicians and budgets in the NHS'. *Financial Accountability and Management*, 4 (3), Autumn, 213–33.

Potter, J. 1988: 'Consumerism and the public sector: how well does the coat fit?'. *Public Administration*, 66 (2), Summer, 149–64.

President's Private Sector Survey on Cost Control (The Grace Commission) 1984: *War on waste*. New York: Macmillan.

Price, C. 1986: 'Parliament', 13–21. In Stewart Ranson and John Tomlinson (eds), *The changing government of education*, London: Allen and Unwin.

Prime Minister 1991: *The citizen's charter: raising the standard*, Cm 1599. London: HMSO.

Prospective Payment Assessment Commission 1986: *Medicare prospective payments and the American health care system: report to the Congress*, Washington DC.

Public Accounts Committee 1981: *Financial control and accountability in the National Health Service*. 7th report, session 1980–81, HC 255, London: HMSO.

Public Accounts Committee 1982: *Financial control and accountability in the National Health Service*. 7th report, session 1982–83, HC 375, London: HMSO.

Pugh, D. S. and Hickson, D. J. 1976: *Organization structure and its context: the Aston programme*. Farnborough: Saxon House.

Pye, A. 1988: 'Management competence in the public sector'. *Public Money and Management*, 8 (4), Winter, 62–4.

Rainey, H. G., Backoff, R. W. and Levine, C. H. 1976: 'Comparing public and private organizations'. *Public Administration Review*, 36 (3), 223–44.

Ranson, S. and Tomlinson, J. 1986: 'An alternative view of education and society', 193–219. In S. Ranson and J. Tomlinson (eds), *The changing government of education*, London: Allen and Unwin.

Rawlings, H. F. 1986: 'Judicial review and the "control of government"', *Public Administration*, 64 (2), Summer, 135–45.

Rayner, L. 1984: *The unfinished agenda*. Stamp Memorial Lecture, London: Athlone Press.

Reed, M. I. 1988: 'The problem of human agency in organizational analysis'. *Organisation Studies*, 9 (1), 33–46.

Reid, R. P. 1988: 'Charter flight', i–iii, Management Education section of *Times Higher Education Supplement*, 25 March.

Rhodes, R. 1987: 'Developing the public service orientation'. *Local Government Studies*, May–June, 63–73.

Richards, S. 1987: 'The Financial Management Initiative', 22–41. In A. Harrison and J. Gretton, *Reshaping central government*, Oxford: Policy Journals.

Robinson, R. 1989: 'New health care market'. *British Medical Journal*, 298, 18 February, 437–9.

Roethlesberger, F. J. and Dickson, W. J. 1969: 'On organizational goals', 51–62. In J. A. Litterer (ed.) *Organizations*, 2nd edn, vol. 1, New York: Wiley.

Rose, R. 1984: *Understanding big government: the programme approach*. London: Sage.

Rose, R. 1988: *Loyalty, voice or exit? Margaret Thatcher's challenge to the civil service*. Glasgow: Centre for the Study of Public Policy, Studies in Public Policy no. 166.

Royal Institute of Public Administration Peat Marwick 1985: *Developing the FMI principles: changes in process and culture*. London: RIPA.

Royal Institute of Public Administration and Arthur Young 1989: *The next steps: a review of the agency concept*. London: Arthur Young.

Rubin, I. S. 1985: *Shrinking the federal government*. New York: Longman.

Sabatier, P. A. 1986: 'What can we learn from implementation research?, 313–25.In F.-X. Kaufmann, G. Majone and V. Ostrom (eds), *Guidance, control and evaluation in the public sector*, De Gruyter: Berlin.

Salaman, G. 1981: *Class and the corporation*. Glasgow: Fontana.

Salaman, G. 1982: 'Managing the frontier of control', 46–62. In A. Giddens and G. Mackenzie, *Social class and the division of labour*, London: Cambridge University Press.

Sayles, L. R. 1958: *Behaviour of industrial work groups*. New York: Wiley.

Scarman, Lord 1986: 'Editorial'. *Public Administration*, 64 (2), Summer, 133–4.

Schliesl, M. 1977: *The politics of efficiency*. Berkeley: University of California Press.

Schneider, W. 1984: 'The public schools: a consumer report'. *American Educator*, 8 (1), Spring, 13–14.

Schon, D. A. 1971: *Beyond the stable state*. New York: Norton.

Searle, G. R. 1970: *The quest for national efficiency*. Oxford: Blackwell.

Shanker, A. 1985: *The making of a profession*. Washington DC: American Federation of Teachers.

Silverman, D. 1970: *The theory of organizations*. London: Heinemann.

Simon, H. A. 1947: *Administrative behaviour: a study of decision-making processes in administrative organization*. New York: Macmillan.

Skocpol, T. 1988: 'A society without a 'state'? Political organization, social conflict and welfare provision in the United States'. *Journal of Public Policy*, 7 (4), 349–71.

Social Services Committee 1982: *Public expenditure on the Social Services*, Session 1981–82, 2nd report, HC306, London: HMSO.

Social Trends 18 1988: London: HMSO.

Soloman, E. E. 1986: 'Private and public sector managers: an empirical investigation of job characteristics and organizational climate'. *Journal of Applied Psychology*, 71, 247–59.

Starr, P. 1986: 'Health for the poor: the past 20 years', 106–32. In S. H. Danziger and D. H. Weinberg, *Fighting poverty: what works and what doesn't*, Cambridge, Mass: Harvard University Press.

Stewart, J. and Clarke, M. 1987: 'The public service orientation: issues and dilemmas'. *Public Administration*, 65(2), Summer, 161–78.

Stewart, J. and Ranson, S. 1988: 'Management in the public domain'. *Public Money and Management*, 8(2), Spring–Summer, 13–19.

Stockman, D. A. 1986: *The triumph of politics*. London: Bodley Head.

Stoker, G. 1988: *The politics of local government*. Basingstoke: Macmillan.

Strong, P. and Robinson, J. 1988: *New model management: Griffiths and the NHS*. Nursing policy studies centre: University of Warwick.

Suffolk Education Department 1985: *Those having torches: teacher appraisal: a study*. Ipswich: Suffolk Education Department.

Taylor, F. W. 1911: *The principles of scientific management*. New York: Harper and Brothers.

Taylor-Gooby, P. 1985: 'The politics of welfare: public attitudes and behaviour', 72–91. In R. H. Klein and M. O'Higgins (eds), *The future of welfare*, Oxford: Blackwell.

Therborn, G. 1981: *The ideology of power and the power of ideology*. London: New Left Books.

Thomas, R. 1978: *The British philosophy of administration: a comparison of British and American ideas*, 1900–39, London/New York, Longman.

Thompson, F. J. 1986: 'The health policy context', 6–12. In C. E. Hill (ed.) *Current health policy issues and alternatives*, Georgia: University of Georgia Press.

Thompson, G. 1987: 'Inflation accounting in a theory of calculation' *Accounting, Organizations and Society*, 12(5), 523–43.

Timmins, N. 1989a: 'Doctors to mount campaign against NHS reform plans'. *The Independent*, 3 March, 5.

Timmins, N. 1989b: 'Costing of hospital care fails to show patient benefits', *The Independent*, 29 May, 6.

Treasury 1986a: *Multi-departmental review of budgeting: executive summary and final central report*. London: H. M. Treasury.

Treasury 1986b: *Using private enterprise in government: report of a multi-departmental review of competitive tendering and contracting for services in government departments*. London: H. M. Treasury.

Treasury 1987: *Flexible pay: a new pay regime for the civil service*, London: H. M. Treasury.

Treasury 1991: *Competing for quality: buying public services*, Cm 1730. London: HMSO.

Treasury and Civil Service Committee 1988: *Civil service management reform: the next steps.* 8th report, session 1987/88, HC 494 I (report) and II (annexes, evidence, appendices), London: HMSO.

Tullock, G. 1976: *The vote motive: an essay in the economics of politics, with applications to the British economy.* London: Institute of Economic Affairs.

Turk, H., Wamsley, G. and Zald, M. 1979: 'The political economy of public organizations: a critique and approach to the study of public administration'. *Administrative Science Quarterly* 24, 151–3.

Universities Funding Council 1992: *Recurrent grant and student numbers for academic year 1992/3*, Circular Letter 4/92.

Urban, W. J. 1985: 'Merit pay and organized teachers in the US', 193–212. In Martin Lawn (ed.) *The politics of teacher unionism: international perspectives*, London: Croom Helm.

US General Accounting Office 1984: A *2-year appraisal of merit pay in three agencies.* GA0-GGD–84–1, 26 March.

U.S. General Accounting Office 1990: *Why and how GAO is reviewing federal college recruiting, Washington DC*: US House of Representatives.

US Systems Protection Board 1989: *The Senior Executive views of former federal executives.* Washington DC: US Printing Office.

US Senate Committee on Governmental Affairs 1984: *Management theories in the private and public sectors:* S.Hrg. 98–1218 before the sub-committee on civil service, post office, and general services, 2nd session, 98th Congress: Washington DC.

US Senate Committee on Governmental Affairs 1986: *President's management legislative initiatives*, S. Hrg. 99–618, 2nd session, 99th Congress: Washington DC.

Ventriss, C. 1989: 'Towards a public philosophy of public administration: a civic perspective of the public'. *Public Administration Review*, 49(2), March–April, 173–9.

Volcker, P 1989: *Leadership for America: rebuilding the public service*, task force report to the National Commission on the Public Service. Washington DC: National Commission on the Public Service.

Walsh, K. 1988: 'The teachers: employment and control'. *Local Government Studies*, 14(1), Jan–Feb, 113–22.

Wamsley, G. L. and Zald, M. N. 1983: 'The political economy of public organizations', 133–141. In J. L. Perry and K. L. Kraemer (eds), *Public management: public and private perspectives*, California: Mayfield Publishing.

Warner, N. 1984: 'Raynerism in practice: anatomy of a Rayner scrutiny'. *Public Administration*, 62(1), Spring, 7–22.

Warner, N 1992: Changes in resource management in Social Services' in Harrison, S. and Pollitt, C. *The Handbook of Public Services Management* Oxford: Blackwell.

Waterhouse, R. 1989a: 'Third of school teachers "looking to resign"'. *The Independent*, 29th May, 3.

Waterhouse, R. 1989b: 'Shame over bad reports "could lead to suicide"'. *The Independent*, 1 June, 3.

Weiner, S. L., Maxwell, J. H., Sapolsky, H. M., Dun, D. L. and Hsiao, W. C 1987: 'Economic incentives and organizational realities: managing hospitals under DRGs'. *The Milbank Quarterly: Health and Society*, 65(4), 463–7.

Weir, M., Orloff, A. and Skocpol, T. (eds) 1988: *The politics of social policy in the United States*. Princeton NJ: Princeton University Press.

Westerlund, G. and Sjostrand, S.E 1979: *Organizational myths*. London: Harper and Row.

White, A. 1901: *Efficiency and empire*. London: Methuen.

Whitley, R. 1988: 'The management sciences and managerial skills'. *Organizational Studies*, 9(1), 47–68.

Whitley, R. 1989a: 'On the nature of managerial tasks: their distinguishing characteristics and organisation'. *Journal of Management Studies*, May.

Whitley, R. 1989b: personal communication with the author, 22 March.

Wildavsky, A. 1969: 'Rescuing policy analysis from PPBS'. *Public Administration Review*, 29 (2), 189–202.

Wildavsky, A. 1973: 'If planning is everything, maybe it's nothing'. *Policy Sciences*, 4, 127–53.

Wildavsky, A. 1979: *Speaking truth to power: the art and craft of policy analysis*. Boston: Little, Brown and Co.

Wildavsky, A. 1988: 'Ubiquitous anomie: public service in an era of ideological dissensus'. *Public Administration Review*, 48(4) 753–5.

Williams, H. W. 1986: 'In search of bureaucratic excellence', *The Bureaucrat*, 15(1) Spring, 16–21.

Wilson, W. (1887): 'The study of administration'. *Political Science Quarterly*, 2, 197–222.

Winner, L. 1977: *Autonomous technology*. Boston: MIT Press.

Winter, M. F. and Robert, E. R. 1980: 'Male dominance, late capitalism, and the growth of instrumental reason'. *Berkeley Journal of Sociology*, 25, 249–80.

Wise, C. 1990: 'Public service configurations and public organizations: public organization design in the post-privatization era' *Public Administration Review*, 50:2, March/April, 141–55.

Wright, M. 1977: 'Public expenditure in Britain: the crisis of control'. *Public Administration*, 55(2), Summer, 143–69.

Zuboff, S. 1988: *In the age of the smart machine: the future of work and power*. London, Heinemann.

Index